POWER TO HURT

Power to Hurt

THE VIRTUES OF ALIENATION

William Monroe

UNIVERSITY OF ILLINOIS PRESS

URBANA AND CHICAGO

Publication of this work was supported by a grant from
the University of Houston.

1   2   3   4   5   C   P   5   4   3   2   1

This book is printed on acid-free paper.

Library of Congress Cataloging-in-Publication Data
Monroe, William Frank, 1952–
Power to hurt : the virtues of alienation / William Monroe.
p.   cm.
Includes bibliographical references and index.
ISBN 0-252-02351-X (alk. paper). — ISBN 0-252-06657-X (pbk. :
alk. paper)
1. American literature—20th century—History and criticism. 2.
Alienation (Social psychology) in literature. 3. Social isolation
in literature. 4. Boredom in literature. 5. Violence in literature.
6. Postmodernism (Literature)—United States. 7. Literature
and society—United States—History—20th century. 8. English literature—20th century—History and criticism. I. Title.
PS228.A6M66   1998
810.9'353-dc21   97-4639
                                                          CIP

As he listened to the cries of joy rising from the town, Rieux remembered that such joy is always imperiled. He knew what those jubilant crowds did not know but could have learned from books: that the plague bacillus never dies or disappears for good; that it can lie dormant for years and years in furniture and linen-chests; that it bides its time in bedrooms, cellars, trunks, and book-shelves; and that perhaps the day would come when, for the bane and the enlightening of men, it would rouse up its rats again and send them forth to die in a happy city.

Albert Camus, *The Plague*

Contents

Acknowledgments

When one takes as long as I have to complete a first book, there are many persons to thank. Let me begin by expressing gratitude to the editors and publishers of a few books and journals, for that is easiest. Versions of parts of this book have appeared in the *Georgia Review, Literature and Theology, Philological Quarterly, The Body and the Text: Comparative Essays in Literature and Medicine,* edited by Bruce Clarke and Wendell Aycock, and *The Good Body: Asceticism in Contemporary Culture,* edited by Mary Winkler and Letha Cole.

As director of my undergraduate thesis at the University of Texas, R. J. Kaufmann was the first to shape, encourage, and support this project. I owe him much more than a title—"power to hurt" was his idea—and more than I can say in the context of acknowledgments. As a luminary teacher his intelligence was matched only by his kindness and an abiding concern for our concerns: he was the pelican who, as in the medieval bestiary, plucks its own breast so that its charges will find nourishment. Other faculty at the University of Texas who provided special assistance were John Trimble, Thomas Seung, Neil Nakadate, and the late Gordon Mills.

My intellectual debt to Wayne Booth at the University of Chicago will be obvious in the chapters that follow. What may be less obvious is my regard for him as a person. Initially awed, I have remained challenged as he continues to teach me to desire better desires. In his good company, both flesh-and-blood and imaginative, there is genuine pleasure: warmth and gratitude and affection. Other faculty at the University of Chicago who helped me in countless and selfless ways were James E. Miller Jr., Gerald Mast, Janel Mueller, Anne Patrick, William Veeder, and James Streeter.

At McMurry University, Gerald McDaniel, Paul Lack, Joseph Stamey, Robert Monk, Faith Downs, Morris Baker, and other valued colleagues helped to create a generous, amiable, and bracing environment for teaching; in addition, the institution gave an inexperienced faculty member the opportunity to develop and offer undergraduate courses whose students, especially Mark Williams, Shelley Pickett, Jon Randall, and Cheri Holdridge, helped to engender and nurture many of the ideas found here.

At the University of Houston, Ted Estess, Samuel Southwell, Lois Zamora, and James Pipkin have provided direct encouragement and support, and a Faculty Development Leave in 1992 assisted the writing of this project. Colleagues on various teaching teams of the Honors College's "Human Situation" course also deserve appreciation: John Bernard, John Danford, Warren Holleman, William Porter, Jack McNees, Warren Frisina, Robert Zaretsky, and, again, Ted Estess have provided more help than they know. English Department and "Common Ground" Institute colleagues have also been supportive both personally and academically: Elizabeth Brown-Guillory, David Mikics, Richard Howard, Daniel Stern, Robert Phillips, Edward Hirsch, Frank Kermode, Roberta Weldon, Carl Lindahl, Linda Westervelt, Peter Gingiss, Irving Rothman, Terrell Dixon, Earl Dachslager, Alfred Arteaga, Linda Narby, Jan Brisack, Cathy Sarkar, Nelda Bristow, Nhu Dzuong, Carolyn Seeks, Linda Lazenby, and the late Michael Cooke.

In 1989–90, a Rockefeller Fellowship at the Institute for the Medical Humanities, a graduate division of the University of Texas Medical Branch–Galveston, revived this project and initiated several others. Mary Winkler, Ronald Carson, Anne Hudson Jones, William Winslade, Thomas Cole, and other institute faculty and staff lent confidence, collegial respect, and friendship at a crucial moment. In June and July of 1990, "Narrative and the Human Sciences," an NEH Institute at the University of Iowa, provided an invigorating forum where notions about performance could be tested and revised. Especially helpful there were Thomas Lutz, Barbara Biesecker, Michael McGee, Bruce Gronbeck, Donald McCloskey, Alan Scult, and Richard Harvey Brown. Back in Houston, actor Tanya Lunstroth, actor-director James Gales, and other members of the Urban Theater Project taught me about theatrical performance and provided generous encouragement on writing and directing.

Other friends and colleagues who have provided support and direction at various times, from graduate school to the present, include Todd Weir, Seth Lehrer, Theodore Lerud, Alvin Snyder, Marlon Ross, Thomas Garvey, Jay Van Santen, Suzanne Poirier, Marshall Gregory, James Phelan, Robert Denham, Thomas Werge, Anne Ponder, Samuel Schuman, David Jasper, Douglas Adams, Mark Leifeste, Randy Burton, Michael Kelly, Carl Moerer, James Reed, and Gregory Scholtz. Some of the many students who offered challenges, special assistance, or inspiration of various kinds include Blake Hurst, Scott Dewey, Jodie Fiore Köszegi, Christian Sarkar, Kimberly Nelson, John Alderman, Bernie Luger, Robert Lichenstein, Amy Potter, Jack Middlebrooks, Colleen Murphy, Mary-Alice Johnson, Vicky Cannon Bollenbacher, Karla Lee, Michael Barnes, Laurie Ellinghausen, Angela Bertino, Bryan Nollett, Kuruvilla Oommen, Monica Jacobs, Michelle Henry, Faisal Shah, Richard Sanchez, Kim Hales, Eric Moya, Thomas Snyder, Dana Dunlap, Anne Ewens, Katherine Carothers, Miguel Segovia, Roxanne Cedeño, and Clarice Annegers.

Richard Martin of the University of Illinois Press was a patient and persistent editor who, despite several detours and setbacks, never lost his enthusiasm for this project. Delaine Foss was an intelligent and supportive assistant when the book was beginning to take shape. More than once James Shapiro offered wisdom and encouragement, helping to get things moving or moving again. Ann Christensen was there with insight and energy when the book desperately needed revision. Krista Carothers thoroughly edited the first complete draft, providing expertise and company when they were needed most. Kerry Neville contributed to the final stages of manuscript preparation with her bibliographic skills, editorial acumen, and sheer determination.

I am indebted to these persons, true collaborators, both personally and professionally, and to many others not named here.

Somehow Helen Marie, my wife, has managed to support us during and after graduate school, to bear and begin rearing four children, and to maintain just enough interest in alienation to keep me from losing faith. She has enabled me to practice other virtues as well, and it is fitting that this volume be dedicated to her.

Prologue

They that have pow'r to hurt, and will do none,
That do not do the thing they most do show,
Who, moving others, are themselves as stone,
Unmovèd, cold, and to temptation slow—
They rightly do inherit heaven's graces,
And husband nature's riches from expense;
They are the lords and owners of their faces,
Others but stewards of their excellence.
The summer's flow'r is to the summer sweet,
Though to itself it only live and die;
But if that flow'r with base infection meet,
The basest weed outbraves his dignity:
> For sweetest things turn sourest by their deeds;
> Lilies that fester smell far worse than weeds.[1]

Shakespeare's sonnet 94 evaluates the wounds of alienation and performance. The poem can be read as a meditation on the "touching" that occurs when virtues are enacted and exchanged. "They that have pow'r to hurt" are able to inspire affiliation, allegiance, admiration, warmth, affection, desire, love. They are the ones who are fascinating, their performances fetching. They have a charisma. They enthrall. But some who possess the power to hurt "will do none": they move others while remaining unmoved and tempt others while remaining cold, aloof, and serene. Because they are ruled by circumspection rather than desire, William Empson calls them "the cold people."[2] In the poem they are "as stone," calculating the costs of their limited affiliations and resisting commitments to people and things. From sonnets such as 20, 25, 139, 144, and 152, we learn that the hypocritical and predatory nature of the world of men and women makes such self-control a necessary means of survival. Those who gush and give their hearts away cannot thrive and do not last—this is the suspicion resonating through this cluster of sonnets. So in 94 the self-protective "lords and owners of their faces" make the better choice. Living and dying unto themselves, celibate, sufficient, and complete, they "inherit heaven's graces, / And husband nature's riches from expense." Having learned to be wary and strategic, presumably burned before, they dare not risk giving in to the love that they inspire. They keep their edge, their advantage—and their distance.

Yet the poet is not content to leave these reluctant performers alone. After the first two quatrains of paradoxical praise, he develops the image of the infected flower, a symbol that implicates the unmoved movers. It is not certain that their way inevitably leads to corruption, but their very coldness, their alienation, puts them in danger. Their refusal, the "No" that they speak to those of us who are mere stewards and common functionaries, makes them vulnerable to a kind of cloistered suffocation. Does their secret keeping and inaccessibility constitute a "base infection," the unlanced, unexpressed festering mentioned in the final couplet? Are the lowly, promiscuous, prolific weeds more valuable and worthy than lilies that, untouched and unplucked, finally "turn" like unused cream? The power to hurt is a "sweet" virtue, but if it remains fugitive it can sour. Hermetic withdrawal and tenacious withholding can take their toll. "Too long a sacrifice / Can make a stone of the heart."[3]

Our literary traditions offer a rich and complex reservoir of those that have the power to hurt and yet do not do the thing they most do show. Like Shakespeare, writers, critics, and ordinary folk share with the Petrarchan poets a fascination with the virtues of alienation. Many of them address, more elegantly and profoundly to be sure, some of the questions behind this book. Is resistance to intimacy a necessary strategy or an indulgent arrogance? Are we more threatened by heedless, hearty, and earnest bonding or by suspicion, withdrawal, and control? How are the virtues of attentive affection and passionate discernment—what Martha Nussbaum calls "love's knowledge"—best cultivated?[4] Through encounters with constancy or spontaneity? Warm and ready familiarity or cool detachment? Often it is a self-sequestered woman who helps us recognize and really feel the high stakes that ride on the answers to these questions. There are, however, ample masculine figurations of colder, paler fires. One thinks of Kafka's renunciations of marriage and his poignant *Letters to Milena*; of Narcissus and Echo or Hippolytus and Phaedra; perhaps of Onan in the Hebrew Bible or John the Baptist in productions of *Salomé*. One thinks also of Søren Kierkegaard's "knight of faith" and his withdrawal from Regina Olsen. But like Kafka, another isolate who nonetheless keeps faith with us, Kierkegaard transformed his personal alienation into a writerly mode of love. "He wrote," John Updike says, "as a lover, having spurned marriage, and the torrent of volumes that follows his break with his fiancée abounds with lover's stratagems: with flirtatious ambiguities, elaborate deceits and impersonations, fascinating oscillations of emphasis, all sorts of erotic 'display.' " Kierkegaard, he says, led "a life of antidotes."[5] His writing became a homeopathic strategy for countering a personal alienation.

Strategies of alienation are not always antidotes, however; many are loveless, paranoid, and pathological. One notable example from popular culture is Stanley Kubrick's General Jack Ripper in *Dr. Strangelove*. Played by Sterling Hayden, Jack Ripper is the violence- and death-loving general who lives with the obsessive fear that women are going to get his "vital fluids." Does the choice come down to this: love and love's knowledge or else incommunicative violence? It is certainly true that a primary motive for violence historically has been the avoidance of contamination and exchange. Jean-Paul Sartre says that violence comes from a scarcity of the interior, and violence does indeed seem closer at hand when another person, or any ethos configured as other, is not allowed *inside*. A means of influence without confluence, violence is a way of domination and control that does not risk intercourse. And resistance to complicated, compromising transactions with the other, though the stance may appear steadfast and conscientious ("noble" in Nietzsche's pejorative sense), can and has evolved toward purgative, "cleansing" violence.

Violence, however, is not the subject of this book. I am interested in crafted literary performances of alienation, not inarticulate anger or belligerent fear. The imaginative refiguration achieved by language, which Jacques Derrida and others have provocatively deemed "violent," is unlike the all-too-chaste pressure, the prodding and pricking without identification and exchange, that marks real violence. Wallace Stevens says that certain poems create "a violence from within that protects us from a violence without."[6] The violence without is a unilateral, antiseptic *Einfluss*; the violence of poetry is a reciprocal identification, a declarative bond with another ethos. It is Gustave Flaubert's "*Emma Bovary, c'est moi*" and T. S. Eliot's Baudelairean "You! hypocrite lecteur! — mon semblable, — mon frère!"

Whatever the violence enacted by poetry, whatever its power to hurt, it comes about through a collaborative performance of readers and writers working within a cultural sensorium. Literary experiences, thus described, are affairs of exchange and interaction analogous to moments of encounter between flesh-and-blood persons. The improvisational element of "meeting" implies that critics who construct readings — presentations of temporal encounters — still have important work to do. When critical readings attempt to describe the qualities or virtues that may be enacted through such meetings, then that work, that criticism, can be characterized as ethical. As an essay in ethical criticism, *Power to Hurt* attempts to describe and classify the virtues of certain literary meetings. I have chosen encounters with literary "performances" of alienation — unfriendly poems, plays, and stories — because they represent strategies that have contributed most to the construction of American modern and postmodern culture, both avant-garde high and counterculture pop, and because they give us the chance to explore the important ethical question, Can literary performances of alienation quicken us, fill us up enough, touch us deeply enough to save us from what Stevens calls the violence without?

"Performances of Alienation," then, is an attempt to bring to performance (by reading "coductively")[7] certain literary works that have the power to make alterity lovely. T. S. Eliot, Vladimir Nabokov, and Donald Barthelme are selected from the canon of twentieth-century American literature, where they represent the oppositionist rule rather than the exception. Since World War I, serious writers in the United States and Europe have by and large been eager to "jab the sore spot" of society.[8] Following Jean-François Lyotard, we can characterize oppositional strategies as "postmodern." Yet the suspicion of grand narratives and totalizing theories, like the practice of cultural resistance and subversion, has always been around. The uncooperative strategies shunted under the postmodern umbrella are apparent and important in Western traditions. Sometimes lurking, sometimes almost dominant, undomesticated voices abide and persist. If we have ears to hear, there are often compelling foreign figures in our midst: Prometheus the thief, Jeremiah the prophet, Socrates the *eiron*, Jesus the parabler. Like Socrates, twentieth-century performers of alienation resist being consumed and homogenized into the polity. Like the Yahwist prophets, they have the power to hurt because they move and enthrall while remaining difficult and disruptive, outside and other. We need a less topical word for them, and though it is, as Raymond Williams says, "one of the most difficult words in the language," *alienation* seems best to cobble together the related literary strategies and performances I examine in this book.[9]

Alienation implies dissatisfaction, discontent, boredom—what R. J. Kaufmann calls *the desire to be elsewhere*.[10] Though the reasons may be vague, the conviction is clear and sharp: the here-and-now is not good enough. At its most subversive, the call of alienation emanates from a transcendent realm beyond historicity or originates in a consciousness superior to the encultured self. While the modes or strategies of alienation are many, they all seem to share the conviction that persons and communities have become estranged from their true destiny or potential. Thus the sulky signs of alienation often imply an intense but diffuse accusation. We often cannot tell exactly where the accusing finger points or what it condemns, but we feel an instinctive doubt and discomfort, perhaps an undifferentiated sense of shame. Something unspecified is wrong, something pernicious that we cannot fully grasp. Standing so accused—vaguely but profoundly—we may adopt our own protective and provocative strategy of alienation. Perhaps it is just such a defensive isolation that threatens the summer flower with base infection.

In the twentieth century, serious writers have been fascinated by the festering sweetness of alienation. Each new movement and mode, and each new generation of writers, has sought to defamiliarize language, disrupt affiliation, and sequester imagination. It has been a long, strange trip, a difficult dancing lesson: we are encouraged to admire, understand, and possess; yet we are held at bay, kept at a distance, perhaps scandalized by a story, poem, or person saying, in the words of Robert Scholes, "Go 'way, I got my own problems."[11] Readers and writers, uncomfortable with their mutual vulnerability, often exchange mixed signals of availability and refusal, invitation and renunciation. Richard Rorty says that *avoiding cruelty* is the principal motive for many of us; indeed, in our time there does seem to be an inclination to withdraw, a reluctance to exploit the power to hurt, even if it is also a power to help and to heal.[12]

Because *alienistic* strategies remind us that our summaries and interpretations are formulaic and full of deceits, evaluating such strategies may seem a wrongheaded, obtuse enterprise. The effort is compromised by the pervasiveness of a culture that, as the anthropologists tell us, does not stop at the skin. Culture is not only the product but also the means of production, not only the target of attack but also the means of critique. So even the most profound alienation will necessarily be expressed using cultural symbols and suspect traditions; even the power to hurt, as practiced by writers, requires the use of words. The sharing of symbols depends on processes that compromise strategies of alienation: encounter, engagement, exchange. Words cannot do their work at a safe distance and values cannot be transferred without involvement.[13] The alienated artist, no less than the enculturated audience, is touched—penetrated as well as enveloped—by the offending and offensive culture. Thus the notion of an "alienistic poem" may well be a paradox, for how can a poet or an audience renounce, obviate, and transcend culture by means of a form that is manifestly, inherently, and doggedly cultural? To make a text that can be recognized, a writer engages an audience, which is other, uses terms and patterns designed to be shared with the other, and, in short, performs for the other. In *The Plague*, for example, Albert Camus exposes the smug and fatal vanity of a happy city; at the same time, he develops a master metaphor designed to be shared with inhabitants of such cities, the very carriers of the disease. *The Plague* is a performance for the complacent sick, intended to save them from their complacency. Somewhat surprisingly, then, the power to hurt is an aesthetic virtue that includes empathy and a willingness to affiliate. Any other kind of hurt comes not from alienistic art but from an impulse to coerce, assault, and brutalize.

The works and writers considered here, like Camus, refrain from wanton assaults on the imagination. I do not believe that Eliot, Nabokov, and Barthelme are sadists, torturers, terrorists, or poisoners of our sensibilities. They are not even spoilers. Since I once considered them to be so, I must conclude that my attitude has been changed by time spent with them. My conversion has not made me a true believer or a zealot, however. My prior concerns, like the speaker's concerns in Shakespeare's sonnet, are not without foundation. For to praise alienation is to praise disconnection and detachment, to say, borrowing Empson's gloss, "It is wise to be cold." Rising above the here-and-now may be remarkable, but everything that rises does not converge. Critical detachment carries the risk of becoming chronic, pathological disaffection. Like Shakespeare, who finally seems certain of the value and "sweetness" of his patron, Mr. W. H., I am sure that the writers examined here are valuable and worthwhile, at least for those who have the requisite energy, encouragement, luck, and leisure—eyes to see and ears to hear. Even their would-be faults, like those of Mr. W. H. (as Empson says), act to preserve and protect them even as they practice publicly the demythologizing virtues of alienation. Their performances are corrosives, however; like any virtue, alienation can have vicious, debilitating manifestations. About such violations, which for substantial numbers of readers are real, I will have more to say in the conclusion.

Despite the corrosive nature of their performances, many alienistic writers, let us say the best of them, create functional responses to dysfunctional cultural situations. This is what it has taken me twenty years to learn: at their best, they contribute and participate and nourish even as they condemn and critique. It now seems probable that the work of such artists actually sustains culture by serving as an inoculation. Their inclusion in the canon underscores the importance of opposition and resistance *within* the tradition. Similarly, our recognition of outsiders such as Jesus and Socrates as "world-historical" testifies to the effectiveness of their performances of alienation. It also testifies finally to their failure to completely keep their distance. Apparently the alienation that becomes art sometimes functions as a homeopathic antitoxin against the alienation that becomes despair or violence. Performances of alienation, in other words, can vaccinate a person or a culture from a full-blown, unperformed, potentially catastrophic alienation. On the other hand, if alienation is not performed, it can become not anticultural but acultural, that is to say, inarticulate, and we move logically and historically closer to flesh-and-blood violence: "It is the artist above all who *realizes* that revolutions—however fresh, violent and destructive, however aspiring, or groping, or contagious—have always *already* taken place; as private murder represents a relation already at crisis or already sundered. Revolution and murder are only the gross cost, assessed too late: the usury of dead institutions."[14] Thus does R. P. Blackmur explain how institutions, systems, and relationships come to violence. Without alienism, alienation.

Admittedly, this quasi-Kierkegaardian repetition (which we can sloganize as "alienation reversed through performance") can be construed as another version of the old formula: potential subversion contained by dominant culture. But the difficulty, complexity, and evasive secrecy of alienistic works underscore the potential variations between performances, whether by speaker or interpreter, writer or reader. And where there is variation, there is potential for transformation. Sonnet 94 is a case in point. I have described it as a work that assesses or evaluates the performance of alienation, but, like a parable's, its lesson is sundered, inconclusive, variable. The poet-speaker has been burned himself, fooled by the worldly ways of love. He cannot, in his more cautious and cloistered mode, simply come out and give advice. Whatever he says, even to the one he loves, he will say indirectly, ironically, alienistically. According to Empson, "You can work through all the notes in the Variorum without finding out whether flower, lily, 'owner,' and person addressed are alike or opposed." By his calculation, there are 4,096 possible movements of thought between these four verbal elements alone, a number he calls "amusingly too great." The poem frustrates the critic bent on neatly capturing it, as well as Mr. W. H., the patron expecting a handy packet of advice. Empson's image for the sonnet is "a solid flute on which you can play a multitude of tunes, whose solidity no list of all possible tunes would go far to explain."[15] How, then, to proceed with the evaluation of performances of alienation except by means of readings, themselves performances of a sort—tentative, temporal, and tenuous but nonetheless clumsily, inefficiently transformative?

In the process of inquiring into literary strategies of alienation and several writers who enact these strategies, I hope to practice a kind of ethical criticism based on a performance paradigm. To the critical readings of part 3, I add an experimental "performative coda" called "Not-Knowing." The piece is intended to be confessional and elegiac and in an unconventional way another attempt at virtue criticism. There a brief personal and professional association with Donald Barthelme gives the lie to a smug depreciation of his work. Again the movement is one of personal conversion through contact and conversation, and thus the coda can be seen as a final exemplum of alienation overcome, an abstract or analogue of the book as a whole. For my hypothesis is that certain alienistic writers grudgingly take up the burden of performance—the doing of creative work with complicit symbols for a complacent audience. If they were politicized and demonstrating in the streets, an unthinkably barefaced activity for them, their slogan might be "Alienation for the Alienated."

Suppose that the resistance, inaccessibility, and detachment of alienistic works were necessary for the ethical cultivation of would-be readers. Then Eliot, Nabokov, Barthelme, and other vexers become teachers of virtue. They are trouble, to be sure, but their trouble is our trouble, and they perform it for us. They speak to and for our historical moment and play, albeit reluctantly, the cultural game. They are hyperconscious that the exercise of imaginative power creates resistance and that the exchange of values generates "ethical friction." But the power to influence and to rhetorically "move" need not be limited to domination, coercion, and control. If it is exercised with care, the artistic imagination can also liberate and strengthen. My experience is that alienation can sometimes be a gift shared in friendship, even the basis of friendship, for alienation shared is alienation overcome. The power to hurt can be a power to heal: the power of art to rouse up its rats again and send them forth to die in a vain but happy city. So, while there will be no earnest argument here for the universal benefit of alienistic writers and their works, I would not be surprised if some readers found in them, as I have, equipment for living.

Notes

1. Stephen Booth, ed., *Shakespeare's Sonnets* (New Haven: Yale University Press, 1977), p. 83.

2. William Empson, *Some Versions of Pastoral* (1935; rpt., London: Hogarth, 1986), p. 93.

3. W. B. Yeats, "Easter 1916," *The Collected Poems of W. B. Yeats* (New York: Macmillan, 1956), p. 179.

4. Martha Nussbaum, "Love's Knowledge," *Love's Knowledge: Essays on Philosophy and Literature* (New York: Oxford University Press, 1990), pp. 261–85.

5. John Updike, "Søren Kierkegaard," in *Atlantic Brief Lives: A Biographical Companion to the Arts*, ed. Louis Kronenberger (Boston: Little Brown, 1971), p. 429.

6. Wallace Stevens, "The Noble Rider and the Sound of Words," *The Necessary Angel: Essays on Reality and the Imagination* (New York: Vintage, 1965), p. 36.

7. My approach to ethical criticism relies on a "performance paradigm" and "coduction," Wayne Booth's notion of collaborative reasoning. These concepts will be elaborated in chapters 1–4.

8. The phrase is William Barrett's, used to describe the aggressive oppositional strategies of "modern art" in his influential book of the fifties, *Irrational Man* (1958; rpt., Garden City, N.Y.: Anchor-Doubleday, 1962), p. 45. See also W. F. Monroe, "'Jabbing the Sore Spot': Alienism and Its Cultural Role," *Georgia Review* 34, no. 1 (1980), pp. 15–37.

9. Raymond Williams, *Keywords* (London: Fontana, 1983), p. 33. Jan Gorak suggests that Williams himself "offers a case study in the psychology and methods of the alienated intellectual" in *The Alien Mind of Raymond Williams* (Columbia: University of Missouri Press, 1988), p. 10.

10. As a student of Kaufmann's at the University of Texas, I heard him use this phrase as a working substitute for *angst:* the desire to be elsewhere. When I inquired about the source, he told me that he developed the equivalence in the process of teaching Kafka and Strindberg in the 1960s (personal correspondence, Feb. 1997).

11. Robert Scholes, *Fabulation and Metafiction* (Urbana: University of Illinois Press, 1979), p. 218.

12. Richard Rorty, *Contingency, Irony, and Solidarity* (Cambridge: Cambridge University Press, 1989), pp. 141–68, 173.

13. Borrowing from the vulgar but mnemonic dialogue in Erica Jong's *Fear of Flying*, we might say that there are no "zipless fucks" in the realm of symbolic transmission; that is, intercourse cannot be limited to sensation without consequences. A literary transaction includes engagement, emotional exchange, empathy, "complications."

14. R. P. Blackmur, "The Great Grasp of Unreason," *Anni Mirabiles, 1921–1925: Reason in the Madness of Letters* (Washington, D.C.: Library of Congress, 1956), p. 8.

15. Empson, *Some Versions of Pastoral*, pp. 89–90.

And there he was this young boy, a stranger to my eyes,
Strumming my pain with his fingers,
Singing my life with his words.
Killing me softly with his song.
  Norman Gimbel (lyrics) and Charles Fox (music), "Killing
  Me Softly with His Song"

She sat stirring her drink and feeling unclose to me. She worries over the way her love for me comes and goes, appears and disappears. She doubts its reality simply because it isn't as steadily pleasurable as a kitten. God knows it *is* sad. The human voice conspires to desecrate everything on earth.
  J. D. Salinger, *Raise High the Roof Beam, Carpenters*

PART I
Virtue Criticism

A poet may believe that he is expressing only his private experience; his lines may be for him only a means of talking about himself without giving himself away; yet for his readers what he has written may come to be the expression both of their own secret feelings and of the exultation or despair of a generation.

  T. S. Eliot, "Virgil"

—(— I

Strategies, Performances, Virtues

Why *virtue* criticism? Not intended as revolutionary or even particularly remarkable, the emphasis on virtue is an effort to "keep the road open," as Lionel Trilling urged his students, between literature and life. Works of literature, like virtues and vices, attitudes and qualities, are connected to action in the world. Poems, stories, and plays are bound up with personal and social commitments and with professional and political practices. These are the well-worn assumptions that led me to consider the virtues enacted by readers and writers when they perform various literary texts. The precise nature of this complex connection, the how and why of the continually evolving bond between world and work, situation and strategy, generates inquiry rather than theory, example rather than formula. This kind of inquiry is by no means new or extraordinary, but the key terms of this approach—strategy, performance, coduction—do point to the inclusion here of something often missing in contemporary theory: agency. By restoring the notion of agency to writing and reading, virtue criticism is an attempt to revive the ancient, pragmatic concerns of criticism, theory, and philosophy—to consider literary works as responses to personal situations, material arrangements, and institutional practices. In other words, poems, stories, and dramas become strategies of understanding and acting, loving and working in the world. As a response to a theory-bound situation, virtue criticism is partly an effort to suggest that "it is possible to live, because it is possible to read, without accepting official versions of reality."[1]

Wayne Booth uses the term *ethical criticism* to designate inquiries that are concerned with the *ethoi* (characters, attitudes, properties, or virtues) of authors, readers, texts, communities, classes, genders, and cultures. It should be clear that my approach to literature owes most to Booth's pioneering work in rhetorical and ethical criticism.[2] Kenneth Burke's discussion of texts as strategies is another obvious resource. In *A Grammar of Motives*, Burke explains how literary works can be considered *acts* within cultural *scenes*.[3] His Dramatistic Pentad and the ancient and medieval sources from which he derives it are the foundation of the paradigm used here: literary works are strategies performed in response to cultural situations. Warwick Wadlington, an admirer of Burke, develops the paradigm in useful ways by including insights from Mikhail Bakhtin and Clifford Geertz and emphasizing the concept of performance.[4] I cannot hope to survey the range of what has gone by various names, including pragmatic, moral, sociological, and rhetorical, as well as ethical, criticism. I do, however, want to lay the foundation for my own version of criticism—a pluralistic, evaluative, and situated mode of reading that I think of as "virtue criticism." Since application is necessary to reveal its powers and limitations, part 3 is an exercise in practical criticism. There I suggest how particular literary works may affect particular readers and try to assess the costs as well as the benefits of perennial strategies of alienation. Here I want to acknowledge and point to some theoretical sources for this approach and in the process suggest the current worth of a criticism that assumes the possibility of agency and maintains a central role for reading and readings.

Burke suggests in *The Philosophy of Literary Form* that it would be useful to see literary works as textual or symbolic strategies with characteristics similar to those of other patterns and plans. As textual strategies, literary works "deal with" situations. That is, they strategically respond to the situations in which and for which they are *written*. Additionally, poems and fictions can be used as responses to situations in which and for which they are *read*. While these imitated (and thus poetic) situations may or may not be "actual," official, lawful, and historical, writers and readers can and do use poetic situations and strategies for psychological, ethical, and political purposes. A story or poem may "depict" a situation, but inherent in that depiction or *imitation*, to use the Aristotelian term, are beliefs, desires, commitments, and value-ridden images. An imitative text not only names a situation, as Burke says, but also names that situation purposively, strategically, and tendentiously. To underscore the bias inherent in any naming of a situation, Burke later uses the term *motive* as the shorthand equivalent of *situation*.

Thus poets and readers figure forth motives when they enact poems. By defining poems as strategies for advantageously "handling" prevalent situations, Burke's approach enables us to relate particular literary works to particular but commonly recognizable circumstances; we thereby avoid impressionism and relativism. Since the experience of situations is made possible by a culture held and constructed socially, textual interpretations cannot be merely idiosyncratic. As Burke says, the situations imitated by a text are real—real not in the sense of preexisting "out there" in the world but in the sense of being held in common by and instantly recognizable to members of the culture. Moreover, similar strategies for handling familiar situations are used by flesh-and-blood individuals and historical communities. Thus, according to Burke, "insofar as situations overlap from individual to individual, or from one historical period to another, the strategies possess universal relevance."[5] His confidence in the relevance and significance of literary works derives from an anthropological observation rather than a metaphysical insight: "Insofar as situations are typical and recurrent in a given social structure, people develop names for them and strategies for handling them."[6] One need not embrace an essentialism, Jungian or otherwise, to agree with Burke that it is convenient for cultures to develop familiar names for recurrent situations and various strategic "moves" for dealing with them. And Burke continually reminds us that the verbal signs (in the form of familiar names) that a culture uses to designate recurrent situations are themselves moves, tendentious and strategic. Thus the familiar "laying bare" of ideological bias, a form of ethical criticism and cultural critique, could look to Burke as readily as to Roland Barthes for its philosophical roots.

The value of Burke's rhetorical and pragmatic approach becomes evident when we want tools to discuss the shaping powers of literary works. To see a poem or story as a strategy is to recognize in it the potential for patterning identities, marshalling qualities of character, and directing human actions and interactions. Stories are seen as symbolic patterns that can serve as potentially useful scripts. Poems and plays become structured plans of sound and sense that can be identified with the goals, intentions, and strategies of flesh-and-blood persons. Clifford Geertz argues that without such symbolic strategies, without what he calls "marching orders," human beings would become "basket cases."[7]

(Like Burke who conjures with *strategy*, Geertz selects a military metaphor suggesting the movement of troops and the advantageous placement of resources.) Take away our cultural scripts and we become inert, unable to perform even rudimentary manipulations of our environment. Without social symbolic patterns, we function significantly less well than animals, who seem to have a "hard-wired" operating system, a ROM, if you will, for surviving and flourishing. For us, however, even so-called survival instincts seem to be culturally programmed and continually reprogrammed. Stories and songs are part of this "Saving" and "Saving As." Thus, shifting back to Geertz's metaphor, stories find their way into our marching orders, our satchel of indispensable cultural scripts. When they do so, they augment and modify the resources that we need for our life campaigns. It is a chestnut to say that literature makes the journey of life richer and more rewarding, but the more compelling case for the survival value of cultural scripts and patterns is rarely pressed. Without symbolic strategies, a life campaign, perhaps human existence itself, may not be possible.[8] Stories and poems can and do protect us—from fear, confusion, enervation, despair, insanity. Like the physician's pharmacopeia, these scripts and patterns constitute our symbolic armamentarium. We use them to confront the intrinsic diseases, alienations, and vicissitudes of human life.

Such claims about the functional value of poems and stories lead to the central questions for virtue criticism. We want to ask, as Wadlington does, "What does the work do for the writer, and what does it do for the reader?"[9] How does this text equip us to cope with perplexity and risk, antagonism and coercion, resistance and stupidity, ignorance and fear? Since various poems and stories constitute diverse responses to more or less common cultural situations, virtue criticism must move beyond theory to the practical criticism of particular texts. A realist might assert: "This work tells us the following truth about the real world." A virtue critic would ask: "What are the virtues of this strategic response? How, by what means and devices, does the text present the situation? What values are examined, proposed, or discovered? How are problems articulated and conflicts negotiated? What specific strategies are employed and how are they enacted by the fiction? What beliefs, values, desires, and images are evoked and what virtues are figured forth? Finally, what's in it for us?" Or, as Richard Rorty puts it, "What sorts of things about what sorts of people do I need to notice?"[10] Can this strategy help me, perhaps, to work without resentment, to love without suspicion, to desire higher and better desires?

To answer such questions one "performs" individual literary works.[11] Each performance of a work figures forth a strategy: a particular pattern of beliefs, values, desires, images, and actions, a "cluster of virtues." Like Booth, Alasdair MacIntyre, and others who have turned to virtue ethics and ethical criticism, I use *virtue* in a broad sense, as a synonym for *attitude* or *quality of character*. Virtues include what are commonly thought of as vices and index the entire range of human powers, propensities, strengths, capacities, and patterns of behavior. Virtues, loaded as they are with desire and judgment, are necessarily tied to actions; particular actions certify and confirm the existence of particular virtues. Burke's definition of attitude — "incipient action" — underscores the important connection between ethos and performance. Good reading, reading that can aptly be called performing, occurs when particular readers aspire to particular virtues through the performance of a particular poem. When performing (with) a text, a reader practices a series of mental stances and maneuvers. These "moves" become part of a reader's satchel of scripts, his or her characteristic repertoire of strategic responses to the world's invitations and disappointments, adoptions and alienations. A virtue critic is a (usually experienced) reader who publicly performs a story to reveal and clarify the virtues of its strategies.

Ideally, such formal, practical criticism proceeds by means of dialogue and conversation. Though virtue criticism has political and potentially historical implications, the conversations here will focus on texts. Through conversations about texts we can often agree that they evoke recognizable situations and develop plausible strategies.[12] For example, if we agree that it strategically names and responds to a common situation, even a complex and difficult poem such as *The Waste Land* can be described as a cluster of attitudes: a "grouse against life," as Eliot himself succinctly put it.[13] To discuss a complex lyric or narrative as a strategy is not to reduce that literary work of art to a monophonic or univocal attitude. Seeing a poem as a finite cluster of attitudes allows for variety, complexity, and even contradiction while at the same time acknowledging limits and the play of difference necessary for meaning and action. Poems and stories, with what Bakhtin calls their heteroglossia, are analogous to the multivalent confederation of persons conventionally identified as one person, a separate individual, one flesh-and-blood human being. The individual, Burke says, is a confederation of "corporate we's"; just so, a poem is a cluster of attitudes.[14] In persons and in poems, organic wholeness need not mean straitened consistency. Thus our foundational assumption is actually quite modest: that a text is as reducible and as irreducible as a flesh-and-blood human being. Depending on the purpose and the context, a reading of a text should be about as coherent and delimited, as complex and nuanced, as a reading of the cluster of virtues

and attitudes known as a person. In all its variegated potential, a given performance of *King Lear* is surely no more complex and multivalent than its myriad-
minded creator, and a reading of *Huckleberry Finn* no more troubling and con-
tradictory than a presentation of Mark Twain—or Samuel Clemens.[15]

This simple insight about the ability of textual strategies to "travel" from one
situation to another is an enabling one for virtue criticism. If literary works are
strategic responses to situations that we can define and designate, then ethical
criticism is or should be a part of the enculturation process and as such an
entitlement. After all, the responsive action of developing and applying strategies, of importing or transporting attitudes from one situation to another, is a
survival skill as well as a creative exercise. "All living organisms," as Burke says,
"interpret the things about them."[16] Seen as critical evaluations, stories and
poems become multivocal resources for naming and responding to situations
and enduring circumstances, such as political arrangements, social hierarchies,
and familial patterns, as well as changing circumstances, such as financial pressures, erotic overtures, the increase or decrease of capacities, the birth of a child,
the loss of a friend. Proverbs, as Burke says, are the more obvious examples of
literature designed as "equipment for living," but more complex literary works
may also be considered, or performed, as proverbial.[17] Norman Maclean's *A
River Runs through It* can plausibly become an elegy for those who are loved
and lost and never understood. As such, it serves as a means of reconciling loss,
but in a way significantly more complex and recursive than a proverb. Similarly, Henry James's *The Ambassadors* can be understood as a painstakingly variegated and elaborated version of what is arguably Burke's proverb of proverbs,
his strategy of strategies: "Keep your weather eye open."[18]

Once we accept Burke's equation—poems are proverbs, proverbs are strategies for handling recurrent situations—the connection between ethical judgments and literature immediately follows. For estimates of good and bad, better and worse, are imbedded in the very notion of strategy. The act of responding
strategically to a situation presumes preferences, the prior existence or ad hoc
construction of goals and purposes. Literary texts help us to embrace, recast, or
reject who or what is present; stories, poems, and plays enable us to recognize,
pursue, or mourn who or what is absent. For example, after brooding for weeks
over a slight, a person's attitude may be changed through a performance of *The
Tragedy of King Lear*. In such circumstances a literary work can recall what is
at stake and re-present brooding as the squandering of relationships, a waste of
life. At such moments, if we are open to the literary "company," it is possible to
reevaluate ourselves and others and to reconsider familiar ideas, habitual pat-

terns, even ideologies and institutions. Profound reevaluations lead us to make fresh resolutions or immediate alterations "accordingly."

We currently speak rightly of multiple worlds and a plurality of cultures, but insofar as situations and traits of character overlap from moment to moment, individual to individual, epoch to epoch, culture to culture, the virtues manifested by textual strategies can be understood as recurrent attitudes with general relevance. A particular reader, for example, may find that a given text can be plausibly performed in such a way that it becomes a usable response to his or her personal situation; another text seems to describe the "current state of affairs," the status quo, with insight and accuracy. Our conviction that a text is "realistic," accurate, or possesses what Northrop Frye calls truth of correspondence matters less than our agreement that usable responses to culturally important situations are figured forth by the text in plausible ways. Such texts possess a "truth of concern" that is of more interest and significance than scientifically verifiable "factual" texts.[19] If the situation imitated by a text has broadly acknowledged significance, then we can look to it for "tentative universality"—that is, a universal applicability that remains hypothetical indefinitely, always susceptible to counter example and never hardening into a conclusion.

The virtue critic's task, then, is not to prove a truth about the text or about its correspondence to the world, but to "put on" a good enough rendition of it, a rendering or performance that a student, conference, or reading audience will assent to and find worthwhile. Thus virtue criticism is a mode of rhetoric and, as such, tentative, vulnerable, and historical in practice. Though he does not use the term, Michael Wood gives us a good definition of virtue criticism even as his evaluation of Nabokov exemplifies it: he calls for a criticism that is "an intense, even intimate dialogue with provocative texts; a report on the adventure of reading. Like all adventures, it has its risks; among the things we shall almost surely lose is our certainty."[20] To remain adventurous and exploratory in our talk about literature—to accept what Wood calls "the risks of fiction"—we would do well to practice "coduction." *Coduction* is Booth's neologism designating a process of inquiry that is dialogic in form and collaborative in practice. Coductive reasoning, unlike inductive and deductive arguments, must always be "corrected in conversations," Booth says, conversations that we enter into with others whose coductions we help shape and therefore trust.[21] Avoiding dogmatic assertions and conclusive declarations, coductive reasoning collapses the distinction between inquiry and explanation—the very synthesis endorsed by Barbara Herrnstein Smith in *Contingencies of Value*.[22] Coductive judgments are auditions rather than declarations, dialogic interactions rather than unilateral determinations. Thus virtue criticism, at least as I hope to practice it, is performative rather than dogmatic: a series of conversations, a regimen of ethical exercises, an invitation to join the flesh-and-blood, heart-and-mind game of proposing correspondences between poems and persons.

NOTES

1. Frank Kermode, *The Art of Telling* (Cambridge, Mass.: Harvard University Press, 1983), p. 70. Kermode attributes a recent iteration of this possibility of rejecting "official versions of reality" to Roland Barthes and the French theorists but notes that D. H. Lawrence anticipated the hope they place in alienistic resistance. Strategies of alienation like those celebrated by Barthes and Derrida, "though now given much attention, are a selection from the set of permanent possibilities" intrinsic to narrative. Indeed, Kermode's definition of a classic is "a text that has evaded local and provincial restrictions" (p. 70).

2. Wayne Booth's *The Company We Keep: An Ethics of Fiction* (Berkeley: University of California Press, 1988) has been particularly helpful.

3. Kenneth Burke, *A Grammar of Motives* (1945; rpt., Berkeley: University of California Press, 1969). Here is Burke preparing to analyze a literary work dramatistically: "To consider [Keats's 'Ode on a Grecian Urn'] as a mode of *action* is to consider it in terms of 'poetry.' For a poem is an act, the symbolic act of the poet who made it—an act of such a nature that, in surviving as a structure or object, it enables us as readers to re-enact it" (p. 447).

4. See especially Wadlington's chapter "Reading and Performance: Reproduction and Persons" in *Reading Faulknerian Tragedy* (Ithaca: Cornell University Press, 1987), pp. 26–49. I have found Wadlington's work on theories of reading to be a broadly applicable synthesis for analyzing the function of literature in the lives of persons and communities.

5. Kenneth Burke, *The Philosophy of Literary Form*, 2d ed. (Baton Rouge: Louisiana University Press, 1967), p. 1. In *The Ethics of Authenticity* (Cambridge, Mass.: Harvard University Press, 1992), Charles Taylor also emphasizes the importance of commonalities—"history, or the demands of nature, or the needs of my fellow human beings, or the duties of citizenship, or the call of God, or something else of this order"—to the development of personal identification strategies (p. 40).

6. Burke, *The Philosophy of Literary Form*, p. 296.

7. Clifford Geertz, *The Interpretation of Cultures: Selected Essays* (New York: Basic Books, 1973), p. 49.

8. Reynolds Price, among others, lists stories among the basic human needs, "second in necessity apparently after nourishment and before love and shelter." A *Palpable God* (San Francisco: North Point Press, 1985), p. 3. For a splendid examination of the

journey of life metaphor, see Thomas R. Cole, *The Journey of Life: A Cultural History of Aging in America* (Cambridge: Cambridge University Press, 1992).

9. Wadlington, *Reading Faulknerian Tragedy*, p. 30.

10. Richard Rorty, *Contingency, Irony, and Solidarity* (Cambridge: Cambridge University Press, 1989), p. 143.

11. Here again I take a cue from Burke: "The reader does not merely *appreciate* a work of art. He *makes* it. He *participates*. The words on the page are like musical notation, and in reading them we *perform*." "Maxims and Anecdotes: II," *New Republic* 94 (16 Mar. 1938), p. 159.

12. We will also sometimes agree that a text figures forth a situation that is so idiosyncratic that it is uninteresting or that the strategic responses implied by the text have so little to recommend them that the text is unworthy of our time or attention.

13. "One of Eliot's friends, Mary Hutchinson, who read *The Waste Land* soon after its completion, said it was 'Tom's autobiography.' Eliot himself said that it was only 'the relief of a personal . . . grouse against life.'" Lyndall Gordon, *Eliot's Early Years* (New York: Oxford University Press, 1977), p. 86.

14. Kenneth Burke, *Attitudes toward History*, rev. 2d ed. (Los Altos, Calif.: Hermes, 1959), p. 264.

15. For a history of various versions of book and author, see Tom Quirk, *Coming to Grips with "Huckleberry Finn": Essays on a Book, a Boy, and a Man* (Columbia: University of Missouri Press, 1993).

16. Kenneth Burke, *Permanence and Change: An Anatomy of Purpose*, 2d ed. (Indianapolis: Bobbs-Merrill, 1954), p. 5.

17. The reference is to Burke's often anthologized chapter from *The Philosophy of Literary Form*.

18. Burke's principal proverb is an imperative analogue to Rorty's interrogative: "What sorts of things about what sorts of people do I need to notice?" This question, Rorty says, is central to the working out of new values through what he calls "a new *public* final vocabulary." *Contingency, Irony, and Solidarity*, p. 143. In one sense a virtue critic is one who offers to give answers, however tentative, to such questions.

19. Northrop Frye, *The Critical Path: An Essay on the Social Context of Literary Criticism* (Bloomington: Indiana University Press, 1971), p. 122.

20. Michael Wood, *The Magician's Doubts: Nabokov and the Risks of Fiction* (Princeton: Princeton University Press, 1995), p. 7.

21. Booth, *The Company We Keep*, p. 73.

22. Barbara Herrnstein Smith, *Contingencies of Value: Alternative Perspectives for Critical Theory* (Cambridge, Mass.: Harvard University Press, 1988), pp. 15–16, 94–102.

⊶— **2**

A Performance Paradigm

In this chapter I will discuss the paradigm of performance as a model for how a reader or writer comes to produce and possess a textual strategy and modify a cluster of virtues. Perhaps *paradigm* is too grand a term for what is being suggested here: it is nothing more than a spinning out of some possibilities inherent in Frank Kermode's passing observation that "to talk about literature is to give a rhetorical performance about rhetorical performances."[1] What precisely happens when readers "take in" a story? What are the cognitive, psychological, and biochemical processes involved in transforming a textual strategy into the attitude of a flesh-and-blood person? These are questions I am not qualified to answer.[2] The means by which an individual or community modifies attitudes, ethical repertoires, and clusters of virtues remains mysterious: reader-response theory and research is by no means conclusive, and its proponents disagree about aims and methods.[3] Again, my elementary, inexact, and rather quaint assumption is that a flesh-and-blood reader is an agent who has the capacity to use a repertoire of virtues to survive, perhaps to flourish — in any case, to "get along." A repertoire of virtues is a repository of plans, moves, and strategies, a cluster of interrelated narratives, beliefs, values, images, patterns, and desires. This repository catalogues the existential choices and courses of action that *press* a given ethos, individual or collective, in a given situation. "Man is a vocabulary," Burke says. "To manipulate his vocabulary is to manipulate him. And art, any art, is a major means of manipulating his vocabulary."[4] "Stamps" such as class, race, and gender do indeed press and impress us; but virtue criticism, concerned as it is with imaginative literature, recognizes the pressures and desires figured and evoked by other symbolic patterns. When narratives are added, an ethos is modified. For instance, when stories such as "Watergate" or "Vietnam" enter the national repository, the virtues of America are changed. By incrementally altering the "pressing repertoire" of an ethos, whether historical society, flesh-and-blood person, or another "corporate we," symbolic strategies such as poems and stories can and do change virtues.[5]

Poems help to make, modify, and maintain persons—we make this assumption while at the same time acknowledging that the process of "reading-in" virtues is a mystery infinitely more complex and at least as hazardous as downloading kilobytes from the Net. When we expose our functional repertoire of scripts and patterns to the inclusion of a powerfully wrought symbolic strategy, we make ourselves vulnerable to displacement and transformation. Will this new program or "application" work like a computer virus or "trojan horse," retarding our processes and disabling other functions? Or will it increase our capacities, allowing us to know and to do marvelous things formerly closed off from us? We can never know in advance exactly what will happen when we open ourselves to encounter even a familiar work. Thus "no one reading suffices," as J. Hillis Miller says. "The work of reading must always start again from the beginning, even in a rereading of a work already read."[6] We simply cannot predict what a text will certainly be or do.

Walker Percy's distinction between "news" and mere "knowledge" provides another angle from which to view the process of participatory reading, with its inherent temporality and vulnerability. News, Percy says, is what is significant insofar as the reader is caught up in the affairs of his or her particular situation "and in so far as he has *not* withdrawn into laboratory or seminar room."[7] The hearer of news is a person—Percy, following Gabriel Marcel, calls him "a castaway"—"who finds himself in a predicament. News is precisely that communication which has bearing on his predicament and is therefore good or bad news." Knowledge, on the other hand, is "'science' in the broadest sense of knowing, the sense of the German word *Wissenschaft*." By definition, such knowledge can be arrived at anywhere by anyone and at any time; yet because it is not grounded in particularity, not situated in space and time, it serves as mere information that is forgotten or stored to be discarded or accessed later. In a particular instance, one reader, practicing vulnerability ("the posture of the castaway") will read a given text as news relevant to her predicament; while another, practicing abstraction ("the posture of objectivity") will discover only information.[8] Hence, as Wadlington cautions, readers and critics in and out of the academy should avoid the casual use of terms such as *makes* or *forces* when discussing the transmission of virtues from persons to texts and from texts to persons.[9]

Are we obliged, then, to spend our energies proclaiming the indeterminacy of texts and the arbitrariness of readings? Or can we speak in useful and interesting (if not authoritative) ways about how fictional experiences affect persons? The problem can be partially circumvented by using technical language and confining our claims to critical constructs: implied authors, implied readers, narrative audiences, authorial audiences, and so on.[10] But formal approaches, even the painstaking and circumspect methods used by narratologists, often ignore this commonsensical insight: readers perform books. Stories and poems are only ink marks on paper until human beings enliven the words through the performative activity we call reading. Thus persons determine the powers and limits of literary texts, not vice versa. As early as 1931, Burke was warning the emerging New Critical coalition that a book can be many things to many people, e.g., "widely read and ineffectual, widely read and influential, little read and ineffectual, little read and influential. It may usher in something of great value; it may 'keep something alive'; it may represent the concerns of a few people living under exceptional conditions. *It may, in fact, do all of these things* at different times in its history, or in its action upon different kinds of readers."[11] Insisting on indeterminacy—observing that a text cannot determine its reception and interpretation—is scarcely new or scandalous. Rather it is literary theory catching up with common sense, as Kermode says in *The Art of Telling*.[12] Similarly, acknowledging the importance of readers does not make evaluative interpretations obsolete or otiose; to the contrary, testing readings in public conversation becomes crucial, auditioning fictions and interpretations indispensable. Writing and reading are typically private, even isolated activities, and we cannot achieve here a coductive, reciprocal evaluation of the sort characteristic of the best literary conversations in classrooms and coffeehouses.[13] Instead, the unspoken appeal, "Does it not seem so to you?" should be understood as implied in the practical criticism of part 3; it is easy, in the long process of writing, to forget the tentative and unpredictable nature of reading.[14]

Nonetheless, we do eventually make choices in our performances and "take our part" in the conversation. We have lives to live, after all, books to read and strategies to enact. Valid caveats need not prevent us from positing, as Burke, Booth, and Wadlington do, the pattern of virtues, the arrangement of beliefs, values, desires, and attitudes, figured forth by a literary work. Virtue criticism should differ, it seems to me, from New Criticism and other formalist approaches that make ambiguity or multivalence or indeterminacy the predictable conclusion of every critical act. To acknowledge that readers will inevitably perform a novel like Kate Chopin's *The Awakening* in a variety of ways (what do we make of the "suicide" that ends the book?) is not the same as claiming that all performances are equally attentive, valid, or valuable. While virtue criticism implicitly acknowledges the importance of historical audiences and interpretive communities, its exponents do not obsess about the variability of interpretations. Literary works will, as Kermode says, "always invite us to plural glosses on the letter, to ingenious manipulations of the codes." But that we "produce rather than consume" textual strategies does not free us from a responsibility to them and to our fellow readers. For literary works also demand that "we liberate them from local and provincial restrictions, including, so far as that is possible, our own."[15] Practical criticism, especially coductive criticism, depends on the possibility of sharing insights about similar situations, responses, and strategies. Thus we maintain the hope that the best readers, or, rather, any person reading at his or her best, will be open to the possibility that any text might become news without being reduced to something merely local and provincial. For example, at age thirty-five a junk dealer in Houston may suddenly recall his high school study of Dante, murmuring, perhaps for the first time with a sense of recognition, the name "Bay-uh-tree-chay." *The Divine Comedy* has become ethically meaningful for him. His memory has allowed him to adopt, to take as his own, a particular textual strategy delineating a cluster of virtues. And this identification with Dante's text can occur even though the poem was experienced, comprehended, and stored away almost twenty years before. At last, or again, he gets it. Knowledge has become news. Even in professional forums, a virtue critic ought to strive for a similar immediacy, a passion elaborated and articulated but not codified and calcified. Virtue critics may build on technical criticism but are not content to stop with information, theory, or even objective interpretations. They too are castaways, performing for castaways. They attempt to show, as precisely as possible, how significant texts can become transformative news for significant numbers of people.[16]

The notion of performance can help us explore the mysterious process whereby stories and poems enter the realm of ethics by affecting us and becoming news—this is my hypothesis and hope. Our intuitions and assumptions about agency suggest that texts do not force their virtues on readers or inject them with attitudes; at the same time, if stories and poems are strategic scripts that contribute to the making and unmaking of persons, then their energy, their power to hurt, is inherent (though latent) in their symbolic figuration.[17] Like other actions, performative reading enters the realm of the ethical when there is both freedom and, as Hillis Miller says, "an imperative, some 'I must' or *Ich kann nicht anders*."[18] "The ethical moment in the act of reading faces in two directions. On the one hand it is a response to something, responsible to it, responsive to it, respectful of it." This something is what we commonly call "the text." The act of reading cannot be ethical, Miller says, if a reader blithely claims "a freedom to do what one likes, for example to make a literary text mean what one likes." Such disconnected freedom makes a travesty of performative reading. On the other hand, we intuit (and henceforth assume) that a person functions as an agent when he or she performs as a reader. For there to be an ethical moment in the act of reading, teaching, or writing about literature, "there must be an influx of performative power" from the reading "into the realms of knowledge, politics, and history." The reading itself can be seen, then, as a collaboration, constrained but not determined by the collaborators—reader, writer, text, culture, theory. To leave room for ethics, as Miller says, "the flow of power must not be all in one direction." In reading, as in any performance with ethical moment, there must be a balance of power.[19]

Louise Rosenblatt's emphasis on the reciprocal nature of literary experiences helps us posit a balance of power between reader and text. As she says, each reading is "a particular event involving a particular reader and a particular text recursively influencing each other under particular circumstances"—a good description of performances in general.[20] Following Rosenblatt's theory of reading as transaction, the performance paradigm that I am proposing emphasizes active participation, an aspiring by particular readers to a cluster of virtues inherent in a particular textual strategy. We take on, we try out, and we pretend to something that we are not, or not yet. Pretending is necessary, because the embrace between the reader and the text requires impersonation, even a certain *hypocrisy* in the etymological sense of "practicing a character." Just as a flesh-and-blood writer performs to achieve a certain persona or voice and make fictions, so the actual reader performs by "playing a role" to bring a literary work to life. Rosenblatt calls this mode of reading an *aesthetic stance*, as opposed to an information-seeking *efferent stance*. When a performing reader willingly joins a performing author through the offices of a text, they engage in play that is also work: ethical stretching, attitudinal exercise—the adoption of virtues. The concept of performance, influenced by Rosenblatt's application of John Dewey's term *transaction,* is meant to point to this reciprocal process of empathy and adoption.[21] "To call forth a literary work of art," Rosenblatt says, "the reader must first of all permit into the focus of attention not only the public linkages with the words but also the personal associations, feelings, and ideas being lived through during the reading."[22] In other words, when a reader performs a strategy with a situation in mind, a text is brought to (a) life.[23] By affecting one life, a performed textual strategy enters the realm of the political and the historical and begins what we might call a journey of dialogic influence.

If performative reading is the adoption of virtues through the offices of a text, then it is obvious that "common readers" practice performative reading and, when called upon, virtue criticism. Recognizing the personal engagement inherent in such reading experiences is, as Rosenblatt says, "vital not only to the solution of various persistent problems in literary theory but, to put it bluntly, essential to the survival of the reading of literature as an active part of our American culture."[24] Robert Coles records the halting literary theory of "Linda," a student who was reading *My Antonia* and *Silas Marner* in his wife's high school English class and trying to "take the books to heart." What did the teacher mean, Coles asks Linda, "take the books to heart":

> She meant that if you "live" with the book a while ("Try to let the book settle in and live in your heads," she'd tell us), then you'll be part of the story, or it'll be part of you, I'm not sure which. Maybe both. She'll take a dull old novel like *Silas Marner* (no one wants to read it, and you wonder why it's on any high school list), and she'll start in with it, teaching it, and soon you're not in some English town a hundred years ago, with an old hermit and his gold and the girl he's got to take care of, you're here in America, and it's your hometown, and you're thinking about people who take advantage of others, and people who become victims, and how sometimes if you've gotten a raw deal, you turn to money, to hoarding possessions; or maybe you're like that because you're not a very good person, but then something happens in your life, and you change. . . . I don't know how to say what happens when you read a good story: it's not TV and it's not reading the paper. It's not fast: you forget what you've seen, because the next flick has come, and you're looking at it. With a novel, if the teacher holds you back and makes sure you take things slowly and get your head connected to what you're reading, then (how do I say it?) the story becomes yours. No, I don't mean "your story"; I mean you have imagined what those people look like, and how they speak the words in the book, and how they move around, and so you and the writer are in cahoots.

Thus Coles represents, perhaps a little breathlessly for those of us schooled in the hard lessons of theory, Linda's "refreshing and exhilarating . . . moral communion." Somehow, "wondrously," Coles says, "a writer's scrutinizing and suggestive images catch hold of a reader's impressionable, yielding sensibility, and thus they become 'in cahoots.'"[25] It is easy to scoff at the lack of technical language and specialized vocabulary, but I think Rosenblatt would applaud Linda's personal engagement and describe hers as a desirable aesthetic stance. Percy would say she has discovered news. Robert Coles and Jane Coles, like countless other teachers of literature, have accumulated qualitative, empirical evidence over the years that readers from diverse backgrounds can and do learn to feel personally for Silas, to suffer "his isolation, his bad luck, and react with anger at the wrongs done him." Though "the novel inspires in each reader a different series of thoughts, memories, [and] images," though "there are lots of Silas Marners," as Linda says in her testimony, many common readers would concur that taking a book to heart is like practicing a kind of love.[26]

The performance paradigm is meant to capture this dance of emotion, the admiration and affection of being "in cahoots," that may be overshadowed by the mercantile connotations of "transaction." Like other dances of intimacy, the performative reader-writer relationship is marked by access, attentiveness, collaboration, and pleasure in one another's company. But performative reading, like loving, is risky business. The cooperation required, Wadlington says, is *hazarded* cooperation. There are, of course, information-seeking modes of reading that do not know the power to hurt, scientistic approaches that "do not do the thing they most do show." We might characterize these "efferent" stances, adapting Booth's distinction, as modes of *over*standing: one cluster of virtues, rather than embraced, is dominated and controlled by means of emasculating analysis and premature critique. Martha Nussbaum characterizes such analytical overstanding as "retentive and unloving—asking for reasons, questioning and scrutinizing each claim, wresting clarity from the obscure." She bases her apt distinction on the kind of text being read (philosophical or literary) and distinguishes between the stance of the philosopher before a philosophical text and the more vulnerable stance of the engaged reader before a work of literature; but by turning her insight only slightly we can say that when we approach a given text (even a narrative or lyric) philosophically, we tend to become "active, controlling, aiming to leave no flank undefended and no mystery undispelled." In such a mode of reading, Nussbaum suggests, it is "not just emotion that's lacking, although that's part of it. It's also passivity; it's trust, the acceptance of incompleteness."[27] Much of our critical work, it seems to me, refuses to accept the insecurity of such incompleteness. There may be something about writing itself that militates against the openness and unpredictability of dialogue and performance.[28] In any case, contemporary theory seems bedeviled by a totalizing tendency to overstand literary texts, and the results are often predictable celebrations or formulaic critiques that do not bear the marks, the wounds, of performance.

Performative reading, on the other hand, requires exposure and entails insecurity. Many of the best performative readings come, not surprisingly, from imaginative writers themselves: Eudora Welty, John Updike, Alice Walker, Donald Hall, David Lodge, Nadine Gordimer, Nabokov, and many others.[29] Daniel Stern fashions a mode of performative reading in his "twice-told tales," fictions wherein he explores the powers and virtues of Nathaniel Hawthorne, Herman Melville, and Franz Kafka, for instance, in his own narrative idiom.[30] Another public reader whom we can justly celebrate as a virtue critic is Frank Kermode, Stern's friend and colleague. Kermode is an immensely productive academic whose criticism is conversational, tentative, and pluralistic — a feeling- and labor-intensive process of discovery and surprise that occurs in historical time. Despite his status (recently certified by Harold Bloom) as one of the twentieth century's great literary critics, Kermode aspires to a role that might be characterized as "engaged and informed amateur": not a dilettante, certainly, but a prepared, hard-working reader, performing in situ with something important at stake. A consummate professional, Kermode nonetheless remains an outsider who eschews the protective jargon and theoretical closure cultivated by academic insiders.[31] Such readers urge us by the example of their (published) reading performances to remain open to experiences of otherness — experiences that are potentially threatening, disconcerting, and transformative. Thus performative reading is a mode of *under*standing, as Booth describes that stance: an unguarded engagement with another's pattern of beliefs, values, desires, and virtues; as such, it shares some of the hallmarks of love. Ann Beattie's "Learning to Fall" can enlist us, according to Nussbaum, in a performative reading that is just such "a trusting and loving activity." Not only does Beattie's character learn to fall in love, but through a certain mode of reading we learn to fall as well: "We read it suspending skepticism; we allow ourselves to be touched by the text, by the characters as they converse with us over time. We could be wrong, but we allow ourselves to believe."[32] Kermode speaks of "forms of attention" and Nabokov sought to teach his students to read "lovingly, in loving and lingering detail."[33] We use the word *love* for certain forms of attention, and certain readings do require the attentions and exposures of love: to read a book with a lover's vulnerability is to bring a new person into your life.

To summarize by means of (somewhat overstated) dichotomies: A performing reader is open to news; a cognitive interpreter is tracking information. An understanding reader is receptive, engaged, and vulnerable; an overstanding theorist is aloof and in control. Readers are prepared to be challenged, confirmed, gratified, frustrated, threatened, and changed by exposure to others — it happens every day. Theory depends on formulas and abstractions to keep its practitioners aseptic and safe. As Wadlington develops the distinction, "Criticism and pedagogy talk about. Reading *does*."[34] Probably, as with loving, we do not expose ourselves to this kind of engagement on a regular basis; like Mr. W. H. addressed in sonnet 94, we cannot always afford to be unguarded and available. But critics who are interested in the potential ethical effects and virtues of texts will strive to be readers who are susceptible to risks and hurts and who, in the words of Nussbaum, "are humble, open, active yet porous."[35] It is this active susceptibility and availability that mark a virtue-shaping and potentially virtue-shaking performance.

In addition to Wadlington, a number of contemporary theorists have applied the concept of performance to literature, and the notion of performance as a mode of presenting a self is found throughout classical rhetoric, notably in Aristotle's delineation of the rhetor's ethical appeal.[36] Marie Maclean, J. Hillis Miller, and Adam Zachery Newton explicitly conjure with the term, as has Richard Poirier in *The Performing Self*, and the 1995 English Institute collection is entitled *Performativity and Performance*.[37] So the term is alive and well and busy being negotiated and contested, as we say. In general, those who want performance to designate only iconoclasms — e.g., performance art — are less useful for my purposes than social constructionists who acknowledge the presence of stubborn restrictions on the performances of texts and persons. It is this dialectical balance between freedom and constraint, agency and determination, that makes a performance paradigm particularly attractive at the present time; it allows for change without suggesting that our negotiated and fashioned performances are created independently, "out of whole cloth." If reading and writing are performative acts that involve the process of trying on, selecting, and habituating oneself to roles, then, as Booth says, "I can hold a fitting of various 'habits,' to see if they enhance or diminish how I/we appear to myself/ourselves."[38] Wadlington, drawing on Geertz and Bakhtin as well as Burke, makes a bold claim for the ethical significance of performance when he asserts that human beings become capable persons, "and *continue* to become capable persons, by enacting personae."[39] Following Wadlington, we begin to see how a performance paradigm can replace ahistorical essentialism, doctrinaire materialism, and abstract theory with contingency, potentiality, and vulnerability. The paradigm also circumvents the synchronically limited analysis of structuralism and allows for amelioration. The upshot of the model is nothing less than the revival of the possibility of agency and a refiguration of the subject or person.

Socially constructed reality proves rather viscous, to be sure, and performances are scarcely unhampered or "free." Even if culture inscribes the subject within scripts, however, various virtues are continually enacted through particular, real-time performances of those scripts. In other words, persons are diverse and they change. Though working with shared cultural scripts, every performer has his or her personal "materials": body, style, memory, accents. In larger cultural scenes as in the legitimate theater, no two human beings perform the same script in exactly the same way. Complex literary strategies are not templates, and cultural scripts do not dictate the exact tenor of their enaction. A good actor will be able to find various resources in a script and in fact will be forced to make exclusive choices about how to play a particular role with a particular company and for a particular occasion. For example, he can play Lear in the first act as fierce and abusive *or else* wounded and sullen. Similarly, he can play Hamlet as vengeful and calculating *or else* disoriented and mad. The choices are mutually exclusive, and to try to do more—to try to bring out every possible attitude that the texts will allow—leads to confusion in the actor and boredom in the audience. The respective scripts of *Hamlet* and *Lear* are literally the same in each circumstance, but each text is rich enough to support a variety of distinct and coherent performances.[40]

For our purposes, then, a performing person is a being-in-progress, embodied and grounded in a particular time and place with access to a variety of plots, scripts, and roles. "It will be the chief and most difficult business of my life," Booth says in *The Company We Keep*, "to grope my way along dimly lit paths, hoping to build a life-plot that will be in one of the better genres."[41] The paths must not be too dimly lit, however; for performances must be publicly enacted to be recognized and realized. As Wadlington says, the rule for any virtue is "use it or lose it."[42] Attitudes, qualities, and capacities that are used are available for use again. Moreover, they can cross over to other theaters, arenas, areas of life. Using begets familiarity; exercise develops capacity. As in antiquity, the development of virtues (and vices) becomes analogous to the development (or dissipation) of physical abilities. Let us take the performance of what Keats calls negative capability as a simple and brief example: A person who suspends judgment and tolerates complexity in his or her imaginative life enacts the virtue of negative capability and adds it to the repertoire, the satchel of scripts. Having practiced negative capability when engaged as a reader, he or she may be able to access the virtue again when engaged as a parent, employer, spouse, or friend.

Particularly valuable for our purposes, the paradigm provides a ready and accessible means of discussing the ethics of strategies, for we are fortunate in having a familiar, nontechnical, and evocative vocabulary for describing, evaluating, and refining the performance of strategies. Our actions—seen as performed *inter*actions—can be sincere or duplicitous, communitarian or narcissistic, supportive or exploitive, cooperative or coercive, promissory or promiscuous, engaged or abstracted. And these dualities merely evoke, they do not exhaust, the range of virtues that they signify. Such a lively, embodied vocabulary unifies *techné* and *areté* and offers a fresh way to combine the aesthetic, the ethical, and the political. By combining aesthetic with ethical analysis, the performance paradigm attempts to do justice to the tentative and artificial status of literary and cultural strategies. At the same time it brings symbolic strategies and personhood more explicitly together by emphasizing that the construction of a person, like the performance of a poem, is a social act as well as an imaginative act. Since this model (in the tradition of George Herbert Mead) conceives of persons as socially constructed, it sets the stakes of performance very high. Any performance, after all, involves an array of risks. Always there is exposure, vulnerability, stage fright, and performance anxiety because there is the continual possibility of failure and shame. A performer's work is finally a public, social event, apprehended and judged by others; if a performer fails, he or she fails before others—by being misunderstood, rejected, or, worst of all, simply not experienced or acknowledged. The shame and rage of Ellison's Invisible Man spikes like a fever when a performance of his humanity goes unrecognized. So in yet another sense the performance model allows for agency: the agency of audience. If a performance is understood as a gift, a rich metaphor that we will explore in the next chapter, then the auditors can refuse the offered gift by disrupting, abandoning, or just ignoring the performance. The complex strategy we call a person is not there, not real, unless an audience *sees* by engaging, affirming, and, in some sense, loving the performer and the performance.

NOTES

1. Frank Kermode, *Not Entitled* (New York: Farrar, Straus, and Giroux, 1995), p. 196.

2. While it seems clear that narratives play a critical role in the development of passions, affections, and "emotional intelligence," the exact biochemical and neurological

processes still seem mysterious, at least to me. In his best-selling *Emotional Intelligence* (New York: Bantam, 1995), Daniel Goleman includes biochemistry and neurology in his interesting discussion of emotions such as empathy, anger, and fear. Following the work of Joseph LeDoux, Goleman identifies the *amygdala*, an almond-shaped structure above the brain stem, as the seat of all passion and affection (pp. 14–22, 312 nn. 2, 3).

3. Kermode renders such moments elliptically and with appropriate reserve: "A great intimacy, never directly expressed but very secure; the nod or glance is enough to signify the happy solemnity, the shared acceptance of a poem, even of a line of verse." *Not Entitled*, p. 195.

4. Kenneth Burke, "Counterblasts on 'Counter-Statement,'" *New Republic* 69 (9 Dec. 1931), p. 101, quoted by Robert L. Heath in *Realism and Relativism: A Perspective on Kenneth Burke* (Macon, Ga.: Mercer University Press, 1986), p. 3.

5. Mark Leifeste, a child and adolescent psychiatrist, introduced me to the work of Douglas Ingram, a psychoanalyst interested in narrative approaches to clinical practice. "There is freedom in moving freely from one story to another," Ingram says, "from 'What an unhappy person I am,' to 'In this brawling life of mine, I may succeed.' It is in the movement among different, often newly authored stories, that a person finds a revitalized repertoire of feelings, behaviors and points of view." "Story Time: The Narrativist Perspective in Analytic Therapy," *Psychiatric Times*, Apr. 1997, p. 49.

6. J. Hillis Miller, *Tropes, Parables, Performatives: Essays on Twentieth-Century Literature* (Durham: Duke University Press, 1991), pp. viii–ix.

7. Walker Percy, *The Message in the Bottle: How Queer Man Is, How Queer Language Is, and What One Has to Do with the Other* (New York: Farrar, Straus, and Giroux, 1975), p. 123.

8. Ibid., pp. 122, 128.

9. Warwick Wadlington, *Reading Faulknerian Tragedy* (Ithaca: Cornell University Press, 1987), p. 62.

10. Some of the best work of this kind is done by Wolfgang Iser in *The Act of Reading: A Theory of Aesthetic Response* (Baltimore: Johns Hopkins University Press, 1978); Gérard Genette in *Narrative Discourse: An Essay in Method*, trans. Jane E. Lewen (Ithaca: Cornell University Press, 1980); Peter Rabinowitz in *Before Reading: Narrative Conventions and the Politics of Interpretation* (Ithaca: Cornell University Press, 1987); and James Phelan in *Reading People, Reading Plots: Character, Progression, and the Interpretation of Narrative* (Chicago: University of Chicago Press, 1989). Phelan has thoughtfully addressed the question of the subjectivity and agency of readers in "On Effects and Audiences," a subsection of an essay entitled "Present Tense Narration, Mimesis, the Narrative Norm, and the Positioning of the Reader" in *Waiting for the Barbarians: Understanding Narrative*, ed. James Phelan and Peter Rabinowitz (Columbus: Ohio State University Press, 1994), pp. 230–33.

11. Kenneth Burke, *Counter-Statement* (1931; rpt., Berkeley: University of California Press, 1968), p. 91, my emphasis.

12. Frank Kermode, *The Art of Telling* (Cambridge, Mass.: Harvard University Press, 1983), p. 128.

13. Gordon Mills describes "the literary classroom" as a rather special and unusual site or structure that makes possible certain rare and valuable modes of conversation and exchange. See especially "Forced Decisions and the Cultural Role of the Literary Classroom," *Hamlet's Castle: The Study of Literature as a Social Experience* (Austin: University of Texas Press, 1976), pp. 238–48.

14. In *Literature against Philosophy, Plato to Derrida: A Defence of Poetry* (Cambridge: Cambridge University Press, 1995), Mark Edmundson reminds us of the dialogic intention of F. R. Leavis—stated but not always manifest—and his contention that critical observations ought to be understood as including the question, "This is so, isn't it?" (p. 26).

15. Kermode, *The Art of Telling*, pp. 70–71.

16. Just as we do not know *how* information becomes news, we seem unable to predict if, when, or for whom information will become news. The mystery surrounding our use and recuperation of literary texts may point to the benefit of sustaining a compendium of commonly read books; it certainly justifies encouraging the formal and informal *reading* of literature, in the empathic, performative sense discussed in this chapter.

17. Wendy Steiner describes the latent or potential nature of the energy possessed by works of art: "Whatever effect art has, it never has literal control. However much we may give ourselves up to art or be moved by it, we can always withdraw ourselves from it, too, because it is only a virtual experience of power." *The Scandal of Pleasure: Art in an Age of Fundamentalism* (Chicago: University of Chicago Press, 1996), pp. 76–77. I have found it helpful to conceive of the virtual or latent power of a text by using the image of a car at rest on the crest of a hill. The pun is convenient and instructive: a text is a *vehicle*, "an agent of transmission" and "a medium through which something is expressed," as my dictionary puts it. The kinetic energy of the vehicle on the hill waits to be brought into being by a "driver." Before a driver arrives to do those things necessary to put the car into motion, however, the vehicle/text already possesses potential energy by virtue of its mass, placement, structure, "automotive" engineering, and stored fuel.

18. J. Hillis Miller, *The Ethics of Reading: Kant, de Man, Eliot, Trollope, James, and Benjamin* (New York: Columbia University Press, 1987), p. 4.

19. Ibid., pp. 4–5.

20. Louise M. Rosenblatt, *Literature as Exploration*, 5th ed. (New York: Modern Language Association, 1996), p. 292.

21. Rosenblatt borrows Dewey's 1949 distinction between *interaction*, which delineates a situation in which separate, unrelated entities act on one another unilaterally, and *transaction*, "used to designate relationships between reciprocally conditioned elements." Ibid., p. 291. Other narrative and imaginative media such as television, film, and music video may come closer to producing interactions in Dewey's sense. That is, media that require less participation and "translation" may unilaterally influence or transport

their audiences, who may be more passive, independent, and consumerlike than performing readers. However, a strong case could probably be made that an active, reciprocal engagement is necessary for *all* symbolic experiences. In any case, my claims pertain only to readers, for even consumers of Harlequin Romances, reading for diversion and relaxation, must translate the ink patterns on the page into imaginary episodes, however formulaic and predictable.

22. Ibid., p. 292.

23. Ibid., p. 293.

24. Ibid. Gordon Mills calls this personal, participatory experience not *transaction* or *performance* but *semblance*. He notes that many other concepts have been used to suggest "the general experience with which we are concerned," and he compiles a short list of related terms. Mills is right to admit that these terms are "by no means synonymous," but they do point in similar ways to the mysterious process that is here called performance. "Aesthetic emotion" (obviously a close variant of Rosenblatt's "aesthetic stance") is, according to Mills, the most common term. Other noteworthy designations include "alert passiveness" and "disinterested intensity of contemplation" (Roger Fry); "intransitive rapt attention" (Eliseo Vivas); "aesthetic quality" (John Dewey); "psychic insulation" (Morse Peckham); "psychical distance" from the practical world (Edward Bullough); an experience in a "transnatural domain" (Michael Polanyi); "analogue" (Jean-Paul Sartre); and "irrealization" (Martin Heidegger). Often in nontechnical reviews and much literary criticism, Mills says, we find a loose application of terms such as "concrete" or "illusion." *Hamlet's Castle*, p. 15.

25. Robert Coles, *The Call of Stories: Teaching and the Moral Imagination* (Boston: Houghton Mifflin, 1989), pp. 63–64.

26. Ibid., pp. 63–66.

27. Martha Nussbaum, "Love's Knowledge," *Love's Knowledge: Essays on Philosophy and Literature* (New York: Oxford University Press, 1990), p. 282. Nussbaum, a philosopher after all, confesses that she is exaggerating the limitations of philosophy to make a point about reading, knowledge, and loving. Wadlington develops a very similar distinction between a "criticism" that only arrives at interpretation and an active mode of "reading" that "entertains the possibility of modifying the audience's sensibility." *Reading Faulknerian Tragedy*, p. 35. But he, too, finally wants an alliance between theory/criticism/interpretation—Nussbaum's "philosophy"—and a performative mode of reading that is more than merely decoding, unmasking, and making sense.

28. Walter J. Ong first explored the sea change from orality to literacy in *Ramus, Method, and the Decay of Dialogue: From the Art of Discourse to the Art of Reason* (Cambridge, Mass.: Harvard University Press, 1983).

29. Certainly Richard Rorty, especially in his readings of Nabokov and Orwell, practices an impressive, systematic virtue criticism. See *Contingency, Irony, and Solidarity* (Cambridge: Cambridge University Press, 1989). My only (partial) reservation about listing Rorty's work as an exemplum of performative reading derives from its "philosoph-

ical" nature: an emphasis on ideas and an "invulnerable" style—oh, and my own disciplinary bias toward "English."

30. See Daniel Stern, *Twice Told Tales: Stories* (New York: Norton, 1990) and *Twice upon a Time: Stories* (New York: Norton, 1992). If we are willing to see certain fictions as unsystematic virtue criticism, then it would seem that certain translations could also be so classified. I am thinking here of a colleague like Richard Howard, a major poet who has done perhaps fifty significant works of translation, and of Robert Fitzgerald, whose performance of Homer's *Odyssey* makes him arguably one of the better virtue critics of our time.

31. I owe this distinction to my colleague David Mikics, who describes Kermode's career as one that gently but persistently opposes "the habits of institutional safety that make reading a sure thing." "Kermode on the Outside Looking In," *Gulf Coast* 8, no. 2 (1996), p. 96. In his autobiography, *Not Entitled*, Kermode underscores his nonconformist perspective by suggesting that students who have actually written "Petrarchan sonnets, villanelles, sestinas, ballades, and so forth, whatever the merit of their performances, actually understand more about poetry than people who haven't." They are likely to be better readers of poems (in the empathic, participatory sense advocated here) and "will know better why poetry is still important" than those more learned academics who may "care very little about poetry" but excel in the disciplines of "philology, linguistics, [and] history, including the history of ideas." "I am almost convinced," Kermode says, that creative writing "is where the study of literature ought to begin" (pp. 196–97).

32. Nussbaum, "Love's Knowledge," p. 282.

33. Frank Kermode, *Forms of Attention* (Chicago: University of Chicago Press, 1985); Vladimir Nabokov, "Good Readers and Good Writers," in *Lectures on Literature*, ed. Fredson Bowers (New York: Harcourt, 1980), p. 1.

34. Wadlington, *Reading Faulknerian Tragedy*, p. 35, my emphasis.

35. Nussbaum, "Love's Knowledge," p. 282.

36. For Aristotle's definition of *ethos*, or ethical appeal, see his *Rhetoric* and Edward P. J. Corbett, *Classical Rhetoric for the Modern Student*, 2d ed. (New York: Oxford University Press, 1971), p. 93. Corbett also provides a short history of classical and modern rhetoric (pp. 594–630).

37. Marie Maclean, *Narrative as Performance: The Baudelairean Experiment* (New York: Routledge, 1988); Miller, *Tropes, Parables, Performatives*; Adam Zachery Newton, *Narrative Ethics* (Cambridge, Mass.: Harvard University Press, 1995); Richard Poirier, *The Performing Self: Compositions and Decompositions in the Languages of Contemporary Life* (New York: Oxford University Press, 1971); Andrew Parker and Eve Kosofsky Sedgwick, eds., *Performativity and Performance* (New York: Routledge, 1995); Erving Goffman, Clifford Geertz, and Victor Turner provide additional insights about the concept of performance that can be adapted for the ethical analysis of literature.

38. Wayne Booth, *The Company We Keep: An Ethics of Fiction* (Berkeley: University of California Press, 1988), p. 268.

39. Wadlington, *Reading Faulknerian Tragedy*, p. 29.

40. I owe this insight to James Gale, former actor-director in residence at the Honors College at the University of Houston.

41. Booth, *The Company We Keep*, p. 268.

42. Wadlington, *Reading Faulknerian Tragedy*, p. 33.

3

Reading, Empathy, Alienation

Virtue criticism and the performance paradigm can be understood as attempts to revisit Coleridge's notion of the reader's "willing suspension of disbelief." But his apt formulation, with its helpful emphasis on the participatory and volitional nature of aesthetic experience, needs to be amplified slightly and pushed beyond the realm of credence and cognition. Each performative reading requires the voluntary suspension of certain qualities in addition to disbelief: those that would prevent us from valuing, desiring, seeing, and feeling what the implied author wants us to value, desire, see, and feel. We might well denote this mode of engagement as empathic. The term *empathy*, common in psychology and in the teaching of speech, theater, and performance, has been widely applied to other practices to suggest a relationship of identification and reciprocity between participants.[1] In a discussion of the theatrical performance of literary texts, Ronald J. Pelias divides the empathic process into three discrete steps—recognition, convergence, and adoption: "Recognition calls for . . . a process of careful scrutiny of the other's perspective. Convergence necessitates identification, adjusting oneself to the world of the other. Adoption demands that the other's unique qualities be incorporated, felt, taken on as one's own." Applied to the practice of criticism, each performative reading, like other modes of performance, would require what Pelias calls a "fresh empathic response" based on recognition, convergence, and adoption.[2] Hence, when a reader performs a work with competence and empathy, an adoptive and affiliative relationship comes into being. The literary critic Peter Rabinowitz describes this empathic encounter as "engaged reading," which he contrasts with "close reading," a mode of interpretative exploitation comparable to Booth's overstanding.[3] A virtue criticism based on this kind of performative reading is, like Burke's "new rhetoric" of identification, a mode of response that stresses willed "consubstantiality" and bilateral cooperation rather than "artsy" persuasion and unilateral interpretation. "In acting *together*," Burke says, distinguishing that cooperative process from acting *on*, "men have common sensations, concepts, images, ideas, attitudes that make them *consubstantial*."[4] The performance paradigm is also like Burke's rhetoric of identification in being "partially dreamlike" and "idealistic"; the notion of identification through performance minimizes "real differences and divisions."[5] This optimistic and therefore vulnerable idealism is related, I would argue, to what Paul Ricoeur calls "a second naiveté." It requires a "second faith," a kind of "postcritical faith," that subverts the hermeneutics of suspicion and makes a trusting performance possible. Borrowing Ricoeur's claim for phenomenological interpretation, we can say that performance is the "instrument of hearing, of recollection, of restoration of meaning" that makes identification possible.[6]

When we read in a performative way, we co-construct and exchange with the writer an imaginative gift: the performance itself, the text brought to life. Through and during the performance, we adopt similar passions, beliefs, and values; we perceive similar images and feel similar desires. There is a little epiphany: we "see." Through such adoptions, trust and confidence momentarily overcome suspicion, opposition, and resistance. Alienation gives way to affiliation and a relationship develops. Like other affiliations, this relationship is supported by voluntary identifications and the exchange of cultural goods. Where there is relationship, virtues are practiced; where virtues are practiced, there is relationship. Virtue criticism attempts to evaluate in ethical terms the characters and attitudes temporarily adopted by readers and writers.

Let us not shrink from stating the obvious: these characters or ethoi, the clusters of virtues practiced in literary relationships, vary. Otherwise, virtue criticism would not be a timeless entertainment in its many ordinary guises (the full range of conversation and gossip about "characters" and "plots") and a principal and perennial mode of education in its more professional manifestations. Despite these obvious variations, however, something like an act of imaginative identification, adoption, or coduction would seem inseparable from empathic, performative reading. The relationship between reader and writer, Booth says, can be seen as analogous to Heidegger's *Sorge*, "a caring about the other, about *l'autrui*, about alterity." Where there is trust and confidence, a reader can attend to the author's various characters and to his or her own various characters "in a way that finally allows a kind of free-flow in both directions, annihilating all anxiety about boundaries."[7] In perverse moods, we may briefly adopt the virtues of an implied author who is manifestly incompetent, lazy, or dishonest. But a sustained relationship with such a one is as difficult as carrying on a conversation with the proverbial Cretan liar. Egoistic and fragile creatures that we are, we look for partners who are persons of coherence and integrity. "In literature as in practical life," as Bernard Harrison says, "we know others, and for that matter ourselves, by the coherence, or lack of it, obtaining between how we present our acts and utterances and what the content of those acts and utterances actually consists in."[8] If performing a text empathically is, in the Nussbaum-Beattie phrase, "learning to fall," if it is allowing another cluster of virtues *inside*, we need to feel confident that we will not be intentionally harmed or deceived. Each shared page, paragraph, and period requires a covenant, a keeping faith with another. Thus performative reading is a "practice" (in the Aristotelian sense elaborated by Alasdair MacIntyre in *After Virtue*) that can be recognized by the following characteristics or virtues: assent, cooperation, adherence, attentiveness, receptivity, creativity, participation, solidarity, benevolence, trust, and, of special importance to us, pleasure in keeping company.[9] As co-performers, readers and writers accept what Wadlington calls the "invitations of language . . . the give and take of reciprocation."[10] They adopt a common practice by willingly submitting to shared standards, agreeing to pursue collaborative ends, and cultivating common virtues. Figures of speech, literary devices, parts of the plot, and language itself become little covenants through which the writer and the audience fashion a relationship. This serenade of artful language leads to moments of pleasure and concern, of "company," the time and "times" friends have with one another. As temporal moment rather than atemporal code, language becomes time and time becomes shared. To sum up: Symbolic communication presumes relationship; relationship consists of interpenetrating and reciprocating auditions and performances; performances enact virtues.

Questions about the quality of these literary relationships, some of which can justly be called friendships, are central to the ethical evaluation of fictions. Booth suggests that some implied authors (or "reading friends") lead us to more in-tense, more generous, and more reciprocal activities. Their stories and poems mold our imaginations into patterns of longing and fulfillment that teach us to desire higher desires. These literary offerings show that life can be worthwhile, as good friendships do, and their makers call us to join not "a coterie, a saved remnant looking down on the fools, slobs, and knaves," but a congregation, a confederation of those willing to perform the text's particular virtues. To other persons enacted by literary performances, we may wish to say good-bye and good riddance. Booth suggests that we test our friendships with literary persons by asking: "'Is the offered friendship in fact what it claims to be?' Is the pattern of life this would-be friend offers in fact one that two friends will pursue togeth-er? Or is this the offer of a sadist to a presumed masochist? Or of a seducer to the seduced? Of a rapist to his victim? Of the exploiter to the exploited? Is this a friend, a lover, a parent, a prophet, a crony, a co-conspirator, an *agent provo-cateur*, a tyrant, a therapist, a sycophant, a suck-up? Or perhaps a sidekick, a lackey, a vandal, a bloodsucker, a blackmailer?"[11] Booth's overarching thesis is that readers and writers develop their characters by spending time with one another. *Hypokrisis* in its simplest form is simply a *reply*, the acting of a part in accord with one's immediate cohorts and surroundings—an insight that may revise our sense of Eliot's provocative "hypocrite lecteur." As readers, as actors, we are continually replying to our environment, responding to the company we keep. Thus, as Booth says, we cannot and should not attempt to avoid the virtue of hypocrisy. Of course, as a pragmatic matter we do well to ask whether our reading, our acting, and our company constitute "hypocrisy upward" or "hypocrisy downward."[12]

Burke identifies the company we keep as fellow actors, and the theatrical metaphor again proves helpful by leading us to Constantin Stanislavski's thoughts on the ethics of the theater in *Building a Character*. There he makes an impassioned plea for trust and reciprocity. One actor, Stanislavski says, is not alone in producing the play; he or she is not solely responsible for construct-ing the scene in which his or her character can perform its characteristics. "In such an enterprise," he says, "one works for all and all for one. There must be mutual responsibility." He is adamant that in theatrical performances, "who-ever betrays that trust must be condemned as a traitor."[13] And indeed, at cru-cial moments in our relationships, whether textual or flesh-and-blood, we do look for persons who will be true to us. We want benevolent and trustworthy friends who will encourage our pursuit of worthy interests and our collabora-tive development of better virtues. Since relational scenes are required for the

enaction of virtues, we need dialogic partners who will join the scenes in which
our dramas of identity are played out. No one person can construct the strategic background within which virtues can be made, modified, and maintained.
For (a) play we need (a) company. We need other persons to acknowledge, resist, challenge, invigorate, and refresh the enaction of our various selves in place
and time. We need partners to audition performances. We need friends to be
ourselves.

Like flesh-and-blood friends, literary strategies help constitute the scenes and
suggest the narratives that make our actions meaningful and our virtues possible. In language reminiscent of Burke's "new rhetoric," Wallace Stevens explains
the poet's relation to his readers as one of identification and consubstantiality:
"I think that his function is to make his imagination theirs and that he fulfills
himself only as he sees his imagination become the light in the minds of others. His role, in short, is to help people to live their lives."[14] Similar words of
identification, intimacy, and friendship have been applied to empathic reading experiences for centuries, such that thinking of books as friends eventually
became a commonplace—now a neglected commonplace, according to Booth.
He suggests the value of modifying the "books as friends" figure—too anthropomorphic—in order to think of stories and poems as *gifts* of a friend. Booth
uses a number of valences to discuss the ethical characteristics of such gifts:
intensity, generosity, reciprocity, coherence, otherness, breadth, concentration.
The literary gift is more or less generous, the time spent with it more or less
intense, more or less reciprocity is allowed for, it offers more or less otherness
to our habitual imaginative patterns, and so on. Accepting a literary gift, an act
of performative co-creation according to our paradigm, reconfigures the relationship between giver and receiver and effects a transfer of goods that have
ethical content by virtue of having symbolic significance. As Virgil Nemoianu
says, the donor "inevitably creates something new in the receiver." Furthermore,
by agreeing or condescending to perform for the receiver, to "gift-make" with
him, the donor inevitably creates something new in herself. In the process of
gifting, as in the performing of stories, a new trait, virtue, or property is (temporarily) called into being. When ethical goods pass between performers and
auditors, a symbol- and value-laden transaction alters the stasis of their imaginations, and both giver and receiver enact clusters of virtues in the process of
exchanging ethical property. There is an adoption, the performance of an
identification, and a new "grey zone of ethical ownership is thus created." This
"grey zone" is the enlivened poem, the enacted bond between donor and recipient, performer and audience, writer and reader. A gift is, in Nemoianu's

words, "an act of sacrifice that is at the same time an act of creation." In language that evokes Stevens, he recognizes in gifts "the creative contribution to another personality." We can adopt these vocabularies of identification, intimacy, and friendship to describe empathic, performative reading as a value transfer that occurs "when material and moral value, donor and recipient, are mated through and in the creative decision of giving."[15]

Most of us yearn for the wholeness of friendships that do not calculate cost or demand equivalence, the exhilarating experience of belonging that comes when benefits flow freely without resistance, resentment, or suspicion. As Nemoianu says, we want friendships to be marked by "a kind of wholeness illustrated by a relation of innocent and unhampered giving and receiving—a frictionless exchange of values."[16] Yet resistance, opposition, and fatigue are inevitably generated when values are exchanged: alienation is the by-product of performance. Neither Lewis Hyde, whom Booth quotes approvingly, nor Booth himself explicitly acknowledges that gifting is wounding, that transmission and exchange generate alienation as well as identification. Nemoianu, while concurring with Booth and Hyde that the concept of gift-making is helpful for understanding the experience of reading and the ethics of fictions, sees alienation as a necessary "auxiliary required by the transfer of values."[17] In other words, alienation is an experience collateral with symbol-mongering. Every story implies an anti-story, every transaction creates a residue of resistance, every benefit incurs a cost. For every cultural action there is a cultural reaction, though not necessarily equal and opposite. Burke, not surprisingly, has anticipated my point in a handy formulation: If motion, then action. If action, then drama. If drama, then victimage. I am simply underlining the obvious: if victimage, then alienation.[18]

If Nemoianu is right about cultural exchange and the transfer of values, then an unblinking consideration of alienation is essential for virtue criticism, a practice that attempts to assess such transfers. Any ethics of reading that ignores alienation will be superficial and fatuous. It will fall victim, moreover, to the totalizing tendency of theory, the "systematicity" of systems. For, like other discursive systems, virtue criticisms categorize, "rubricize," and control. Theories, even untidy, pluralistic theories, will tend to homogenize the resistant, the recalcitrant, and the disruptive. Thus a virtue criticism that overlooks alienation will miss what Nemoianu calls *the secondary*, a potent source of "relaxation and defeat" and a perennial source of renewal and refreshment. The secondary, he says, "finds artistic expression through disorder, relaxation, and idleness. Negligence, tolerance, and procrastination are its allies, lack of energy and purpose provide it with strength." The function of the secondary is to play "the adjunct role of grumbling, objecting, qualifying, keeping open doors, envisioning possibilities, and nursing dreams."[19] *Alienism* and *alienistic* are terms I use to refer to those verbal and symbolic strategies, impulses, and performances that "dance" the secondary. Like Nemoianu's term, *alienism* can associate fictions not only with persuasive, theoretical, and imaginative discourse but also with recurrent nonliterary motives, attitudes, and strategies for living: antinomianism, physical or emotional withdrawal (hermitism and various modes of "dropping out"), some patterns of psychotropic substance use ("tripping out"), some "appearances of resistance" (long hair? no hair? tattoos? body piercing?), some instances of passive aggression, anorexia, depression, borderline personality disorder, and other performances described in the *DSM-IV*.[20]

If the exchange of values creates fatigue and resistance, then culture becomes the breeding ground of alienation. All communication is strategic, hence tendentious, hence manipulative. As Burke says, "a way of seeing is also a way of not seeing."[21] A way of saying is also a way of not saying. We assent, we submit, we understand, but at some level, often visceral and unconscious, alienation begins to grow. Alienistic artists are hyperconscious of the hurt that comes when virtues are performed and adopted, and they yearn for a respite from participation in cultural processes. Were it possible, they might well prefer injecting virtues into an audience by means of a safer procedure, less messy and "septic" than art. As writers, however, they are performers; they cooperate, engage, and participate. As an other-directed act of symbolization, the uncoerced making of imaginative literature reconfigures all the players within a matrix of empathy and affiliation. Somehow, despite the inescapable compromise—the mediation and "sophistication" of their virtues—skittish players continue to show up with their gifts of performance, their stories, plays, and poems.

What Nemoianu says about the reciprocal relationships created through gifting is true of other mutual performances: gifts and alienation can be bound together "with tolerable comfort." Exchanging performative gifts and experiencing alienation are not mutually exclusive categories or even wholly distinct temporal moments. Unlike Booth and Hyde, Nemoianu acknowledges that alienation eventually erodes the "glorious flowering" associated with gift-making. Yet alienation is not a simple antagonist of performance; it is a function, even a functionary, of performance. The frustrations of alienation *are* the wounds of performance; frustration, alienation, and agon are therefore inseparable from the exchange of values and the transfer of gifts. If we recognize frustration as what Blackmur calls "a *fundamental* condition of life," then alienation will be understood as "fate, tragedy, damnation, the Cross, the other side of every infatuation."[22] At the same time, the performance of alienation refigures fate through representation, recognizes comedy within tragedy, transcends damnation, and celebrates the distance that makes "falling" in love possible and, if one would live with passion and vulnerability, necessary.

A good instance of the complementarity of empathy and antagonism can be found in the Beatles—the group was an emblem of mutual performance as well as alienation when it exploded on the cultural scene in the 1960s. The band endured its own well-documented conflicts and divisions, and the residue, perhaps, of one such episode is recorded on *The Beatles Anthology 1*, released in 1995. John Lennon utters something directive off-microphone, to which Paul McCartney replies, ". . . and if I don't, well it's just too bad, isn't it?" The group tries to get started on a song, but break it off, and there is another indecipherable comment from John. The tension has broken, though, and now Paul's exasperated retort is a fond "You're daft, Jack." On Paul's count, "the boys" begin a sustained version of "Eight Days a Week."[23] Thus do performances spring from the seedbed of alienation.

Hearing such a studio session and intimately knowing the familiar "perfect harmony" that results, we suddenly realize that alienation is subject to its own processes, that it shares in temporality, becoming, and change. It is true that every empathic performance, like every gift, sows the seeds of its own alienation in the evanescent process of joining two or more identities. But the corollary is also true: every alienation traces, records, and certifies a relationship as it prepares for a fresh and reconfigured one. Alienation is the seedbed of adoption, the dissolution that makes fresh affiliations possible, the absence that makes presence imminent.[24] Edwin Dobb, writing about the threshold experience of kissing, says that emotional separations and physical partings have taught him that romantic love "endures only if it continually transforms itself, that transformation is achieved through the rapture of arrival, and that there is no arrival without a departure of one sort or another. . . . Romance is rhythm. We exhale so as to inhale again. We withdraw so as to approach anew."[25] If these rather homely examples of alienation yielding to identification and performance can be extrapolated to the realm of cultural criticism, then the historicist slogan "subversion contained" could be more hopefully configured as "alienation alienated." Thus, Nemoianu says, an "optimist" could construe alienation as "a mere tool" that assists with the ethical transfer inherent in gift-making and, I would add, in performance generally.[26] Conceived linearly, we have the temporal alternation of alienation and performance (with its virtues of empathy and adoption), one cooperatively making way and giving way to the other. But perhaps a third dimension and an ancient metaphor borrowed from the craft of weaving provide a still better model: alienation and performance, we can say, make up the warp and woof of human situations.

If alienation is an implement or medium of performance, a tool that makes possible the transfer of values, then somehow it should be incorporated into the work of any ethical criticism that attempts to describe the transfer of values. Positing agencies and strategies behind performances is one means of incorporating alienation into a theory of ethical criticism. The observer who discerns a *performed* alienation recognizes that an insight, intuition, pattern, epiphany, or impulse has been shared with an instigating agent, a cluster of virtues. This agent-with-virtues or person—made and maintained through performance—encourages us to identify with the alienation that she has known and, in the case of literary works, painstakingly figured forth. Her crafted performance of alienation is her offered gift and carries with it the implicit promise that the time we spend will be worth our while. Maybe the instigating author set out to threaten and estrange, to create danger and perplexity, but by condescending to join and identify with us, she arms us to confront perplexity, to face threats, and to take risks.[27] Her performance may be troublesome, but trouble, alienation itself, can be a gift when it is shared. Thus the value and virtue of an alienistic utterance is likely to be found not in its message, meaning, or interpretation but in the traces of agency in performance itself: if someone is there, alienation can be endured. Trouble is tolerable with company. "The terrors of alienation are lessened," Nemoianu says, "by a long, hard look at the gift of gift-making"—that is, by scrutinizing the implications of performance.[28]

From the standpoint of a recalcitrant alienism, however, *any* empathic adoption is suspect; any merging with another cluster of virtues, any compromise with the world's debased sensorium, diverts and distracts the anticultural impulse.[29] Thus the performance paradigm cannot help but deny strategies of alienation, collected here under the rubric of alienism, the full potency of their disorder, idleness, and resistance. A teacher or scholar who casts an alienistic performance as the enaction of a strategy has already begun a process of domestication. Alienation's power to hurt gets harnessed by "clerks" for "education" or another recognized good, and for this domestication society often compensates them. Hence it is only fair to admit that one of our central concepts, "strategy of alienation," cancels itself out: to conceive of alienation as "a strategy among the strategies" is to dilute and "de-alienate" it. Burke himself regretted that his term *strategy* sounded too rigid, earnest, and premeditated. (But "method" is no better, he says, because it suggests an overly "methodical" process.)[30]

Here again Burke reveals his suspicion of "artsy," manipulative rhetoric and indulges a life-long alienistic impulse to resist the constraints of systems. The alienistic motive, a motive sympathetic to Burke and elaborated throughout his ouvre, might well be defined as a suspicion of the methodical and the systematic, a resistance to strategies, theories, and abstractions as such. Since critical readings invariably discover strategies behind even the most alienistic performances, a natural competition develops between alienism and criticism, with its consolidations, comparisons, and categories.[31] A plausible virtue criticism will acknowledge the competition and face up to its hard lesson: even as reader and writer affiliate through performance, the persuasive and manipulative dimension of their affiliation sows the seeds of a fresh alienation. One might say: the more persuasive and artsy the performance, the more imminent the boredom; the more manipulative the strategy, the more extreme the alienation.

In a curious and heartening way, though, the looming imminence of alienation makes virtue criticism (and other strategies of identification) necessary and important. As Burke says, "If men were wholly and truly of one substance, absolute communication would be of man's very essence"; and, we might add, virtue criticism would be pointless. In other words, if art worked "automatically" and unerringly for everybody, then evaluative visitations and revisitations would not be necessary. But such is not the case in our postlapsarian world: the identifications of virtue criticism need to be "affirmed with earnestness" precisely because there *is* alienation. If we are to be honest and searching in our ethical criticism, we must "confront the implications of *division*," as Burke says, even as we celebrate the powers of identification, adoption, and empathy. "One need not scrutinize the concept of 'identification' very sharply to see, implied in it at every turn, its ironic counterpart: division."[32] We have need of performances—critical as well as poetic—precisely because alienation is the beast in the cultural jungle, always lurking, always *springing*. I shall return to this paradox—that artful identifications both recreate and re-create alienation—in the chapters that follow and most explicitly in the conclusion. It is one of the principal assumptions of *Power to Hurt* and meant to be implicit throughout.

NOTES

1. For applications of empathy to the practice of medicine, see *The Empathic Practitioner: Empathy, Gender, and Medicine*, ed. Ellen Singer More and Maureen A. Milligan (New Brunswick: Rutgers University Press, 1994), and *Empathy and the Practice of*

Medicine: Beyond Pills and the Scalpel, ed. Howard M. Spiro (New Haven: Yale University Press, 1993).

2. Ronald J. Pelias, *Performance Studies: The Interpretation of Aesthetic Texts* (New York: St. Martin's Press, 1992), p. 96.

3. Peter Rabinowitz, "Against Close Reading," in *Pedagogy Is Politics: Literary Theory and Critical Teaching*, ed. Maria-Regina Kecht (Urbana: University of Illinois Press, 1992), pp. 230–43.

4. Kenneth Burke, *A Rhetoric of Motives* (Berkeley: University of California Press, 1969), p. 21.

5. Kenneth Burke, "Interaction: Dramatism," in *The International Encyclopedia of the Social Sciences* (New York: Macmillan, 1968), vol. 7, p. 450.

6. Paul Ricoeur, *Freud and Philosophy: An Essay on Interpretation*, trans. Denis Savage (New Haven: Yale University Press, 1972), p. 28.

7. Wayne Booth, *The Company We Keep: An Ethics of Fiction* (Berkeley: University of California Press, 1988), p. 266.

8. Bernard Harrison, "Rhetoric and the Self," *Inconvenient Fictions: Literature and the Limits of Theory* (New Haven: Yale University Press, 1991), p. 214.

9. Opposing qualities such as suspicion, resistance, and alienation may also arise, but a "touching," some point or moment of engagement and communion, is logically required for a performance. Alasdair MacIntyre underscores the importance of relationship to a practice such as the practice of writing/reading. "Every practice," he says, "requires a certain kind of relationship between those who participate in it." *After Virtue: A Study in Moral Theory*, 2d ed. (Notre Dame: University of Notre Dame Press, 1984), p. 191. In a widely anthologized essay entitled "Voice as Summons for Belief," Walter Ong makes a similar point about the promissory nature of the relationship inherent in the practice of publication: all writers, Ong says, are implicitly claiming to be offering something "worth our while." *Literature and Belief*, ed. M. H. Abrams (New York: Columbia University Press, 1958), pp. 80–105.

10. Warwick Wadlington, *Reading Faulknerian Tragedy* (Ithaca: Cornell University Press, 1987), p. 62.

11. Wayne Booth, "'The Way I Loved George Eliot': Friendship with Books, a Neglected Critical Metaphor," *Kenyon Review*, n.s. 2 (Spring 1980), pp. 26–27.

12. Booth's approach to ethical criticism (following Aristotle) posits the self as a confederation of selves or a cluster of virtues that persists over time but remains in dynamic flux. Thus one's character is never set but always under construction and subject to change, for good or ill. Transformations of the self, then, require a pretending or trying on of new virtues, new characters, until they become comfortable, established, and habitual. In street slang, "you fake it 'til you make it."

13. Constantin Stanislavski, *Building a Character*, trans. Elizabeth Reynolds Hapgood (New York: Theatre Art Books, 1949), p. 249.

14. Wallace Stevens, "The Noble Rider and the Sound of Words," *The Necessary Angel: Essays on Reality and the Imagination* (New York: Vintage, 1965), p. 29.

15. Virgil Nemoianu, A *Theory of the Secondary: Literature, Progress, and Reaction* (Baltimore: Johns Hopkins University Press, 1989), pp. 140, 141, 144.

16. Ibid., p. 151.

17. Ibid.

18. Burke, "Interaction: Dramatism," p. 450.

19. Nemoianu, A *Theory of the Secondary*, pp. 202, 203.

20. *Diagnostic and Statistical Manual of Mental Disorders*, 4th ed. (Washington, D.C.: American Psychiatric Association, 1994). The *DSM-IV* is the manual used in the diagnosis of psychological pathologies.

21. Kenneth Burke, *Language as Symbolic Action: Essays on Life, Literature, and Method* (Berkeley: University of California Press, 1966), p. 49.

22. R. P. Blackmur, "The Great Grasp of Unreason," *Anni Mirabiles, 1921–1925: Reason in the Madness of Letters* (Washington, D.C.: Library of Congress, 1956), p. 6.

23. "Eight Days a Week (sequence)," "Eight Days a Week (complete)," *The Beatles Anthology 1*, Apple Corps Ltd./EMI Records Ltd., 1995, CDP 7243-8-34445-2-6.

24. By now it should be clear that the virtues shared through mutual performances are ephemeral. The temporal performative moment is one of concord and solidarity, but the moment does not last, the identification deteriorates, and (some degree of) distance and alienation return. Alienation, then, heralds empathic mutual performance just as empathic performance is followed by relative estrangement.

25. Edwin Dobb, "A Kiss Is Still a Kiss," *Harper's*, Feb. 1996, p. 43. Burke's notion of rhetoric as identification suggests a similar alternation of alienation and love. After defining communication as "a generalized form of love" (p. 37), Burke defines love as "a communion of *estranged* entities." A *Rhetoric of Motives*, p. 177, my emphasis. "There can be courtship," he says, "only insofar as there is division. Hence only through interference could one court continually" (p. 271).

26. Nemoianu, A *Theory of the Secondary*, p. 151.

27. As Burke says, literary strategies can arm us "to confront perplexities and risks." *The Philosophy of Literary Form*, 2d ed. (Berkeley: University of California Press, 1967), p. 297.

28. Nemoianu, A *Theory of the Secondary*, p. 151.

29. *The Theory-Death of the Avant-Garde* (Bloomington: Indiana University Press, 1991) is Paul Mann's exploration of how theory inevitably leads to the circumscription and "death" of avant-gardes.

30. Burke, *The Philosophy of Literary Form*, p. 60.

31. It can be argued that there is a competition between any literary performance and any critical discourse seeking to explain or categorize it. Indeed, Nemoianu argues that literature by its nature is a "secondary" as opposed to a "principal" practice, and as such it evinces what I am calling alienistic virtues: playfulness, indirection, negligence, privacy, unconcern, license, humor, amusement, tolerance, independence, irony.

32. Burke, A *Rhetoric of Motives*, pp. 22, 23.

4

Virtue Criticism as Cultural Criticism

Why virtue *criticism?* Why a critical as opposed to a theoretical approach? It is indeed comforting to be identified with theory if theory is defined as that which stands against and scrutinizes the manifest exploitations, injustices, and mendacities of culture. Culture and theory, however, need not be poised in opposition. Following Nemoianu, we may recognize theory as one of the progressive consolidations of culture, a function of what he calls "the principal." Certainly insofar as theory is comprehensive, inclusive, and efficient ("totalizing"), it functions to reduce and simplify. Yet the critical practice we need at the present time, according to observers Barbara Herrnstein Smith and Mark Edmundson, is contingent evaluation, a mode of analysis and assessment that does not rest on authoritarian claims, a priori determinations, or totalizing theory.[1] In *The World, the Text, and the Critic,* Edward Said calls for a "secular criticism" *between* culture and theory. Virtue criticism is a mode of evaluation, "secular" in Said's special sense of that word, that recognizes the importance of aesthetic experience and insofar as possible privileges it.[2] By conceiving of aesthetic experience as temporal and performative, virtue criticism resists the predictable reductions of theory and hopefully checks for cultural gaps or seams.

Performances of alienation hold special promise for discovering such openings or *poria*. That we can discern and evaluate alienistic motives (irony, anarchy, license, disorder, asceticism, opacity, hermeticism, rebellion, irrationality, inferiority, immorality, inefficiency, and bad taste, among others) suggests that somehow the impulse to dispose of such motives is not completely successful. After cultural power does its consolidating work, something important is left over. Market capitalism, marxism, Leninism, democratic socialism, positivism, logocentrism, ethnocentrism, patriarchy—whatever their various mechanisms for domination and control, monolithic ideologies have not been able to purge alienation and its performance from the culture.

Theory, located by Said on the other "side" of criticism from culture, is typically more efficient. Insofar as it is elegant, abstract, and tidy, theory is more consistent and coherent than any worldly culture could ever be. Matthew Arnold predicted that literature would eventually replace religion, but he surely never suspected that literary theory could become as indignant, demanding, and pietistic as religion. When he said that "most of what now passes with us for religion and philosophy will be replaced by poetry," surely he was not anticipating the reduction of "poetry" to deductive, formulaic approaches, what Edmundson calls "streamlined theoretical models."[3] It does seem that when theory begins to resemble a positivist, illiberal religion, it neglects its alienistic promise. Virtue criticism, as we have seen, is bedeviled by its own totalizing impulses. As a responsive, impressionistic cultural criticism, however, it is willing to muddle through with inefficient, pragmatic, localized, situated inquiry. Part of the critic's job, as Said says, is "to find resistances to theory, to open it up toward historical reality, toward society, toward human needs and interests."[4]

My hope, then, is that virtue criticism will contribute to the practice of a more liberal cultural criticism with its own alienistic motive: resisting the efficient consolidations of theory. We would certainly want neither to avoid theory, even if that were possible, nor to replace one set of reductions with our own. Nonetheless, it is possible to grant, as Smith does, the contributions of theoretical systems without ignoring "the experiences and activities that constitute the valuing and evaluating of literature." These experiences are "important components of the system," Smith says, "what keeps the system 'alive'—active and continuous rather than still and stagnant."[5] In an effort to value and evaluate, we assume that performed literary works become engenderers, makers, and

refiners of selves. Maker-author, made-poem, and maker-reader are constitut-
ed and constituting characters. Together they, *we*, construct a relationship and
"have a time." When they are not being performed, poems and stories persist
as quiescent strategies, scripts that can be called on, revisited, and incorporated into life campaigns. Thus stories and poems, enlivened through performance, have the power to enable and empower, to disable and exclude, to constitute, dissolve, and reconstitute persons and communities.

The performance paradigm is itself, of course, an instance of theorizing, but
the observations and insights made possible by conceiving of poems and stories as participatory moments in the lives of persons are implicitly qualified and
stubbornly contingent. By trapping meanings in the present, the concept of
performance inevitably opposes the systematicity of theoretical endeavors. The
very topicality and temporality of performances, according to Benjamin Bennet, makes them "stick in the craw" of totalizing theory.[6] At any given moment
we inevitably read, not as omniscient or ideal readers, but "from *some* perspective," as Smith says. This perspective, though limited, is real; the moment of
performance, though transient, is real; and "our experience of the value of a
work"—coterminous with our performance of it—"*is* its value." Furthermore,
the performance that gives us access to the value of a work also allows us to
"estimate its probable value for others," because the perspectives and performances of others, "the total economy of *their* existence," may, as Smith says,
"be quite similar to that of our own."[7] Other persons being other, one responsible method of testing for similarities would seem to be offering coductive critical performances, grouped and given context by descriptive ethical categories,
here called strategies. Using assumptions such as these, virtue criticism may be
able to contribute to the valuing and evaluating of literature while resisting
theory's powerful but potentially deleterious efficiencies.

In principle, there is no limit to the number of strategies that we can identify,
label, and cobble together into ethos groups: the process is comparative and ongoing. If we think of strategies as clusters of performances, then we need (and
therefore construct) a different strategy for every significant character or ethos
we encounter—every person and every book we come to know and care about.
This is not to say that we have no need of theories; we do need principles of
classification and comparison, for we do not find it useful or wise to see each
strategic ethos as *sui generis*. As beings who try to keep our weather eye open and
continually ask, "What sorts of things about what sorts of people do I need to
notice?" we find it helpful to develop names for strategies that share similar
motives, qualities, and virtues. We evaluate the dean and the president as, say,

"visionary," though they differ in so many other ways. Some faculty colleagues are clever, others bitter, still others detached. This friend is sought out for unquestioning support, another for a critical "reality check."[8] Burke suggests that literary works could also be classified according to their capacities for certain existential functions: lamenting losses, affirming allegiances, exposing contradictions, meeting threats, reconciling conflicts, replenishing resources, expiating guilt, revealing secrets, celebrating heroics, renouncing corruption, justifying the ways of God,[9] and so on. If we concern ourselves with twentieth-century literature, there will certainly be a large and multiplicitous category consisting of strategies that evoke alienation.

The larger and more recognizable a group of strategies becomes, the more likely that a consolidating and unifying theory will be developed to explain, organize, and define the cluster. What we call our "sites of negotiation" or "sites of struggle" are often rhetorical battles over how to name and define a cluster of strategies, or over whether to include or exclude a particular strategy (or a particular performance of a strategy) in an already-defined category. *Feminism* and *postmodernism* are contemporary examples of such contested terms or categories since both have been applied to a vast number of disparate strategies and performances. And whether this or that strategy or performance *is* feminist or postmodernist matters to a great many people. Summing up, then: Performances are topical and temporal moments that imitate (or figure forth) strategies. Similar strategies can be grouped together according to their properties, motives, and virtues. Strategy groups that have economic, social, political, or cultural importance eventually become recognized as ethos groups—the "isms" behind the "asms" of performance.

Of the many possible ethos groups within the broad category "strategies of alienation," I identify and discuss only three isms in detail: gnosticism, aestheticism, and parabolism. Gnostic strategies have occurred at many different times and places, but for a term to be most useful as a name for a group of strategies, it ought not be applied too freely. Thus it would seem that *gnostic* ought to describe movements, stances, texts, and ethoi that share significant characteristics with (but not necessarily a direct intellectual lineage from) historical Gnosticism.[10] Historical Gnosticism made alienation a spiritual virtue by asserting the existence of a pristine spark of divinity in those who felt an unappeasable aversion for the Greco-Roman world. By analogy, modern gnosticisms also claim spiritual superiority and express their alienation from the dominant cultural patterns of our time. Aestheticism has also been an important strategy of alienation in the twentieth century, one that was inherited and adapted from some of the Romantics and Aesthetes of the nineteenth. *Aestheticism*, as the term is used here, denotes a sequestering of the purely literary or aesthetic imagination from practical activity and mundane mental processes. Performers of aestheticist strategies attempt to extricate at least part of consciousness, the aesthetic "part," from the aggrandizing and victimizing activities of culture. The third kind of strategy examined here is the parabolic. Parabolic strategies pursue the goals of authenticity as discussed by Charles Taylor and Lionel Trilling before him.[11] Because they are formally provocative and thematically oppositional, such strategies are often called *postmodernist*; but *parabolic* is useful because it explicitly points to the corrosive and corrective motives of parable—subverting myths and disrupting foundational narratives.[12] Samuel Beckett's *Krapp's Last Tape*, for example, works as parable by undermining Krapp's unreflective faith in reality and his conventional expectation of improvement and progress. Krapp's attempt to locate himself in the world, to narrate himself by means of archived affiliations and reconstituted memories, is debunked by Beckett's parable. Thus parabolic strategies, like other strategies of alienation, alert us to the delusions inherent in modes of representation and remind us of the Derridean violence inherent in social bonds and congregations.

These three groups of strategies can be united under the rubric *alienism* because they implicitly or explicitly repudiate affiliation, allegiance, and congregation.[13] Other strategies of alienation could be explored, of course, but gnostic, aesthetic, and parabolic strategies have been prevalent, some would argue predominant, in twentieth-century canons. I have tried to describe these ethos groups in part 2 to suggest a context for the literary performances evaluated in part 3: Eliot's *The Waste Land*, Nabokov's *Pale Fire*, and Barthelme's *Snow White*. These and the alienistic works that are discussed in less detail exemplify a perennial, compelling, and tonic response to the delusions of culture. Alienated and alienating writers have often discovered the negative by constructing various strategies of opposition and renunciation. Recognizing the costs exacted by cultures, they remain suspicious of dominant psychological, aesthetic, and historical patterns and processes; their alienistic works imply that remaining apart is better than pandering to a repressive interpretive community. These "alienists" take the measure of our madness, sometimes by calling it forth. They help restore (natural? genetic? God-given?) resistance and immunity using mysterious and frequently dangerous homeopathic techniques. Most importantly, they do not abandon us; they show up to play, participate, and respond. They strategize and perform. They "go on."

This "going on" is critical when we turn to evaluation. It is important to look not only at *what* is said but also at *how*—and to keep in mind that there *is* saying. For it is by means of their formal qualities that strategies of alienation support action and proffer themselves for use. Formally they become ethical; through their workings they become news. In *Narrative Ethics*, Adam Zachery Newton ably develops the importance of the connection between intersubjective relationship, and ethics, and "Saying." He sees "narrative structure and form as ethical relation," and by emphasizing "Saying over and above Said," properly identifies the virtues of particular performances as the source of ethics in narrative. "Narrative is performance or act," Newton says, "purgative, as in Turgenev's 'The Country Doctor,' malignant, as in Camus's *La chute*, historically recuperative, as in A. B. Yehoshua's *Mr. Mani*, erotic and redemptive, as in *The Thousand and One Nights*, obsessive and coercive, as in Coleridge's *Rime of the Ancient Mariner*."[14] Like the tellers of these diverse tales and their authors, we employ plot, character, thought, music, and spectacle (or, rather, their homespun equivalents) in ways analogous to Aristotle's "maker" to bring our personal strategies to performance. As pragmatic evaluators, what we want to know, in life as in art, is how the elements of story are brought to performance and for what apparent purpose—in the service of what immediate and general strategies.

This union of technique and telos, implicit in the performance paradigm, leads to critical work that includes examples. Like formal and analytical approaches, virtue criticism emphasizes particularity and close attention to texts; its critical judgments are supported by readings—textual evidence and synthesizing warrants. The readings that make up part 3, however, should not be mistaken for New Critical formalism. The positivist metaphors of formalism are easily distinguished from the contingent, coductive metaphors of virtue criticism. Instead of deciphering, we are engaged in auditioning; instead of "digging for the truth" we are "trying on for size"; instead of interpreting a text, we are mutually performing with a friend.[15] The work of the book is not the definition, description, or elaboration of theory but the practice of virtue criticism through contingent valuations. The performance paradigm should remind us that the other *is* other, that as readers and writers, storytellers and story evaluators, we are adopting affiliations, pretending to identifications, aspiring to virtues. If this approach succeeds, the ethical placements and evaluations should seem contingent, unguarded, and vulnerable as well as analytical, responsible, and plausible. The worth of virtue criticism and the performance paradigm derives as much from an engaged, coductive style of inquiry as from the resulting evaluations. Practicing that dialogic method and constructing those usable judgments are the related aims of this book.

NOTES

1. See Barbara Herrnstein Smith's *Contingencies of Value: Alternative Perspectives for Critical Theory* (Cambridge, Mass.: Harvard University Press, 1988). Mark Edmundson explores the ancient antipathy between poetry and philosophy, literature and theory, in "Prologue: An Ancient Quarrel," *Literature against Philosophy, Plato to Derrida: A Defence of Poetry* (Cambridge: Cambridge University Press, 1995), pp. 1–29. In a *Harper's* essay adapted from this prologue, Edmundson suggests that "with the onset of theory, the critical contingency is fast disappearing. There are now plenty of poets and no end of philosopher/theorists, but art's public defenders, writers whose first allegiance is to the aesthetic experiences that have shaped them, are becoming ever more rare." "Theory's Battle against the Poets," *Harper's*, Aug. 1995, p. 28.

2. Edward Said, *The World, the Text, and the Critic* (Cambridge, Mass.: Harvard University Press, 1983), pp. 1–30, 178–225.

3. Matthew Arnold, "The Study of Poetry," in *Essays: English and American*, ed. Charles W. Eliot (New York: P. F. Colier and Son, 1910), pp. 65–66. Edmundson, "Theory's Battle against the Poets," p. 30.

4. Said, *The World, the Text, and the Critic*, p. 242.

5. Smith, *Contingencies of Value*, p. 16.

6. Benjamin Bennet, "Performance and the Exposure of Hermeneutics," *Theatre Journal* 44, no. 4 (1992), pp. 440, 431.

7. Smith, *Contingencies of Value*, p. 16.

8. Some friends, usually not many, will know and trust each other so well and so completely that they can "say anything," as the 1989 film title has it. But we know that even those we love the most have lapses and imperfections and sometimes disappoint us, as we do them.

9. This classification already exists, of course; we call such works "theodicies."

10. In this chapter and throughout the book, *Gnosticism* is used to indicate the historical Gnostic movements of the first centuries of the Common Era; *gnosticism* is used as a heuristic term for an attitude or strategy that can be employed to explain the motives of fictional characters and authors as well as flesh-and-blood human beings.

11. See Charles Taylor, *The Ethics of Authenticity* (Cambridge, Mass.: Harvard University Press, 1992), and Lionel Trilling, *Sincerity and Authenticity* (Cambridge, Mass.: Harvard University Press, 1972). In early drafts I used *authenticism* to designate this group of strategies.

12. The subversive function of parables is described by contemporary scholars and theorists of religion such as John Dominic Crossan, Sallie McFague, Robert Funk, and the influential participants in Funk's Jesus seminar on New Testament parables. "Open" parables are sometimes distinguished from "closed" parables, though most scholars simply use the term *parable* or *parabolic* to designate literary, political, or theological openness or subversiveness. A colleague wondered whether *parabolic*, in addition to the

demythologizing functions of parable, might also refer to the curve made when the appropriating gaze glances off a resisting text. And, while the analytic geometry may not be precise, both usages speak to a particular sort of "displacement." Thus sonnet 94, seen as a parabolic strategy, does bend back the embracing curve of interpretation. For a somewhat fanciful comparison of comets, parabolas, and parables, see J. Hillis Miller, *Tropes, Parables, Performatives: Essays on Twentieth-Century Literature* (Durham: Duke University Press, 1991), pp. 135–36.

13. See W. F. Monroe, "'Jabbing the Sore Spot': Alienism and Its Cultural Role," *Georgia Review* 34, no. 1 (1980), pp. 15–37, for a more thorough discussion of this heuristic term.

14. Adam Zachery Newton, *Narrative Ethics* (Cambridge, Mass.: Harvard University Press, 1995), p. 7. Newton is interested in "the ethical consequences of narrating story and fictionalizing person, and the reciprocal claims binding teller, listener, witness, and reader in that process." As a virtue critic who shares some affinities with Wadlington, Nussbaum, and Booth, he suggests that "one faces a text as one might face a person, having to confront claims raised by that very immediacy, an immediacy of contact, not of meaning" (p. 11). In his criticism, however, Newton looks primarily to Stanley Cavell, Emmanuel Levinas, and Mikhail Bakhtin and sets his "project at quite a distance from the work of Wayne Booth and Martha Nussbaum." "Humanism with a (Post)Social Face: A Reply to Daniel Schwarz," *Narrative* 5, no. 2 (1997), p. 210. See also Daniel R. Schwarz, "Performative Saying and the Ethics of Reading: Adam Zachery Newton's *Narrative Ethics*," *Narrative* 5, no. 2 (1997), pp. 188–206.

15. For a more thorough elaboration of the distinction between analyzing texts and performing (with) persons, see William Monroe, "Performing Persons: A Locus of Connection for Medicine and Literature," in *The Body and the Text: Comparative Essays in Literature and Medicine*, ed. Bruce Clarke and Wendell Aycock (Lubbock: Texas Tech University Press, 1990), pp. 25–40, and William Monroe, Warren Holleman, and Marsha Holleman, "Is There a Person in This Case?" *Literature and Medicine* 11, no. 1 (1992), pp. 45–63.

It's good when your conscience receives big wounds. . . .
I think we ought to read only the kind of books that wound
and stab us. If the book we're reading doesn't wake us up with
a blow on the head, what are we reading it for? We need the
books that affect us like a disaster, that grieve us deeply, like
the death of someone we loved more than ourselves, like being
banished into forests far from everyone, like a suicide. A book
must be the axe for the frozen sea inside us.
    Franz Kafka to Oskar Pollak, 27 January 1904

Depending on others, as we all do, the language of "yes" is our
native tongue. The language of refusal, the music of courage,
the poetry of "no"—they're all foreign languages; hard to learn.
    Daniel Stern, "Bartleby the Scrivener by Herman Melville"

PART 2
Strategies of Alienation

The wounded surgeon plies the steel
That questions the distempered part;
Beneath the bleeding hands we feel
The sharp compassion of the healer's art.
   T. S. Eliot, "East Coker"

--⟨— **5**

Necessary Troublemakers

A few years ago a friend, excited about this project, was rebuffed by a more skeptical colleague: "Alienation? What's new about alienation?" Well, nothing and everything. Words come in and out of fashion, and for a long time *subversion, resistance, otherness,* rather than *alienation,* have been in the air. In any case, we do seem to feel the special allure of alienation, to possess what Thomas Mann calls a "sympathy with the abyss."[1] And Franz Kafka's parables of alterity bear, as W. H. Auden says, "the same kind of relation to our age that Dante, Shakespeare, and Goethe bore to theirs."[2] Within theory and criticism, countless books and articles celebrate alienation, though the words used are more likely to be *marginality* or *oppositionist.* We might even speculate that most influential writers of theory and criticism implicitly cast themselves as alienated, isolated, perhaps even endangered resisters of hegemonic forces. Their strategy, like mine, is an attempt to partake of the incorrigible newness, the inexhaustible freshness, of alienation.

On the other hand, there is nothing new about alienation. Paul Zweig finds strains of intransigent resistance throughout Western cultures. He places Jean-

Jacques Rousseau, Søren Kierkegaard, Herman Melville, Charles-Pierre Baudelaire, Stéphane Mallarmé, Paul Valéry, and Friedrich Nietzsche in the subversive tradition, joining there the historical Gnostics, the Manicheans, the medieval cult of the Free Spirit, and countless orthodox and unorthodox religious
mystics. Zweig argues that the affirmation of the self at the expense of the body
politic may constitute not a response to specific historical conditions but rather "a traditional refusal to accept, not only *these* conditions, but any conditions
whatsoever."[3] In *Sacred Discontent*, an analogous study focusing on scriptural
rather than secular literature, Herbert Schneidau documents the persistence
of what he calls "Yahwism." In "In Praise of Alienation," the gateway chapter
of Schneidau's study, he uses the Hebrew Bible, the New Testament, and other canonical writings to show that an enduring strategy of alienation remains
firmly ensconced *within* the Judeo-Christian tradition.[4] As a cultural historian,
Nemoianu is less concerned about citing particular texts than Zweig and
Schneidau are, but his claim is similar to theirs. He believes that literature, by
its very nature, is beneficially subversive of the inertial and exclusive forces of
"the principal," his synonym for the pitiless consolidations of history. If an unblinking consideration of alienation is essential for a cogent and plausible virtue criticism, then it would seem that virtue critics are indeed fortunate to have
strategies of alienation readily available in every historical period.

Manifestly varied as well as ubiquitous, strategies of alienation often share
hallmarks and etiologies. Alienistic patterns of response and compensation are
sometimes fashioned in resistance to the rapid and sanguine advance of one
civilization and sometimes out of frustration with the oppressive stasis of another;
yet motives and even imagery recur. Prison imagery, for example, can be found
throughout Western traditions. Gibbon describes the homogeneity of the late
Roman Empire, the Pax Romana, as a prison, vast yet confining and airless.
Fredric Jameson reminds us that it was Plato himself who recorded the most
famous and persistent story of the world as prison chamber: the "Myth of the
Cave" in book 7 of *The Republic*.[5] In the cave or chamber, Socrates says, are
"men who have been *prisoners* there since they were children, their legs and
necks being so fastened that they can only look straight ahead of them and cannot turn their heads." They know nothing "of themselves or their fellows save
the shadows thrown by the fire upon the wall of the cave opposite."[6]

The Myth of the Cave tells us that what we know with our culturally mediated tools of perception and analysis is not the ground of knowledge; what we
experience is not reality itself, but something foisted upon us by our collective
symbolic system. Even Platonic metaphysics, rivaled only by René Descartes's

dualism as the alleged source of our logocentric cultural and political ills, implies that the best way to live is to escape the prison-house of culture. More proximate to us, the prevalence of prison images in nineteenth-century literature is noted by Lionel Trilling, who suggests that writers began "to think of the prison not as a political instrument merely but as the ineluctable condition of life in society." William Wordsworth, Matthew Arnold, and Charles Dickens, according to Trilling, anticipate Freud's view of the human mind as its own punitive confinement once the social impress has been applied.[7] The use of *prison* to describe the characteristically human situation can be found in divergent sources within various civilizations; its prevalence suggests that a certain attitude toward the world—that it is a vast confinement, an enormous, stifling corruption—is a recurrent strategic response to social arrangement.

Confining prisons and deceptive caves imply that there is something else, something better, *not here*. Thus the very expression of alienation implies the existence of a transcendent sphere. Alienation makes no sense and has no force without the possibility of transcendence. As we will see in the following chapters, this sphere may take the form of a secret metaphysical cosmos, a sequestered bower of aesthetic sufficiency, or an incompletely revealed prophecy of disruption. As Zweig suggests, the very presence of an alienated persona on the scene becomes evidence of resistance, an incipient performance with political implications. But the alienistic performance may also have metaphysical implications: it implicitly condemns what is while intimating the superiority of an unseen realm beyond the ken of society and the *res publica*.[8] Strategies of alienation, according to Trilling, include a dream of places or conditions above and beyond the manifest culture that "establishes its prisons in the family life, in the professions, in the image of respectability, in the ideas of faith and duty, in . . . the very language itself."[9] That we are trapped within the linguistic-symbolic or some other overarching system is a conviction espoused by Platonists and neoplatonists, gnostics and Manicheans, Freudians and Lacanians, Derrideans and Foucauldians.[10] Freedom from life—from one's culture, one's language, one's own mind—this is the dream of alienation, and it is never far to seek in human experience.

Perhaps subversive dreams and transcendent impulses are never more effectively domesticated and contained than in museums. Here art's cultural packaging, so oppressive to the ironical and the alienated, is pervasive—and, since "beneficial," that much more difficult to circumvent. In an often cited episode of *The Last Gentleman*, Walker Percy dramatizes the deadening effects of well-meaning cultural structures and bureaucratic systems. Will Barrett, ever the keen, ironical observer, notes that "happy people were worse off in their happiness in museums than anywhere else." In the great museums, the items on display, each representing a "particle of culture," smother the substance and spark of art, artist, and viewer:

> the air was thick as mustard gas with ravenous particles which were stealing the substance from painting and viewer alike. . . . Let everything be done properly: let one stand at the correct distance from a Velázquez, let the Velázquez be correctly lighted, set the painting and viewer down in a warm dry museum. Now here comes a citizen who has the good fortune to be able to enjoy a cultural facility. There is the painting which has been bought at great expense and exhibited in the museum so that millions can see it. What is wrong with that? Something, said the engineer, shivering and sweating behind a pillar. For the paintings were encrusted with a public secretion. The harder one looked, the more invisible the paintings became.[11]

It is this encrustation, a *presentation* experienced as domesticating and eviscerating, that the alienistic impulse desires to overcome. In our time that impulse, frustrated at the very moment of performance and gratification, has led to ever more outrageous manifestations, to ever more recondite expressions, and, eventually, to withdrawal and to silence.

Certainly the twentieth century supplies an ample bibliography of canonical examples of alienistic strategies, including first and most notably those texts associated with modernism. The texts of Joseph Conrad, Henry James, James Joyce, T. S. Eliot, Ezra Pound, Gertrude Stein, Virginia Woolf, Franz Kafka, and Samuel Beckett scrutinize and often challenge the comforts of traditional identifications. Modernism, as a strategy of alienation from modernity, alerts us to the arbitrariness of society's "arrangements," heightens our sense of sacrifice, and awakens us to the costs of seeing ourselves and our world in one way and not another. At this juncture, it may be necessary to remind ourselves that modernism and modernity are not best understood as cooperative partners. In fact, the complexity of the relationship between the artistic modes that we identify as modernist and the forces, processes, and practices of modernity has inspired the creation of a journal, *MODERNISM/modernity*. In the same corrective vein, Kimberly Benston points to the conflict between modernity, which he associates with the epistemological certainties of Descartes, Immanuel Kant, and the Enlightenment, and modernism, a subversive stance that opposes those dominant certainties. "Modernism," he writes (in a *PMLA* section devoted to performance), "refers to cultural practices produced self-consciously through struggle against modernity's conceptual regime." Some modernist strategies and practices are outright revolts "against modernity's sway"; others avoid positivist certainties with more complexity and ambivalence. In any case, Benston says, modernism is a cluster of oppositional strategies that often includes elements of suspicion and hostility toward the dominant cultures of modernity.[12]

Benston's observation is supported by points made by Irving Howe in the late 1960s. In "The Idea of the Modern" Howe expresses what was then a widely held understanding among cultural critics: that *modern writing* or *modern art* were intertwined if not synonymous with *opposition*. To the modern writer, Howe says, artistic expression requires the explicit renunciation of morality, which seems blatantly "counterfeit; taste, a genteel indulgence; tradition, a wearisome fetter. It becomes a condition of being a writer that he rebel . . . against the received ways of doing the writer's work."[13] Thus even narrative itself, the force and momentum of "and then, and then," — what Kermode calls the *tick-tock* of plot[14] — would need to be broken so that rebellion and renunciation could manifest themselves in form as well as theme. The world is not worth remaking: by now, as Howe says, it is seen "as hopelessly recalcitrant and alien." The modernist mode, he says, is marked by a polemical, unyielding rage against the prevailing culture.[15]

As early as World War II, Erich Auerbach was developing his conviction that Joyce, Woolf, and others who have come to be known as giants of modernism were engaged primarily in strategies of alienation. *Ulysses, To the Lighthouse,* and other multiple-consciousness novels are often "confusing," "hazy," and "hostile." "We not infrequently find a turning away from the practical will to live," Auerbach says, "or delight in portraying it under its most brutal forms. There is hatred of culture and civilization, brought out by means of the subtlest stylistic devices which culture and civilization have developed, and often a radical and fanatical urge to destroy."[16] We do well to remember that the best and most discerning contemporary readers understood modernism's project as cultural subversion rather than construction.

Anti. Opposition. Against. Such terms point toward the method, purpose, and theme of postmodernism as well. Postmodernists arguably differ from modernists in the development of a more acute sense of the cost of *any* position, even a strategy pitting the artistic imagination of modernism against the certainties and institutions of modernity. Like some earlier alienistic strategies, some postmodernist writing seems not to be against anything in particular. Its texts assiduously avoid preference or evaluation as such. Insofar as they can, some postmodernist writers practice a mode against all modes, a voice, if such a thing is possible, without a statement. The table of contents for Philip Stevick's postmodern anthology *Anti-Story* effectively demarcates the suspicions of so-called postmodernist writers and the cultural categories that they renounce:

AGAINST MIMESIS
AGAINST REALITY
AGAINST EVENT
AGAINST SUBJECT
AGAINST THE MIDDLE RANGE OF EXPERIENCE
AGAINST ANALYSIS
AGAINST MEANING
AGAINST SCALE.[17]

This scatter-shot mode of resistance is not, however, limited to postmodernism. Trilling—who is, like Auerbach, dubious of the alienistic turn in culture—notes that we would have trouble naming "any great writer of the modern period whose work has not in some way, and usually in a passionate and explicit way," pursued and elaborated the "standing quarrel" between the self and culture. There is scarcely any major literary figure, he says, "who has not expressed the bitterness of his discontent with civilization, who has not said that the self made greater legitimate demands than *any* culture could hope to satisfy."[18]

One distinguished cultural critic who unreservedly praises such strategies of alienation is Ihab Hassan. In "The New Gnosticism: Speculations on an Aspect of the Postmodern Mind," Hassan discerns in those he identifies as postmodern a "universal consciousness," a passion for mystical, "im-mediate" experience that functions as the source "of imagination and change in our time."[19] Admitting that his statement needs qualifying, Hassan nonetheless generalizes in a useful way about modern literature: "From the great modernists—Valéry, Proust, Rilke, Kafka, Joyce, Yeats, Pound, Eliot, Stevens, etc.—to the enigmatic postmodernists—Beckett, Borges, Genet, Butor, Cortazar, Barth, etc.—the tendency of literature has been to escape itself, to subvert or transcend its forms, to re-imagine imagination; and, as it were, to create a state of unmediated literary awareness."[20] *Escape, subvert, transcend, unmediated*—after a quarter century these remain contested terms that compel attention and focus theoretical discourse.

In the remainder of his list of representative authors Hassan states the alienistic qualities of particular authors with more specificity:

the playful "ultimacy" of John Barth's *Chimera*; the entropic indeterminacy of Thomas Pynchon's *The Crying of Lot 49*; the pop or "dreck" surrealism of Donald

Barthelme's *City Life*; the oneiric death-denying abandon of Robert Coover's *The Universal Baseball Association*; the epistemological introversion of Rudolph Wurlitzer's *Flats*; the self-reflexive exuberance of Raymond Federman's *Double or Nothing* and its typographic laughter; and the regenerative narrative blanks of Ronald Sukenick's *Out*.[21]

Hassan acknowledges that "these fictions are distinct, and their postmodern authors even more so," but he suggests that these authors, with William Burroughs, share something crucial: "a complex desire to dissolve the world." It is not that Pynchon and Barthelme and Federman all use cultural symbols, or what Hassan calls "signs of the earth," in the same way or for the same purposes. Some alienistic writers, for example, banish the hazards of the real world by creating alternative horrors that seem even more threatening; some try to banish boredom by reinventing or re-presenting it. For Hassan the value of such textual solvents, as we might call them, and the function that unites them is a capacity to "abolish the terror, dreariness, and hazards of given things by FANTASY."[22] By "*given* things," I take Hassan to mean the patterns of culture experienced as deadening, the matrixes of imprisonment suffered by an alienistic sensibility trapped in a disappointing world. Through FANTASY—the capitals suggest something unconventional, perhaps transcendent—his alienistic writers remain in the game, reconstructing "an absurd or decaying or parodic or private" world that is, after all, part of a social symbolic system.[23]

Hassan borrows the term *gnostic* to describe his motley crew of resisters, and I will try to put the term to good use in the next chapter. *Alienism*, however, is intended as a broader consolidating term. *Gnostic* is valuable for designating a particular kind of strategy, attitude, or motive, but its connotations are finally too passive to do justice to aggressively oppositional works and too spiritual and apocalyptic to describe others. *Alienistic* seems a better heuristic term because it suggests a common rhetorical purpose enacted within various ethical, social, and political contexts. It helps us see more readily some cultural functions that are shared by diverse literary texts and other verbal and nonverbal strategies. The term is also flexible enough to suggest the effect of symbolic *in*action, the theoretical terminus of mere noise or unpunctuated silence. But this is only a theoretical terminus, for actual alienistic works, if only because they are *works*, cannot dispense entirely with rhetorical functions or social identifications. They embody the recognition, in Wadlington's words, that "something must be said in a certain way in order for anything to get said at all"—and even "for something *not* to get said."[24] Symbolic renunciations of the world must be couched in the language of the world. "The words of the poet are not puppets," Burke says, "but acts. They are a function of him, and he is a function of them. They are a function of society, and he is a function of society."[25]

Burke's work helps to explain why there will always be exclusions, costs, unhappy by-products, and septic side effects of cultural practice. Patterns, languages, affirmations, and institutions are examples of "terministic screens," and by screening they "let in" but "keep out," delimiting what can be apprehended and appreciated. Burke notes that André Gide's awareness of the costs of any cultural vocabulary leads him to distrust symbolic action per se: "the carrying out of one possibility . . . necessarily restricts other possibilities."[26] It is a formal necessity, as James Kastely explains Burke's position, that "language generates property, empire, and division. Injustice did not just happen . . . but was logically entailed by the nature of language, which requires difference or division as a condition for its possibility." Thus restrictive and exploitive "hardenings" cannot be avoided: they derive from the hierarchical nature of language itself. Injustice and empire are "not only a result of a moral or political failure" but also "an inevitable outcome of the operation of language."[27] Wadlington, deeply influenced by Burke, explains how strategies generate exclusions: "Every statement pays its price, in a progression of narrowing possibilities and widening exclusions. . . . Every statement precludes in its duration and form some other thing that might have been said. In the largest sense, only one thing can be said at a time, no matter how polyphonic the utterance; the idea's specific formulation, sound, and rhythm delimit other possibilities for what comes next."[28] Utterance of any kind has a punitive dimension. Any performance, any practice, creates what we may call the *exclusion problem*. Wadlington encourages us to see that the problem goes beyond literary texts and genres to a more comprehensive terministic screen: "the thickened and extended statement, the total interwoven system of communications, called a culture."[29]

Even unsophisticated audiences are implicitly aware of the mendacities of culture, the conspicuous and covert deceits, conceits, and myths that are and have been used as devices of order. Modernist and postmodernist writers typically recognize that all symbolic and political actions have a punitive dimension and a sacrificial aspect. The repression implicit in any affirmation, no matter how general and inclusive; the privileges and preferences hidden in every nomenclature, no matter how conscientious and encompassing; the hierarchy supported by any culture, no matter how enlightened and cosmopolitan—the twentieth century and its cultural performers have made us painfully aware of the costs of symbolic strategies. This suspicion, and often renunciation, of the twentieth-century world—with its exploitation, war, mechanization, conspicuous consumption, and pervasive mendacity—has been compelling. What man or woman of sensitivity and conscience would not be *against* such a world and opposed to the cultural forms and genres that support and take sustenance, however indirect, from that world? We might well look in desperate hope to strategies of alienation.

But where would we look for them? Though rarely acknowledged by critics of "Eurocentrism" and traditional canons, there are many strategies within the tradition that expose the lies and victimage inherent in Western cultures. Such alienistic works have, moreover, proven psychologically compelling and aesthetically successful with twentieth-century audiences. For instance, we would not stand for a cheaply affirmative, cockle-warming *King Lear;* in that sense Jan Kott is quite right to cast an alienistic Shakespeare as our contemporary.[30] We seem to need and seek out works that take up the task that Kafka said had been laid upon us: discovering the negative. That alienistic strategies—imaginative, critical, and theoretical—command attention and admiration seems obvious. The evidence of their paradoxically "successful reception" is everywhere. Since 1910 or so we have set aside for marginal and resisting voices special recognition; there has been a continual exposure of the costs of our cultural arrangements. My hunch is that, as beneficiaries of these cultural arrangements, those of us who are ensconced as makers and interpreters of culture sense that there is much of which to be ashamed. Two related benefits of strategies of alienation for us are, first, a recognition of the negativities of the milieu in which we thrive, and, second, an imaginative or symbolic discarding of shame-producing cultural advantages. "Life-affirming" literature offers few benefits for a privileged audience engorged and sated with the efficient functionings of culture. The special benefit of alienism for virtue criticism lies in its capacity to touch us precisely at those moments when we are most bogged down in familiar myths, static patterns, and "uplifting" cultural performances. Thus, as we have seen, alienistic works can be plausibly imaged as gifts.

There is often a trick to these gifts, however, because they come from an unpredictable, disconcerting friend who in many ways resembles a Trickster. The alienistic Trickster may bring gracious offerings, but her dazzling public performances and inscrutable intentions remain troubling. Wadlington explains the Trickster's ambiguous fascination and seductive, culture-shattering role: "Whether he is seen, according to social and historical circumstances, as demiurge, culture hero, savior-god, devil, shaman, or comic rogue, the Trickster

has a profound fascination, abrogating as he does in his tricks and self-decep-
tions all restrictions, rules, and taboos, manipulating the untouchable, and freely
tapping the unchecked powers of the unconscious or the afterworld by means
of illusion and metamorphosis."[31] The author of an alienistic work is a kind of
trickster figure. He or she sees things differently, hearkens to a secret voice or
daimon, and maintains a mysterious connection to an alien otherworld. In
countless social, political, and historical situations, such disconcerting trouble
and resistance to the ways of the world has proven culturally tonic, and its literary analogues rightly compel attention and esteem.

Just as there is a trick to the giving, there is a trick to the receiving. The trick
is to accept the Trickster's gift of alienation without succumbing to it. The gift
of alienation is an awareness of the presence of plague and a recognition that
we are and have always been plague bearers. By participating in the machinations of culture, we are part of the hurtful game played by Camus's power elite,
"the men who wear the red robes," "the most eminent of the plague stricken."[32]
And if alienistic artists cannot be free of a complicity with culture, certainly the
political, economic, administrative, and commercial "players" are much more
deeply implicated, smug as they must surely be and feeling stupidly at home.
But some of the nobles have accepted the Trickster's gift. Some of them do not
feel at home; they are not as "noble" and smug as we conveniently presume.
Rather, they have become painfully aware of the hurtful power of culture and
the part they play in its ugliness. Some of them, in fact, are able to persist in
publicly validated labor only because their acute sense of alienation enables
them in some paradoxical way to go on. Listen, for instance, as George F. Kennan—"one of the most remarkable Americans of the twentieth-century," according to the *Atlantic*, "a Pulitzer Prize–winning author of rare literary gifts, a brilliant diplomatic historian, a former ambassador to Yugoslavia and the Soviet
Union," and "The Last Wise Man"[33]—describes graduation day at a large
American university:

> May 8, 1977
> Sunday morning in a wretched motel, waiting for the commencement ceremo-
> nies. The motel barricaded like a fortress against the fresh air and sunshine of the
> spring morning. Not a window open. Everything locked up tight, the air-condition-
> ers roaring incessantly. Unventilated corridors, smelling of stale tobacco. An over-
> crowded cafeteria, with sloppy service. And through the sealed-up windows, a scene
> of asphalted desolation such as only the American developer, given his head, can
> produce: a Ford dealer's enormous headquarters, lying amid its parking lots like
> an island in a sea; warehouses; factory chimneys; tall buildings in the distance; a

bank, empty, still, and similarly barricaded by vast empty parking lots; sloping sides
of turnpike elevations; but not a tree, not a pedestrian, not a sign of actual life
except, here and there, a moving car, its occupant likewise walled off against nature in his own tiny, lonely, air-conditioned world. Not a touch of community; not
a touch of sociability. Only the endless whirring and roaring of the air-condition-
ers, the wild wasting of energy, the ubiquitous television set, the massive bundle
of advertising pulp that masquerades under the name of a Sunday newspaper. All
unnatural; all experience vicarious; all activity passive and uncreative. And this
wasteland extending, like a desert, miles and miles in every direction. A fine end
of the world we have created in the American city.[34]

As a disaffected poet Eliot may utilize subtler stylistic devices to express his
grouse against the "Unreal City"; but even *The Waste Land* scarcely commu-
nicates a darker vision of the modern polis than this short articulation of alienation. My point in introducing a statesman and diplomat (who is also an author and intellectual) is to suggest that Kennan may serve as a plausible model
for the alienistic performer. He continues to practice, to produce, and to work
on behalf of his civilization, despite an acute awareness that it is largely a wasteland at the "end of the world." Maybe he was able to sustain his varied professional and personal life by means of just such private and personal expressions
of renunciation and alienation. "Men and women *figure* their dreadful situation," Richard Brodhead says of twentieth-century writers, "and, by figuring it,
resist it."[35] In Camus's novel, it is Dr. Rieux who lives to fight on against terror
by *playing his part*. Unlike Tarrou, whose purity and sharp insistence on de-
marcations eventually destroy him, alienistic performers understand that they
are "unable to be saints"; they knowingly, if reluctantly, spread the ravaging
disease known as culture. Their knowledge leads them into trouble but, significantly, not into victimhood: by their powers of figuration they respond as agents,
becoming troublemakers, trouble-performers. The more generous and able
among them refuse to "bow down to pestilences" and, despite the rapacious
processes, institutions, and habituations they observe and even preserve, they
"strive their utmost to be healers."[36]

The potentially immunizing, antiviral action of alienistic literature has been
remarked by a number of commentators. Modern alienistic art may, in the words
of William Barrett, open "our eyes to the rejected elements of existence" and
redeem us "from the brute march of power."[37] Or, as Malcolm Bradbury says,
alienism may play a constructive cultural role by "shattering false visions and
blind delights."[38] Burke discerns a cultural utility in Gide and other disruptive
performers, extolling the irony, novelty, experimentalism, vacillation, and

conflict they practice and celebrate.[39] Strategies of alienation can have, as Ellen Pifer says *Pale Fire* does, a "liberating effect on the reader" and can lead, in the words of Jonathan Culler, "to that questioning of the self and ordinary social modes that has always been the result of the greatest literature."[40] Indeed, a world of perfect adjustment, universal solidarity, and unadulterated identification really would constitute the end of history.

While the ambassador and the jurist are compromised by their deeds, the alienistic artist is compromised by poetics. By using artifice and rhetoric to engage the imagination of readers, alienistic strategists implicate their performances in the very culture that they so eloquently renounce. The performer who still speaks to his or her community is a maker of that community—hence implicated in the goods and evils, the "advantages" and depreciations of that community. Effective performers may be led by the alienistic impulse, in Zweig's words, "close to the danger point of silence, yet not beyond it." Not beyond it: a distinction can be made between the effective artist and the culturally lost or absent. "The hero's ordeal," like that of Eliot's questing figure in *The Waste Land*, "is worth nothing if he cannot find his way back among men to tell what he has done. Between the hero and the madman there is this difference: the hero carries not only his own solitude but the solitude of his countrymen as well. Even at the farthest point of his journey, he is sustained by the community to which he will return. The madman, one might say, is a hero who has lost his way; the hero, a madman who can and will still speak to us."[41] The writers examined in this book do return to speak to us. Their urgency of vision, performed, becomes a concern for civilization.

We do well to remember that the ethical value of strategies of alienation extends to all personal and professional theaters, including the academy. The questioning of self, social arrangements, hierarchies, and power relationships does not stop at our door. Cornel West, who includes himself in critiques of cultural habits and practices, makes this point eloquently. "The humanity of black people," he says, "does not rest on deifying or demonizing others."[42] We should be willing, he says, to subject our own presumptions and perspectives to scrutiny. Those of us in the academy have become fond of thinking of ourselves as outsiders, subalterns, and prophets; we fancy that we speak truth to power, play Nathan to David, and scandalize presidents, politicians, and the likes of George F. Kennan with "Thou art the man" accusations. But we are bound up with our local disciplinary cultures; we, too, become encrusted with familiar subject matters, legitimated by technical vocabularies, and authorized by power relationships. Our celebrations of subversion can become comfortable and controlling habituations. It is convenient for alienistic art and oppositional criticism to take on the prestigious role of outsider and embrace an easy authenticity. "In less critical circles," as Paul Mann says, "art is always free, one is always 'exterior to power,' the outside is wherever one stands."[43] Thus are alienists naturally but foolishly led to assume that they have no part in cultural exploitations. "Between them and me," we say of those naive, incarcerated denizens of the world, "a high wall and a deep ditch." Yet, as Brodhead explains, consistently alienistic writers will practice a self-critical and "wary circumspection," recognizing "that the apparently liberated or subversive may be complicit in maintaining a repressive order."[44]

It follows, then, that practitioners of theory and cultural critique can themselves benefit from the tonic challenges of gnostic, aesthetic, and parabolic strategies. In the 1960s, Irving Howe was already warning that resistance and alienation could be easily co-opted: *"modernism must always struggle but never quite triumph, and then, after a time, must struggle in order not to triumph."*[45] Howe's warning was prophetic, for even strategies of alienation, at the moment of cultural performance, begin the process of joining the bureaucracy. Probably that bureaucratization is what leads contemporary theorists to equate oppositionist modernism with imperial modernity. A strategy is "bureaucratized," as Burke explains, when it is formalized in the "language and habits, in the property relationships, the methods of government, production and distribution, and in the development of rituals" of a given culture—including, we might add, an academic culture.[46] As early as the 1950s, Lionel Trilling was speaking of a disenchanted academic culture that was already becoming formulaic and predictable in its adversarialism: professors were engaged, he said, in "the socialization of the anti-social, or the acculturation of the anti-cultural, or the legitimization of the subversive."[47] Critical strategies, however oppositional and democratic, can and do become ossified and *sophisticated.*[48]

Thus readers of the *New Yorker*, the *Chicago Review*, or even *Unmuzzled Ox* who are comfortably habituated to the strategies of Faculty Lane and Graduate Circle need ironies and disruptions no less than readers of the *Saturday Evening Post* or the *Wall Street Journal* who are ensconced on Main Street or River Oaks Boulevard. Without the renewals of alienation, inhabitants of self-validating institutions may conveniently forget the punitive but comfortable consolidations of their local cultures. Any guild or subculture will encourage protective and parochial practices by hearkening to what Frye calls "myths of concern." These are symbolic strategies that hold a polity together; part of their function is to resist voices of doubt or dissent. "Concern," Frye says, "so far as it is a feeling, is very close to anxiety, especially when threatened."[49] Frye likens the myth of concern to Arnold's "Hebraism" and contrasts it with the "myth of freedom," a cluster of resistances that we might justly claim for our "strategies of alienation" rubric. According to Frye, without a myth of freedom to leaven it, a myth of concern "becomes the most squalid of tyrannies, with no moral principles except those of its own tactics, and a hatred of all human life that escapes from its particular obsessions."[50]

A guild, a coterie, even the congregation of selves that Burke calls a "corporate we" can become obsessed with its own myths of concern and evolve into a tiny Pax Romana. Hence, as Kastely argues, there is a need for alienistic strategies that function to keep "new languages and their consequent desires impure." The impure and the comedic are necessary dialectical "hecklers" of any language, any discursive or structural pattern, however "new," democratic, and inclusive. "We need to cultivate bad taste," Kastely says, "we need to become comedic."[51] So the challenge, despite what we constantly hear, is not to find methods and processes and procedures that are more efficient and consistent. The task that is laid upon us is not TQM ("Total Quality Management"), CQI ("Continuous Quality Improvement"), or any of the other totalizing theories that are supposed to make life and work better and more fulfilling. R. P. Blackmur points to the uniform motion of the twentieth century and identifies it as the source of our "torpor"—not the running down of things but "the spread of momentum." Foolishly concerning ourselves with friction and entropy, as though we were in the process of losing structure, energy, and organization, "actually we have been as busy, as violent, and as concentrated as the antheap." Momentum efficiently diffused throughout a system is experienced paradoxically as a loss of spirit, energy, and significance; the system itself comes to resemble the vast but oppressive homogeneity that spawned the Gnostics and countless other *remnants*. "We are torpid," Blackmur says—boggy, disaffected, alienated—"because we are glutted with energy": the obsessive, aggrandizing energy of the antheap.[52]

It is when we are most enervated, symptomatically showing what Blackmur calls our "incapacity for fresh idiom," that we most need the homeopathic treatment of alienism.[53] In *The Last Gentleman*, Will Barrett sees a fine American family succumbing to the apathy and alienation spawned by a great New York museum: they go "weaving along . . . all handsome as could be," but miserable, sunk in their everyday happiness and "bogging down." They seem to be irredeemably well-adjusted when a falling skylight disrupts their complacency: "*KeeeeeeeeeeeeeeeeRASH*, first a rusty clank from above like a castle drawbridge, then a cataclysm. . . . Glass powdered to sugar . . . covered the family, too. They stood for an age gazing at each other, turned into pillars of salt; then, when they saw that no one was hurt, they fell into one another's arms, weeping and laughing."[54] Thus a sudden threat rescues them from their sluggish conformity. Unknowingly trapped in what is quite literally a prison-house of cultural space, lost to themselves and each other, they are refreshed by danger. Through a shattering, disorienting experience, they momentarily recover a sense of time, of place, of self and other. By being nearly killed, they are ironically saved.

We should all be so lucky. Without the danger, the transgression, and the broken frame—sources of alienism's freshening power—we may gradually forfeit our capacities to see, to feel, to function at all. But by attending to alienistic strategies and performances, we, too, may hear and feel a cataclysmic crash. The properly arranged archives of our imaginations may be shattered as we miraculously come to ourselves once again. This role of constructive invigoration is the ethical contribution alienistic performers make to culture in spite of themselves. When a culture is most efficient, they become necessary troublemakers.

NOTES

1. Thomas Mann, *Death in Venice*, trans. H. T. Lowe-Porter (New York: Vintage, 1954), pp. 13, 72.

2. W. H. Auden quoted by Monroe K. Spears in *The Poetry of W. H. Auden: The Disenchanted Island* (New York: Oxford University Press, 1963), p. 179.

3. Paul Zweig, *The Heresy of Self-Love: A Study of Subversive Individualism* (1968; rpt., Princeton: Princeton University Press, 1980), p. 252, my emphasis.

4. Herbert N. Schneidau, *Sacred Discontent: The Bible and Western Tradition* (Berkeley: University of California Press, 1976), pp. 1–49.

5. Fredric Jameson, "Beyond the Cave: Modernism and the Modes of Production," in *The Horizons of Literature*, ed. Paul Hernadi (Lincoln: University of Nebraska Press, 1982), pp. 157–82.

6. Plato, *The Republic*, trans. H. D. P. Lee (Harmondsworth, Middlesex: Penguin Books, 1955), book 7, pp. 278–79, my emphasis.

7. Lionel Trilling, *The Opposing Self* (New York: Viking, 1955), pp. 53–55.

8. Zweig, *The Heresy of Self-Love*, p. 252.

9. Trilling, *The Opposing Self*, p. xi.

10. Jameson uses the image of incarceration to discuss contemporary structuralism in *The Prison-House of Language: A Critical Account of Structuralism and Russian Formalism* (Princeton: Princeton University Press, 1972) and thereby suggests some of the scandals of structuralist analysis: its emphasis on the synchronic at the expense of the diachronic, its inability *as a system* to account for linguistic and cultural change, and its "arbitrary and absolute decision" to analyze reality in terms of linguistic systems.

11. Walker Percy, *The Last Gentleman* (New York: Ivy Books, 1966), pp. 19–20.

12. Kimberly W. Benston, "Being There: Performance as Mise-en-Scène, Abscene, Obscene, and Other Scene," *PMLA* 107, no. 2 (1992), p. 448, n. 1.

13. Irving Howe, "The Idea of the Modern," in *The Idea of the Modern in Literature and the Arts*, ed. Irving Howe (New York: Horizon, 1967), p. 14.

14. "The clock's *tick-tock* I take to be a model of what we call a plot, an organization that humanizes time by giving it form; and the interval between *tick* and *tock* represents purely successive, disorganized time of the sort we need to humanize." Frank Kermode, *The Sense of an Ending: Studies in the Theory of Fiction* (New York: Oxford University Press, 1967), p. 45.

15. Howe, "The Idea of the Modern," pp. 16–17, 13.

16. Erich Auerbach, *Mimesis*, trans. Willard Trask (1946; rpt., Garden City, N.Y.: Anchor Press/Doubleday, 1957), p. 487.

17. Philip Stevick, *Anti-Story: An Anthology of Experimental Fiction* (New York: Free Press, 1971), pp. v–vi.

18. Lionel Trilling, *Beyond Culture: Essays on Literature and Learning* (New York: Viking, 1965), p. 118, my emphasis.

19. Ihab Hassan, *Paracriticisms: Seven Speculations of the Times* (Urbana: University of Illinois Press, 1975), pp. 144–45.

20. Ibid., p. 140.

21. Ibid., p. 141.

22. Ibid.

23. Ibid.

24. Warwick Wadlington, *The Confidence Game in American Literature* (Princeton: Princeton University Press, 1975), p. 315.

25. Kenneth Burke, *Attitudes toward History*, rev. 2d ed. (Los Altos, Calif.: Hermes, 1959), p. 336.

26. Ibid., p. 225.

27. James Kastely, "Kenneth Burke's Comic Rejoinder to the Cult of Empire," *College English* 58, no. 3 (1996), pp. 309–10.

28. Wadlington, *The Confidence Game*, p. 315.

29. Ibid.

30. Jan Kott describes Peter Brooks as giving us a Shakespeare who "is violent, cruel and brutal; earthly and hellish; [a Shakespeare who] evokes terror as well as dreams and poetry." Jan Kott, *Shakespeare Our Contemporary* (Garden City, N.Y.: Anchor/Doubleday, 1966), p. 352.

31. Wadlington, *The Confidence Game*, p. 16.

32. Albert Camus, *The Plague*, trans. Stuart Gilbert (New York: Modern Library, 1948), p. 227.

33. *Atlantic*, Apr. 1989, cover, p. 2.

34. George F. Kennan, "Sketches from a Life," *Atlantic*, Apr. 1989, p. 60.

35. Richard Brodhead, "Cluster on Modern Fiction," *PMLA* 106, no. 2 (1991), p. 206.

36. Camus, *The Plague*, p. 278.

37. William Barrett, *Irrational Man* (1958; rpt., Garden City, N.Y.: Anchor-Doubleday, 1962), pp. 59, 11.

38. Malcolm Bradbury, *The Social Context of Modern English Literature* (New York: Schocken, 1971), p. 115.

39. Kenneth Burke, *Counter-Statement* (1931; rpt., Berkeley: University of California Press, 1968), pp. 104–5.

40. Ellen Pifer, *Nabokov and the Novel* (Cambridge, Mass.: Harvard University Press, 1980), p. 118; Jonathan Culler, *Structuralist Poetics: Structuralism, Linguistics, and the Study of Literature* (Ithaca: Cornell University Press, 1975), p. 129.

41. Zweig, *The Heresy of Self-Love*, p. 257.

42. Cornel West, "Race Matters," lecture, National Collegiate Honors Council, St. Louis, Mo., Oct. 28, 1994.

43. Paul Mann, "Invisible Ink: Writing in the Margin," *Georgia Review* 39, no. 4 (1985), p. 816.

44. Brodhead, "Cluster on Modern Fiction," pp. 206–7.

45. Irving Howe, *Decline of the New* (New York: Harcourt, Brace, and World, 1970), p. 6, Howe's emphasis.

46. Burke, *Attitudes toward History*, p. 225.

47. Trilling, *Beyond Culture*, p. 26.

48. For elaborations of this point, see Murray Krieger, *The Institution of Theory* (Baltimore: Johns Hopkins University Press, 1994), and Mark Edmundson, *Literature against Philosophy, Plato to Derrida: A Defence of Poetry* (Cambridge: Cambridge University Press, 1995). Krieger, like Edmundson, sees a struggle between imaginative literature and philosophical theories that seek a kind of imperial domination of them.

49. Northrop Frye, *The Critical Path: An Essay on the Social Context of Literary Criticism* (Bloomington: Indiana University Press, 1971), p. 37.

50. Ibid., p. 55.

51. Kastely, "Kenneth Burke's Comic Rejoinder," pp. 309–10.

52. R. P. Blackmur, *Anni Mirabiles, 1921–25: Reason in the Madness of Letters* (Washington, D.C.: Library of Congress, 1956), pp. 6–7.

53. Ibid., p. 6. In the "Poetic Categories" section of *Attitudes toward History*, Burke uses an extended footnote to discuss the homeopathic virtues of the literary form he calls "the Elegy, or Plaint." "The 'allopathic' style," according to Burke, "confronts the threat of danger with an antidote of assurance," whereas the homeopathic style seeks "to *attenuate* a risk (to control by channelization) rather than to *abolish* it (to control by elimination)" (pp. 44–45). Burke would agree that there is "an ingredient of homeopathy" to be found in many strategies in addition to the elegy. Or, said another way, there is an elegiac element, a note of plaint, to be found in many alienistic-homeopathic strategies.

54. Percy, *The Last Gentleman*, p. 20.

6

"Heaven's Graces": Gnostic Strategies

There are forms of estrangement, patterns of disappointment, virtues of reticence, strategies of resistance. If remarkable and influential strategies of alienation are many and various, then it is likely that all historical epochs have fostered what Freud called *Unbehagen* and those persons whom we may call "strange ones." These discontents invite us by their presence and their performances to recognize the costs of the political and communal identifications that civilize us. Once we have felt the sacrifices of civilization, how should we respond? What ethoi should we adopt and construct? Eliot's St. Narcissus embodies—or attempts to disembody—one recurrent strategy of withdrawal:

> He could not live men's ways, but became a dancer to God.
> If he walked in the city streets, in the streets of Carthage
> He seemed to tread on faces, on compulsive thighs and knees,
> So he came to live under the rock.[1]

For the holy man or woman who draws apart, congregation is forever joined to exploitation and oppression; merely by walking, by working, they cannot help but "tread on faces, on compulsive thighs and knees." A multitude of poets, intellectuals, sages, and writers of every variety have eloquently expressed and often personally enacted similar if less drastic estrangements from their cultures. In an afterword to *The Nag Hammadi Library in English*, Richard Smith identifies a group of gnostic writers that includes William Blake, Herman Melville, Hermann Hesse, Laurence Durrell, Jack Kerouac, Allen Ginsberg, and Carl Jung.[2] There is also ample evidence that Ezra Pound, *il miglior fabbro*, as Eliot calls him, was directly influenced by *Pistis Sophia* and *The Hymn of Jesus*, two Gnostic texts translated and commented on by Pound's friend and mentor George R. S. Mead.[3] Like many other sophisticated strategies of alienation, gnostic strategies can be understood as responses to unhappy situations, responses that lament the relentless need for strategic responses.

Identification, like adoption and affiliation, is a functional antonym of *alienation*. Whereas alienation suggests separation, division, and contest, identification is rooted in sameness, similarity, and communion. In discussing "identification" in *Attitudes toward History*, Burke describes a strategy of renouncing corporate or group associations entirely, an attempt to escape polity, to transcend community. This alienistic strategy created a dilemma for "wised-up" individuals at the end of the Greco-Roman era: "As Hellenism drew to a close, and the disorders of the state made it impossible for the earnest man to identify himself with the emperor (as the Stoics had done) many of the 'enlightened' were enfeebled by the attempt to avoid all identification whatever. And in thus attempting to reject any corporate identity, they automatically despoiled themselves (with inanition, emptying, boredom, alienation as the result)."[4] In their obsession to avoid impure identifications, some of the most conscientious and circumspect people of Latinity abandoned the characteristic Roman public life. The Gnostic movement, the most potent of these abnegations, was a diffuse yet comprehensive phenomenon that influenced many Greek and Jewish sects, as well as pre-Christian and early Christian religious thought.[5] The scholarship of Hans Jonas did much to explain the attractiveness of this syncretic religion for inhabitants of the twentieth century as well as the first centuries of the Common Era. Harold Bloom has more recently argued that gnosticism (in combinations with Enthusiasm and Orphism) remains the de facto religion of the United States.[6] Moreover, numerous critics and commentators—notably Cleanth Brooks and Eric Voegelin as well as Hassan and Zweig—use *gnostic* to designate what we have called an ethos group, a strategic category within which characters, authors, and movements can be placed.[7] Some scholars of comparative religion, including Rosemary Radford Ruether and Elaine Pagels, look to historical Gnosticism as a powerful and perennial countervailing theology, beneficially subversive of the patriarchal orthodoxies of the West.[8] Gertrude Stein in *Tender Buttons* and Elizabeth Cady Stanton in *The Woman's Bible*, according to Lisa Ruddick, also developed feminist perspectives and secretive styles of expression that have parallels in "the gnosticism of the early Christian era and in medieval mysticism."[9] But as early as the 1950s, Jonas was already describing the fascinating similarities between ancient Gnosticism and twentieth-century strategies of alienation. *The Gnostic Religion*, according to Pagels, "remains, even today, the classic introduction" to Gnosticism.[10]

Jonas's comparison suggests the possibility of using *gnosticism* as a generic term signifying an aversion to worldly communities—an aversion that is perennial, if usually peripheral, in the West. Central to all versions of historical Gnosticism is a radical distinction between the material and the spiritual, between the world and God. Unlike orthodox Christianity, which retained a certain reverence for the human body and the fallen but divinely created world, the Gnostics denounced the mutable world, its laws, and its customs as utterly evil and foreign to the "knowing" among humankind. Basic to Gnosticism, Jonas says, "is the feeling of an absolute rift between man and that in which he finds himself lodged: the world."[11]

Gnostic cosmogony ingeniously posits an unseeing and ignorant Demiurge as the creator of the corrupt and corrupting world. Such a cosmogony is made necessary because "the true God cannot be the creator of that to which selfhood feels so utterly a stranger."[12] The possession of knowledge (*gnosis*) distinguishes the spiritual one from the environment and sanctions a privative mood: the gnostic of whatever age is the knowing one in the midst of the unknowing, the light in the midst of darkness. Just as the true and hidden God is alienated from the created universe, so a gnostic *pneuma* is a foreign, divine spark of otherness, temporarily trapped within a perniciously encultured world. The true gnostic will therefore be forever estranged from what Heidegger called the "they-world," and this state of not belonging, of *Unbehagen*, is seen as the assertion of the authentic freedom of the self.

If the Gnostics' sense of alienation gave rise to their notions of an antiworldly God and *pneuma*, it also engendered a derisive attitude toward those homely ones who accommodate themselves to the world to succeed on its terms. Just as the Gnostic cosmogony posited a radical dualism between God and the Demiurge, the Gnostic theology drew a sharp distinction between the saved and the damned. Centuries later, some Calvinistic Christians would see the earmarks of election in worldly success; the Gnostics, conversely, cultivated their estrangement, for failure in the world signified their superiority and their salvation. And this individualistic soteriology was manifested in anti-ecclesiastical practices and a suspicion of organizing structures. The Gnostic movement was widespread but ill-defined; it amounted, really, to a kind of adversary culture, dependent on a larger tradition for its strategy of alienation. The Gnostic vision, in sum, sees the world and its inhabitants as categorically impure, and salvation within it, no matter how the world may be improved or reformed, remains impossible.

If we view the historical Gnostics as fabricators of responses to the flux and confusion of a dubious world, then we can expect strategies similar to historical Gnosticism to emerge at other historical moments. In fact, in his early article "Gnosticism and Modern Nihilism," Jonas's express purpose is to identify correspondences between first- and second-century Gnosticism and similar twentieth-century attitudes. In this vein, he reminds us that Oswald Spengler declared our world to be "contemporaneous" with the Greco-Roman world of the first Christian centuries.[13] Zweig is concerned with the strategy of "subversive individualism, and the curious persistency with which it reappears throughout all European history." For him, the alienation of the Gnostics "from worldly experience, their antisocial doctrines, [and] their extreme spiritual self-reliance" anticipate certain strategies of modernism and existentialism.[14] *The Waste Land*, as I argue in part 3, can be profitably read as the performance of just such a strategy.

For Eliot, the gnostic impulse eventually resolved itself in an exaltation of Lancelot Andrewes and "The Idea of a Christian Society": a world of high culture that would foster classic works of art shaped by a refined, intellectual religion. But the poet of *The Waste Land*, as Calvin Bedient observes, is "like the Hinayana Buddhist who goes apart from others to save his purity, as opposed to the Mahayana Buddhist who would establish a Pure Land for the many."[15] Writing immediately after World War I, which signified for many the collapse of an entire culture that was "too assertively, too hopelessly, itself," in Burke's words, the flesh-and-blood Eliot may well have sensed a cultural or personal need for a gnostic transcendence of the world.[16] Lyndall Gordon suggests that throughout his early years Eliot was driven by a vague but unquenchable need for perfection, a need manifesting itself in dualistic transcendence. He "made body and soul enemies and set up the uncompromising dichotomy that ordered his early life." According to Gordon, Eliot toys with the role of martyr, "emphasizing the martyr's abandonment of the ways of other men." In his early poems he sets up a metaphysical choice by opposing "the notion of an Absolute or Pure Idea or Soul over against ordinary experience." His strategy, she says, is proving to himself "that women, time, society were the Absolute's enemies"; in "The

First Debate between Body and Soul," written in January 1910, he calls on the Absolute to rescue him from demeaning physicality and corrupting sensory experience.[17]

Modernity has put the serious artist in a problematic rhetorical situation. Poems that uphold and preserve seem deadening props of oppressing institutions. A gnostic renunciation and transcendence, conversely, may very well awaken a powerful aesthetic and spiritual response in readers confined within an airless, stultifying prison-house. It is not surprising, then, that the twentieth century has spawned countless stories of gnostic aliens. Usually their renunciation manifests itself in asceticism, as it does in many of Eliot's pre–*Waste Land* poems. On the other hand, a similar gnostic strategy can be enacted through transgression and indulgence. Careless immersion in the world's evil is held to be an equally efficacious strategy of renunciation.

In his essay "Baudelaire," as well as throughout *The Waste Land* itself (as we will see in chapter 10), Eliot endorses licentiousness as a mode of renunciation. "Baudelaire" is of course postconversion for Eliot, but he had long been fascinated by the virtue of committing damnable transgression. In "Prufrock" we find an impatience with the path of moderation and accommodation, and in the epigraph to "The Hollow Men," a preconversion poem that is thematically consonant with *The Waste Land*, the poet rues the death of Kurtz, Conrad's dark overreacher: "*Mistah Kurtz—he dead. / A penny for the Old Guy.*" Eliot is clearly attracted to the license associated with apotheosis, and Kurtz's apocalyptic vision of civilization—"The horror, the horror!"—was to serve as the epigraph to *The Waste Land* before Pound's editing made the poem less explicit and expansive. Kurtz is, of course, a figuration of Faust, the great overreacher of the West; and the recurring character of Faust combines secret knowledge, antinomian excess, pessimism about the world, and an attempt at personal transcendence. In other words, Faust and Kurtz are gnostic figures, potent and transgressive magicians in the tradition of Simon Magus, the great Gnostic heretic. Simon "was known in Latin surroundings as Faustus, the favored one," according to Zweig, and the Simonians were the originators of a "libertine gnosis," a peculiar state of grace which "seems largely to have been translated in terms of sexual liberation."[18] Simon the Gnostic, for whom the sin of simony is named, claimed a special divinity, a personal exaltation and apotheosis that was unavailable to the many. His consort, Helena, came to be identified with Helen of Troy—the goddess conjured up by Doctor Faustus so that he could indulge in acts of sexual transgression.[19] For his violations of the natural order, Marlowe's Faustus is conveyed by Mephistophilis to hell.

For the Gnostics, however, "a man who has opened the right doors in his spirit" is not accountable to conventional morality.[20] Damnable transgressions by the knowing ones only serve to confirm their divinity and provide evidence "of a higher dispensation"—as the sins of Baudelaire and Kurtz do for Eliot. Simon asserted that he was not what he appeared to be, a magician and a libertine, but the very Son of God.

In *Being and Nothingness* Sartre declares that the desire to be God is anything but a historical aberration. "The best way to conceive of the fundamental project of human reality" according to Sartre, "is to say that man is the being whose project is to be God."[21] It is other people who remind us that we are not God, that we must compromise, that coexistence requires flawed polities, imperfect social arrangements, and unjust economic systems of transference and exchange. "*L'enfer*," Garcin says in Sartre's *Huis-Clos*, "*c'est les Autres*."[22] There are elements of the Faustian project to be God and the Baudelairean strategy of excess in *The Waste Land* just as there are in "The Hollow Men." A bang is better than a whimper: "The worst that can be said of most of our malefactors, from statesmen to thieves, is that they are not men enough to be damned."[23] The gnostic *fabbro* desires to be unmediated, metacultural, and antinomian; his or her gnostic strategy may well suggest that the vicious and vapid ways of the world can be best overcome by using them up.

Typically, however, the gnostic way is one of denial: asceticism contains, cloisters, and withholds, and gnosis is characteristically a secret knowledge. Whether ascetics or libertines, though, gnostic aliens can be found in the works of many writers and philosophers. Allan Tate lists a number of writers that Richard Smith does not mention, including Lautréamont, Arthur Rimbaud, Mallarmé, the Surrealists, Hart Crane, Wallace Stevens, and Dylan Thomas.[24] He draws on the work of Jacques Maritain and Raïssa Maritain to distinguish the symbolic imagination, which he apprehends in Dante, and the angelic imagination, which he sees epitomized in Poe. In "The Angelic Imagination," Tate characterizes Poe as a "forlorn demon" and describes the heresy and idolatry of separating the language of poetry from "the grammar of a *possible* world."[25] From Poe's destructive tendencies and from the suicides of other writers we learn that lives as well as works often testify to the irresistible and otherworldly nature of the gnostic call.[26]

What attracts writers to gnostic strategies? Platonic metaphysics suggests that the best salvation comes to the few who have escaped the prison-house of culture. One could argue, in fact, that a gnostic impulse already within Platonism reemerged a millennium later in the dualisms of the Neoplatonists. According to Jonas, the agitation of the first centuries of the Common Era naturally gave rise to "a general religion of the period," characterized by dualism, transcendence, and anticipatory eschatology.[27] But a more direct and panhistorical explanation comes from Pagels, who quotes the Gnostic *Gospel of Philip:* "You saw the spirit, you became spirit. You saw Christ, you became Christ."[28] In *Holy Feast, Holy Fast,* Caroline Walker Bynum describes the phenomenon of medieval fasting as a strategy of alienation by women who feared co-optation by an encompassing church. These pious "hunger artists" also sought escape from the bonds of immanence: they wanted, "without compromise or moderation, to imitate Christ."[29] And indeed, the modern gnostic strategy of alienation aims at a similar, though less sectarian, escape from the physical ugliness, moral depravity, and spiritual emptiness of the encultured world. Such a large and multifarious group may not have much in common, but this we may hazard: gnostic strategies seek apotheosis. "Poe as God" is the apt subtitle of Tate's essay on the angelic imagination.

At their best, gnostic strategies offer a room of one's own, a place of solace and quietude for authors and readers who cannot abide affiliating with a world of senseless war, comfortable conformity, luxurious emptiness, and life-in-death. The professional life of Professor Ioan Culianu certainly invites the speculation that his study of gnostic transcendence was a strategic response consistent with his twenty-year exile from Romania, just as his outspoken disgust for its new regime was connected to his neofascist-style political assassination.[30] For countless political, intellectual, and cultural exiles, the greatest impetus for the cultivation of gnostic strategies in the twentieth century has been its uninhabitable nature. Sharp divisions between good and evil and spirit and flesh, a tradition of mystical apotheosis beyond the prison-house of stultifying conformity, and a sequence of antinomian attempts to "exhaust the flesh"—these gnostic strategies have exerted a powerful appeal for modern writers. As Pagels says in summarizing Jonas's position, the gnostic worldview combines "a philosophy of pessimism about the world . . . with an attempt at self-transcendence."[31]

Jacques Barzun characterizes this intractable discontent as a desire to replace mediating civilization with a wholly *unconditioned* life.[32] Yet we do not live except under conditions. Even the recluse who abandons the *res publica* must practice some social or corporate identifications—even the hermit's role may be a social one. Their effort to avoid sociality led the Gnostics to cluster in small enclaves, often in the various "deserts" of the ancient world; their corresponding effort to avoid corporate or group identifications led them to create alternative, otherworldly identifications of mystical self-regard. In practice, though, the Gnostic prophet could no more cure his followers of their impulse to identify with shared corporate attitudes than can the modern psychoanalyst who, according to Burke, "cures" his patient of a faulty identification "only insofar as he smuggles in *an alternative identification*."[33] Smuggling in, for example, an otherworldly identification might well be accomplished by a story or poem—that is, by the enaction or performance of a strategy or pattern of gnostic desire. General culture can never be sufficiently otherworldly to qualify as gnostic; it is always bound up with economics, politics, and ordinary people. But particular cultural artifacts—Stein's *Tender Buttons*, some of Pound's *Cantos* and "The Flame"—have been described, somewhat paradoxically, as gnostic poems. Whether *The Waste Land* qualifies as a poem that "smuggles in" a gnostic strategy of alienation is a question that must wait until part 3 and the findings of formal analysis, a necessary portion of the coductive work of virtue criticism.

NOTES

1. T. S. Eliot, "The Death of St. Narcissus," quoted by Lyndall Gordon in *Eliot's Early Years* (New York: Oxford University Press, 1977), p. 94. According to Gordon, Valerie Eliot reported "that Eliot could not remember the date of 'St. Narcissus', but it may have been early in 1915" (p. 91, n.).

2. Richard Smith, "Afterword: The Modern Relevance of Gnosticism," in *The Nag Hammadi Library in English*, 3d rev. ed., ed. James M. Robinson (San Francisco: Harper and Row, 1988).

3. Angela Elliott, personal correspondence, 26 Feb. 1987. See also her "Pound's 'Isis Kuanon': An Ascension Motif in *The Cantos*," *Paideuma* 13, no. 3 (1984), pp. 327–56, and "Pound's Lucifer: A Study in the Imagery of Flight and Light," *Paideuma* 12, nos. 2–3 (1983), pp. 237–66.

4. Kenneth Burke, *Attitudes toward History*, rev. 2d ed. (Los Altos, Calif.: Hermes, 1959), p. 264.

5. Hans Jonas, *The Gnostic Religion: The Message of the Alien God and the Beginnings of Christianity*, 2d rev. ed. (Boston: Beacon Press, 1963), pp. 31–47.

6. Harold Bloom, *The American Religion: The Emergence of the Post-Christian Nation* (New York: Simon and Schuster, 1992), pp. 49–50.

7. See, for example, Cleanth Brooks, "Walker Percy and Modern Gnosticism," *Southern Review* 13, no. 4 (1977), pp. 667–87; Eric Voegelin, *Science, Politics, and Gnosticism: Two Essays* (Chicago: Regnery, 1968); and John F. Desmond, "The Scriptural Tradition and Faulkner's Gnostic Style," *Southern Review* 25, no. 3 (1989), pp. 563–68.

8. Rosemary Radford Ruether, *Sexism and God-Talk: Toward a Feminist Theology* (Boston: Beacon, 1983); Elaine Pagels, *The Gnostic Gospels* (New York: Random House,

1979). Pagels is sympathetic to historical Gnosticism's inclusion of "God the Mother" as a beneficial supplement to an exclusive God-the-Father tradition.

9. Lisa Ruddick, *Reading Gertrude Stein: Body, Text, Gnosis* (Ithaca: Cornell University Press, 1990), p. 3. Ruddick speculates that Stein and Stanton also duplicate "the idea one finds in some branches of historical gnosticism, that the snake was our benign tutor who was then discredited by the patriarchs as evil" (p. 249).

10. Pagels, *The Gnostic Gospels*, p. xxxi.

11. Jonas, *The Gnostic Religion*, p. 435.

12. Ibid., p. 436.

13. Hans Jonas, "Gnosticism and Modern Nihilism," *Social Research* 19, no. 4 (1952), p. 433.

14. Paul Zweig, *The Heresy of Self-Love: A Study of Subversive Individualism* (1968; rpt., Princeton: Princeton University Press, 1980), p. vi.

15. Calvin Bedient, *He Do the Police in Different Voices: "The Waste Land" and Its Protagonist* (Chicago: University of Chicago Press, 1986), p. 218.

16. Kenneth Burke, *Counter-Statement* (1931; rpt., Berkeley: University of California Press, 1968), p. 105.

17. Gordon, *Eliot's Early Years*, pp. 24, 23. For Eliot, the enemies of perfection identified by Gordon are *time*, especially as manifested through bodily decay, and *women*, especially as manifested through sexuality (pp. 24–28).

18. Zweig, *The Heresy of Self-Love*, pp. 21, 19.

19. E. M. Butler, *The Myth of the Magus* (1948; rpt., Cambridge: Cambridge University Press, 1979), pp. 78, 82–83. For an encyclopedic survey of Faust figures, see Butler's *The Fortunes of Faust* (1952; rpt., Cambridge: Cambridge University Press, 1979).

20. Jonas, "Gnosticism and Modern Nihilism," p. 19.

21. Jean-Paul Sartre, *Being and Nothingness: An Essay in Phenomenological Ontology*, trans. Hazel E. Barnes (New York: Philosophical Library, 1956), p. 566.

22. Jean-Paul Sartre, *Huis-Clos* (Paris: Gallimard, 1947), p. 62.

23. T. S. Eliot, "Baudelaire," in *Selected Prose of T. S. Eliot*, ed. Frank Kermode (New York: Harcourt, Brace, Jovanovich, 1975), p. 236.

24. Allan Tate, "The Angelic Imagination: Poe as God," *Collected Essays* (Denver: Alan Swallow, 1959), p. 437. Another tracker of modern gnostics is Jefferson Humphries in *The Otherness Within: Gnostic Readings in Marcel Proust, Flannery O'Connor, and François Villon* (Baton Rouge: Louisiana State University Press, 1983). In *Flannery O'Connor: The Imagination of Extremity* (Athens: University of Georgia Press, 1982), Frederick Asals also identifies O'Connor as a gnostic writer (p. 58). For Asals, *Wise Blood* expresses a deeply Manichean or Gnostic vision (p. 240, n. 39). When gnostic tendencies are discovered everywhere, however, the term loses its heuristic value, and thus the sorting into categories should proceed gingerly. I believe, for example, that Asals and Humphries are wrong to classify O'Connor as a gnostic writer for reasons developed in "Flannery O'Connor and the Celebration of Embodiment," in *The Good Body: Asceti-*

cism in Contemporary Culture, ed. Mary G. Winkler and Letha B. Cole (New Haven: Yale University Press, 1994), pp. 171–88.

25. Tate, "The Angelic Imagination," p. 437, my emphasis.

26. Listing authors who can be construed in general terms as gnostic is dangerous because almost anyone who has apprehended the threat of the world or the danger of the corruption of the true self can be included. There may be some value, however, in naming again some of those writers identified by Zweig and Ihab Hassan: Rousseau, Kierkegaard, Baudelaire, Nietzsche, Valéry, Proust, Rilke, Kafka, Joyce, Yeats, Beckett, Borges, Genet, Butor, Cortazar, Nabokov, Barth, Pynchon, Barthelme, Coover, Wurlitzer, Federman, Sukenick, Burroughs, and Bowles.

27. Jonas, *The Gnostic Religion*, pp. 31–32.

28. Pagels, *The Gnostic Gospels*, p. 134.

29. Caroline Walker Bynum, *Holy Feast and Holy Fast: The Religious Significance of Food to Medieval Women* (Berkeley: University of California Press, 1988), p. 218.

30. Culianu's magnum opus is *The Tree of Gnosis: Gnostic Mythology from Early Christianity to Modern Nihilism* (San Francisco: HarperCollins, 1992). In it he surveys Gnosticisms from Valentinus to Nietzsche, emphasizing the dualistic contrasts between good and evil, spiritual and material. For a report on his political murder, see Ted Anton, *Eros, Magic, and the Murder of Professor Culianu* (Evanston, Ill.: Northwestern University Press, 1996).

31. Pagels, *The Gnostic Gospels*, p. xxx.

32. Jacques Barzun, *The Use and Abuse of Art* (Princeton: Princeton University Press, 1975), p. 67.

33. Burke, *Attitudes toward History*, p. 264, Burke's emphasis. It is in the context of this discussion of "Identity, Identification" that Burke says, "the so-called 'I' is merely a unique combination of partially conflicting 'corporate we's'" (p. 264).

7

"Sweetest Things": Aesthetic Strategies

All art practices a strategy of alienation. The motive for art, at least as we have come to understand that motive since the nineteenth century, includes originality, and originality implies antagonism to what already exists. Even conventional art—the aesthetic or imaginative making, expressing, or imitating of something—implies that another articulation, iteration, or version is needed or desirable. In its more revolutionary forms, Zweig tells us, the artistic impulse "springs from the same moral ground as Marx's revolutionary politics": the sense that something else ought to be the case. But the development of revolutionary art is often quite different from the development of revolutionary politics. Strategies such as Formalism, Romanticism, and Aestheticism, all revolutionary in their time, cast suspicion on accessible, straightforward, sincere works of art. The aesthetic realm, instead of being seen as a place of political and historical engagement, becomes recognized as "a bulwark for the individual *against* the pressures of his social milieu." "From the late eighteenth century on," according to Zweig, "the individual resisted those influences which otherwise would have diminished his humanity, i.e., 'alienated' him" by cultivating himself aesthetically.[1] The pattern is this: an artistic soul, appalled at what civilization has become, retreats to a higher culture accessible only to those who are willing to put aside their political and parochial agendas, their worldly desires, in favor of transcendent beauty itself.

Estranged, alienated, and motivated by resistance as much as by the love of beauty, modernist and postmodernist writers have often cultivated marginality through eccentric, arcane forms and even through silence—the absence of form. The English novelist Malcolm Bradbury notes a withdrawal from politics and history that is characteristic of serious writers: "Instead of acting within history and culture, the artist must, if he is to survive, escape from it."[2] Bradbury sees writers abandoning the common realm and art giving up its claim to be "a general activity of intelligence." He notes the desire among those he calls formalists to produce "a highly specialized and arcane form of knowledge," what we might identify as an *aesthetic* gnosis, rather than a religious or cosmic one.[3] Perhaps Archibald MacLeish's formulation that art should not mean but *be* is partly motivated by a desire to remain uncontaminated by history and culture. "We cannot stir a finger in this world without the risk of bringing death to someone," Tarrou says in *The Plague*.[4] Bradbury, Trilling, Howe, and more recently Mark Krupnick and Giles Gunn concur: much of modern writing purposely abandons the middle-brow appeals, intelligibility, and social "connections" that would threaten it with co-optation.[5] The motive, as articulated by José Ortega y Gasset, is to be "purified of life": to cease to be generally or generically human.[6] This disconnection is the primary intention of aesthetic strategies of alienation, not an unfortunate side effect.

In *Counter-Statement*, Burke sketches the abiding conflict between the practical and the aesthetic. "On the side of the practical," Burke locates "efficiency, prosperity, material acquisitions, increased consumption, 'new needs,' expansion, higher standards of living . . . in short, ubiquitous optimism. Enthusiasm, faith, evangelizing, Christian soldiering, power, energy, sales drives, undeviating certainties, confidence, co-operation, in short, flags and all the jungle vigor that goes with flags." Against the practical, Burke aligns what he calls the aesthetic—qualities remarkably similar to the "secondary" qualities that Nemoianu identifies. Burke's list underlines the alienation intrinsic to the strategy of aestheticism: "inefficiency, indolence, dissipation, vacillation, mockery, distrust, 'hypochondria,' non-conformity, bad sportsmanship, in short, negativism. Experimentalism, curiosity, risk, dislike of propaganda, dislike of certainty—tentative attitude toward all manners of thinking which reinforce the natural dogmatism of the body." Burke concludes: "The practical: patriotism—the aesthetic: treason."[7]

Burke does not mean to assert that the practical and the aesthetic function equivalently in human affairs. The political value of the aesthetic is limited to "keeping the practical from becoming too hopelessly itself." Writing in 1931, Burke was well aware of the "at the present time" nature of his argument. The disruptive independence of the aesthetic is defensible, he says, "because it could never triumph. Certainties will always arise, impelling men to new intolerances." A reaction more than a position, the aesthetic way opposes certainties and convictions. It is "anti-practical, anti-industrial, anti-machine because the practical, the industrial, the mechanized is so firmly entrenched." Burke links the aesthetic with a suspicious, inefficient, cantankerous, unpredictable democracy: therein lies its ethical and political importance. The aesthete is the democrat, the negativist, the oppositionist who seeks "by wit, by fancy, by anathema, by versatility—to throw into confusion the code which underlies commercial enterprise, industrial competition, the 'heroism' of economic warfare," or any new method, market, materialism, or efficiency yet to be invented by the progressive optimists of the future. According to Burke, the aesthetic principle is committed to nothing less than "the de-Occidentalizing of the West."[8]

◄— Joyce's Exemplary Aesthete

In *Counter-Statement* Burke was making a polemical book, almost a tract, and in it he does not thoroughly consider the less *counter* and more *disinterested* motives that we rightly associate with aestheticism. Burke has often been charged with not being sensitive enough to the relevant differences between high art and, say, advertising slogans, and he readily acknowledges the truth of such charges. Moreover, in *Counter-Statement* he is more concerned with what another Burke called the *sublime*, a troubling and disconcerting mode distinguishable from the *beautiful*. So for a portrait of a pure, apolitical, and transcendent aesthetic we must look elsewhere.

For anglophone readers, James Joyce created the definitive exemplar of the isolated and disinterested aesthete in the character of Stephen Dedalus. In *A Portrait of the Artist as a Young Man*, Stephen's aesthetic epiphany comes, significantly, when he is alone—"alone and young and wilful and wildhearted, alone amid a waste of wild air and brackish waters." In this scene Stephen observes but does not pursue a girl who, "when she felt the presence and the worship of his eyes her eyes turned to him in quiet sufferance of his gaze, without shame and without wantonness." Stephen contemplates her not with the gaze of desire but with the gaze of disinterested art. The sight of the girl causes Stephen's "soul, in an outburst of profane joy," to cry out in its new awareness. But Stephen's epiphany drives him away from rather than toward his fellow creature: he sets off "far out over the sands, singing wildly to the sea." Though the girl's "eyes had called to him," he feels not the pull of life, of humanity in conflict and fructifying congregation, but the insistent, otherworldly call of art. In his independent celebration there is "no human figure near him nor any sound borne to him over the air."[9]

Stephen's aesthetic epiphany, like his earlier religious epiphany, offers him "a secret knowledge and secret power" that promise him separateness and se-curity from the flux of the contentious and competitive world.[10] Like the cold people of Shakespeare's sonnet, he becomes unmoved and to temptation slow. Like a gnostic hermit, he draws physically apart from humanity and cultivates a divine disinterestedness. His senses become unresponsive as his aesthetic epiphany becomes a strategy of withdrawal similar to gnosticism. But Stephen's strategy of alienation differs from gnosticism in its special emphasis on art and artist. His private call does not come in the form of religion or theosophy but derives rather from "idle curiosity," Burke's synonym for the aesthetic. His du-alism is not between flesh and spirit but between egoistic desire and the aes-thetic imagination in pure and untrammeled possibility.

Stephen's friend Lynch, in contrast, demonstrates an eminently personal and passionate approach to imaginative patterns. No alienist he, Lynch's strategies will all be directed toward incorporation, coupling, and the satisfaction of ap-petites. Lynch, in name as well as attitude, suggests unbridled desire: the de-sire to seize the work of art, to take it as his own, to "lynch" or "execute" a text through the process of interpreting it. "Though I did eat a cake of cowdung once," he says mockingly to Stephen, "I admire only beauty." He thereby re-veals both his awareness of Stephen's pure aestheticism and his own counter-emphasis on physicality. Stephen explains the stasis of mind that results from the *apprehension* of the beautiful: Aquinas, he says, chooses the word *visa* be-cause it "is clear enough to keep away good and evil which excite desire and loathing." But desire is exactly what Lynch brings to his experience of art: "give me the hypotenuse of the Venus of Praxiteles," he tells Stephen. And when Stephen tries to philosophize, saying, "Let us take woman," Lynch interjects fervently, "Let us take her!"[11]

Thus Joyce's narrative begins to suggest that "lynching" a work of art may complement the process of "moving others": aesthetic pleasures and experiences can be integrated with ordinary and customary patterns of belief, value, and desire. Confronted with Stephen's aesthetic speculations, Lynch gruffly dismisses them, observing that Stephen's theoretical walling up of the imagination has "the true scholastic stink." More politicized than his modernist comrade, Lynch thinks that "prating about beauty and imagination in this miserable God-forsaken island" is unseemly and callous. The depersonalized and depoliticized work of art, according to Lynch, is nothing more than a method the artist can use to escape responsibility for the practical results of his creation. Lynch holds even God to account for his poor craftsmanship: "No wonder the artist retired within or behind his handiwork after having perpetrated this country." Thus Lynch's response to an aesthetic work is not, in Burke's sense, aesthetic: he wants a work of art, as he wants God's own Ireland, to accommodate him, and he is critical of all "works" that do not.[12]

Lynch's appetitive acquisition of art is clearly suspect; his mixing of memory and desire makes him incapable of "the luminous silent stasis of esthetic pleasure," the pure disinterested "enchantment of the heart" exalted by Stephen as the proper response to beauty.[13] Yet Lynch's admittedly gross appetite competes with Stephen's dispassionate aestheticism for our attention and our alliance. In the first place, the implied author's treatment of Lynch and Stephen, as Booth argues in *The Rhetoric of Fiction*, is mitigated by Stephen's pomposity and forced self-confidence.[14] By default, then, Lynch is more appealing in *Portrait* than Buck Mulligan is in *Ulysses*, for example. Moreover, as flesh-and-blood readers rather than scholastic interpreters, we may well identify with Lynch. As lazy readers we are egoists who are fond of asking, as Lynch does with his entire social, political, and libidinal personality, "What's in it for me?" As better readers, perhaps, we will want to ask less immediately self-serving questions of the handiworks and performances that we encounter. But even Goethe, certainly aware of the special power of art, suggested that looking and seeing are processes of assimilating and commingling.[15] Joyce lets us know that Lynch is on to something when he asks about art's relevance to life and commingles aesthetic experience with general experience. He understands that the power to hurt means breeding lilacs out of the dead land, making beauty from social and political stuff.

Still, the alienistic motive for a secure and separate haven remains. A great many artists and critics have sought to isolate and protect the aesthetic sensibility from the quotidian world and its busy functionaries. Like the gnostics, aesthetics such as Stephen seek to relinquish their mundane personalities and prejudices. Instead of asceticism, antinomianism, or metaphysical detachment, the means becomes aesthetic experience. Stephen's disquisition is one of the more famous descriptions of the alienistic virtues of artistic detachment: "The personality of the artist, at first a cry or a cadence or a mood and then a fluid and lambent narrative, finally refines itself out of existence, impersonalises itself, so to speak. . . . The artist, like the God of creation, remains within or behind or beyond or above his handiwork, invisible, refined out of existence, indifferent, paring his fingernails."[16] Like Stephen, Oscar Wilde might have been gainsaying Lynch when he wrote that "Beauty is that which does not concern us."[17] And, like gnosticism, this particular mode of isolation and resistance, what I am calling the aesthetic strategy, has been for many a compelling and perennial alternative.

◄— Aesthetic Strategies Then and Now

The social preeminence of myths of concern and their correspondent virtues of concern suggests, however, that a powerful part of us remains preoccupied not with beauty but with that which does concern us. By "virtues of concern" I mean such qualities as possessiveness, competitiveness, avid practicality, and the obsessive reaching after fact and reason indicted by Keats. Roger Fry, another champion of disinterested detachment and negative capability, complains that the aesthetic sensibility is weak compared with the pragmatic sensibility that dominates most people.[18] His lament is tied to classic, late nineteenth-century Aestheticism, which held that the mind must surely be composed of different "parts," the pure *imagination* and the grosser *understanding*. The understanding—functionally related to Booth's overstanding—was dominated by parochial concerns and instrumental motives. Like many similar schema about the mind's or soul's partitions, Aestheticist theories can be traced to the German Romantic philosophers.[19] Drawing on the thought of Friedrich Schiller, Friedrich von Schelling, Goethe, and especially Kant, Aestheticist theory isolated the mental function that apprehended aesthetic beauty and called it the imagination, while the balance of an individual's mental or spiritual functions was assigned to the understanding. The imagination, then, processed sensuous, aesthetic experience. The concept was that the aesthetic was distinguishable from the ethical and the practical, that the purely formal was not historical, social, or political, but somehow transcended all of these. Aestheticist theory exalted artistic works that appealed to only that "part" of the perceiving mind that was purified of "not art." Since there was an independent imagination, the exclusive function of which was aesthetic apprehension, artistic works themselves could remain essentially discrete from other sorts of mental, physical, political, and economic products and constructs.

The isolated imagination, free from pragmatic tasks, could be developed and cultivated; the result would be heightened sensitivity and passionate experiences. Nature might be the source of this inspiration, but more likely it would be art itself. Walter Pater's conclusion to *The Renaissance* suggests what is at stake. "Our one chance," he says, "lies in . . . getting as many pulsations as possible into the given time." The danger is that nature or the lower forms of culture will confuse the imagination with feelings and perceptions that are not purely aesthetic. "The poetic passion, the desire of beauty, the love of art for its own sake"—these are likely to yield the highest passion, a peculiarly aesthetic wisdom. "For art," he says, "comes to you proposing frankly to give nothing but the highest quality to your moments as they pass, and simply for those moments' sake."[20] This exquisite sensitivity of the imagination depends on its isolation from the "multiplied consciousness" of everyday life.

The Aestheticist separation of the imagination from the practical intellect ("understanding") obviously marks a break with the notion that various kinds of verbal and symbolic production and apprehension are generically similar and continuous. Wilde, for example, insisted that "a separate realm for the artist" was necessary for true aesthetic creativity and was "characteristic of all great imaginative work and of all great eras of artistic creation."[21] The artist and his or her works are "of the imagination," which is a realm foreign to the quotidian world. Thus in "The Critic as Artist," Wilde notoriously describes the world as inferior art: sterile, inane, and not a proper residence for the imagination. Aestheticism, as R. V. Johnson explains, holds the realm of the imagination to be much more than merely separate or different; rather, the imagination does not refer back to actuality "in any way." The aesthete, whether creator or critic, "stands for the separation of one human interest—the aesthetic—from others, such as the religious, the philosophical, the moral."[22] And, we might add, the political, the economic, the social, the sexual.

The progressive contraction of the aesthetic has been noted and often regretted by writers such as Saul Bellow. He laments the reduction of what is considered proper to the literary realm and frequently criticizes the isolation of modern literature as he did upon receiving the National Book Award for *Herzog* in 1965: "Literature has for several generations been its own source, its own province, has lived upon its own traditions, and accepted a romantic separation or estrangement from the common world."[23] Yet Bellow seems unaware of the implicit ethical urgency of this estrangement. If there has been an increasing separation of imaginative works from the common world, it may be part of a centuries-old strategy of resistance to modernity's violence, exploitive efficiencies, and persistent materialisms. The uncompromising parochialism of Stephen Dedalus's family, church, and country make him only too aware of the dangerous partisanship and intolerance brought about by "lynching" strategies of production and interpretation. His characteristic musings, always hypothetical, may evoke nothing more than "a thoughtenchanted silence," but they will not lead to a hasty blow and the avenging response—or what Nabokov calls "filthy murder."[24]

M. H. Abrams makes it clear that Aesthetes such as Wilde and James Whistler were already following many others who wanted to establish the imagination as distinct from the emotions, the intellect, and the understanding. Thomas Carlyle's vision of the "Poet as Hero," for example, and John Stuart Mill's separation of poetry from eloquence amount to a similar sequestering of the imagination. Carlyle emphasizes the otherworldly quality of poetry by recalling that in Roman antiquity, *vates* was used to designate both poets and prophets.[25] Further, the artist's godlike superiority is suggested by Carlyle's use of a celestial metaphor to describe genius: "Genius has privileges of its own; it selects an orbit for itself." Ordinary folk with their "progressive," increasingly commercial culture are "mere star-gazers" who must cease to object or cavil at Genius and begin to observe it and calculate its laws.[26]

Abrams neatly summarizes the intellectual progression that culminates in the aesthetic strategy of alienation: "The revolution is complete, from the mimetic poet, assigned the minimal role of holding a mirror up to nature, through the pragmatic poet who, whatever his natural gifts, is ultimately measured by his capacity to satisfy the public taste, to Carlyle's Poet as Hero, the chosen one who, because he is 'a Force of Nature,' writes as he must, and through the degree of homage he evokes, serves as the measure of his *reader's* piety and taste."[27] The detached artist is a force of Nature, but of a peculiarly otherworldly and supercultural kind. Nature, for Carlyle, is a transcendent rather than immanent force, and Abrams's choice of *homage* and *piety* to indicate the appropriate quality of attention underscores the divine authority of the true poet. Our culture's understanding, its everyday system of domination and control, do not and cannot contain works of a superior imagination. Such, at least, is the hopeful conviction of aesthetic strategies.

Structuralism, in its concern for the products of an independent imagination, is one kind of aestheticism. As Culler explains in *Structuralist Poetics*, structuralist theory values the detachment of the literary text from the pragmatic, the utilitarian, and the personal. From a structuralist perspective, the kind of interpretation practiced by Lynch represents a coarse, hasty, and inappropriate application of the purely imaginative and formal—the aesthetic—to the diurnal, "thematic" realm of life. As a relative of aestheticism, structuralism avoids such "premature closure," what Culler elegantly calls the "unseemly rush from word to world," and thereby allows the reader to reside "within the literary system for as long as possible."[28] The text seen as literary system becomes sequestered, a "world elsewhere"[29] that can play an alienistic role by resisting the reader's efforts to appropriate or "recuperate" it. By making itself unavailable for assimilation, the structuralist text critiques rather than reflects or explains the inhabited world. Culler, describing structuralism in 1975, does not differ so very much from Carlyle describing the work of genius 150 years before. The best imaginative work resists the reader's efforts to "understand" it, to interpret it in terms of his or her prejudicial motives, beliefs, values, and desires— to "naturalize" the text, in Culler's words. And it is this resistance to naturalization, this cultivated separation of the literary imagination from the conscience and the intellect, that aestheticism shares with structuralism. Structuralism, Culler says, "insists that literature is something other than a statement about the world."[30] The work of aesthetic genius, or any work viewed with the proper aesthetic detachment, maintains a celestial orbit and thereby resists being "lynched."

R. V. Johnson describes the influence of aestheticism on artistic practice as "a tendency . . . not merely away from moral didacticism . . . but from any sense on the artist's part that he is called upon to speak for or to his age at all."[31] Likewise, structuralism has its favored pantheon of texts—the "most challenging and innovatory texts," according to Culler, "which are precisely those that are difficult to process according to our received modes of understanding."[32] And yet Culler follows Goethe in acknowledging that to look and see is to mix, measure, compare, and commingle. Whether we call it recuperation, naturalization, or performance, the adoption of the text is inevitable: the "structuralist dissatisfaction with naturalization does not entail an ability to go beyond it," Culler says. Eventually, as we continue to read, we assimilate; we make judgments about the images, actions, and characters; we improvise and perform the text in terms of our own accumulated experiences and enabling commitments. A structuralist approach is valuable, according to Culler, because it postpones naturalization and thereby ensures that our appropriation occurs "at a higher and more formal level."[33]

From Burke we learn that aesthetic strategies are unconventional, provocative, and politically challenging; from the Romantics and the Aesthetes we learn that they are playful, original, and creative; from the structuralists and formalists we learn that they are precise and disinterested. This antirecuperative preference for the higher and more formal suggests that the performing self of an aesthetic strategy, while creative, is not an imperial self arrogantly recasting things to further its own projects.[34] Patience, disinterested receptivity, negative capability, cool precision—these are virtues of aestheticism, not the unbridled heat of "strong reading." But how can splendid creativity and attentive precision be united in one ethos? We can understand the potential relatedness of precision and creativity (often competing rather than complementary virtues) by recognizing the underlying metaphysics of an aesthetic strategy such as Nabokov's. In an immensely useful piece of scholarship, Vladimir Alexandrov reconstructs the lost conclusion to Nabokov's "The Art of Literature and Commonsense" from a 1941 version of the same lecture: "A creative writer, creative in the particular sense I am attempting to convey, cannot help feeling that in his rejecting the world of the matter-of-fact, in his taking sides with the irrational, the illogical, the inexplicable and the fundamentally good, *he is performing something similar in a rudimentary way to what the spirit may be expected to perform, when the time comes, on a vaster and more satisfactory scale.*"[35] These sentences immediately follow an affirmation that "one's individual secret" outlives "the process of earthly dissolution." As Alexandrov explains, the "earthbound artist" can make "contact with a more real, transcendent realm."[36] Here the aesthetic strategy closely resembles gnostic sentiments and diction: he likens the work of the creative artist, whether reader or writer, to the actions of the immortal soul or otherworldly *pneuma*, when it finally attains its proper spiritual realm. To access this otherworld from the ordinary world, the creative artist must exercise precision as well as originality; receptivity as well as creativity; attentiveness as well as spontaneity.

Alexandrov believes that Nabokov's sense of the otherworld, of *potustoronnost*, was suggested by Petr Uspinskii, a dualistic thinker who influenced many intellectuals and artists in Russia and Europe during and after World War I. Uspinskii, as Alexandrov explains, was a dualistic mystic who believed that "normal existence consists of mechanical responses to various random events." Normal existence, that is, corresponds to the "hylic," or earthy, realm of appetites and aversions. Like other dualistic thinkers, Uspinskii believed that the enlightened could transcend the normal state of perception, cultivate a higher form of consciousness (which he called the "fourth dimension"), and in the process serve a higher metaphysical realm.[37] Heidegger is another important philosopher of art who sees poetry as able to provide access to the metaphysical. He associates poetry with a special power: the power of language to bring *Being* "into the open," as Steven Cassedy explains.[38] Language is "the house of Being," and poetry illumines the realm of Being by *unconcealing* it. Moreover, many commentators—John Macquarrie is a convenient example—take Heidegger's philosophy of aesthetics to be a thinly veiled metaphysics or even a theology in which "Being" is equivalent to "God."[39] According to our definition, then, Uspinskii's dualism and Heidegger's metaphysical aesthetic are influential examples of aesthetic strategies that, like gnostic strategies, ally themselves with the not-here and not-now. They are alienistic strategies, furthermore, because they advocate a potentially saving art that transcends the mundane they-world of common sense and common understandings by providing access to a higher dimension or by revealing Being itself. No matter the term used, aesthetic strategies regret the need for bringing a work of art "back" or "down" to the ordinary world. Thus aestheticism's ethical dimension derives from its claim, asserted in a multitude of ways, that the most beneficial texts are sequestered, "writerly," and adamantly independent. By repairing to the implicitly transcendent realm of the imagination, readers and writers can reduce their collaboration with the machinations of modernity.

NOTES

1. Paul Zweig, *The Heresy of Self-Love: A Study of Subversive Individualism* (1968; rpt., Princeton: Princeton University Press, 1980), p. 251.

2. Malcolm Bradbury, *The Social Context of Modern English Literature* (New York: Schocken, 1971), p. 102. Bradbury employs the term *formalism*, a category that shares some qualities with alienism but does not suggest the willful formlessness of some alienistic literature.

3. Ibid., p. 104.

4. Albert Camus, *The Plague*, trans. Stuart Gilbert (New York: Modern Library, 1948), p. 228.

5. See Mark Krupnick, *Lionel Trilling and the Fate of Cultural Criticism* (Evanston, Ill.: Northwestern University Press, 1986), and Giles Gunn, *The Culture of Criticism and the Criticism of Culture* (New York: Oxford University Press, 1987).

6. José Ortega y Gasset, *The Dehumanization of Art, and Other Writings on Art and Culture*, trans. Willard A. Trask (New York: Doubleday, 1956), quoted by Bradbury in *Social Context*, p. 104.

7. Kenneth Burke, *Counter-Statement* (1931; rpt., Berkeley: University of California Press, 1968), pp. 111–12.

8. Ibid., pp. 112–15. Having made his case this forcefully, Burke characteristically refrains from dogmatizing the aesthetic strategy of resistance. The de-Occidentalizing that he advocates "is justified only while the West remains so thoroughly Occidental; the Orient might well cultivate many of those very tendencies which the Occident should discourage" (p. 115). Alienation, especially when strategically aligned as alienism, has its vices as well as its virtues, and I turn to these explicitly in the conclusion.

9. James Joyce, *A Portrait of the Artist as a Young Man* (1916; rpt., New York: Compass-Viking, 1969), pp. 171–72.

10. Ibid., p. 159.

11. Ibid., p. 208.

12. Ibid., p. 215.

13. Ibid., p. 213.

14. Wayne Booth, *The Rhetoric of Fiction* (Chicago: University of Chicago Press, 1961), pp. 323–36.

15. On Goethe, see M. H. Abrams, *The Mirror and the Lamp: Romantic Theory and the Critical Tradition* (1953; rpt., New York: Norton, 1958), p. 303.

16. Joyce, *A Portrait of the Artist*, p. 215.

17. Oscar Wilde, *Intentions* (London: J. R. Osgood, McIlvaine, 1891), quoted by Johnson in *Aestheticism*, p. 81.

18. Roger Fry, *Vision and Design* (London: Chatto and Windus, 1920), p. 10.

19. See, for example, the genealogy of Aestheticism in Irving Singer, "The Aesthetics of 'Art for Art's Sake,'" *Journal of Aesthetics and Art Criticism* 12, no. 3 (1954), pp. 343–59.

20. Walter Pater, "The Renaissance," *Walter Pater: Three Major Texts (The Renaissance, Appreciations, and Imaginary Portraits)*, ed. William E. Buckler (New York: New York University Press, 1986), p. 220.

21. Oscar Wilde, "English Renaissance of Art," *Essays and Lectures* (London: Methuen, 1909), p. 128, quoted by Singer in "The Aesthetics of 'Art for Art's Sake,'" p. 351.

22. R. V. Johnson, *Aestheticism* (London: Methuen, 1969), pp. 39, 61.

23. Bellow's acceptance speech was adapted and published in *Saturday Review*, 3 Apr. 1965, p. 20.

24. Joyce, *Portrait of the Artist*, p. 213; Vladimir Nabokov, *Strong Opinions* (New York: McGraw-Hill, 1973), p. 116.

25. Thomas Carlyle, *On Heroes and Hero Worship*, in *The Works of Thomas Carlyle*, ed. H. D. Traill (New York: Scribner's 1896–1901), vol. 5, p. 80.

26. Thomas Carlyle, "Jean Paul Friedrich Richter," in ibid., vol. 26, p. 20.

27. Abrams, *The Mirror and the Lamp*, p. 26.

28. Jonathan Culler, *Structuralist Poetics: Structuralism, Linguistics, and the Study of Literature* (Ithaca: Cornell University Press, 1975), p. 130.

29. The phrase comes from Richard Poirier's title, *A World Elsewhere* (New York: Oxford University Press, 1965).

30. Culler, *Structuralist Poetics*, p. 130.

31. Johnson, *Aestheticism*, p. 12.

32. Culler, *Structuralist Poetics*, p. 129.

33. Ibid., p. 160.

34. In *The Performing Self: Compositions and Decompositions in the Languages of Contemporary Life* (New York: Oxford University Press, 1971), Poirier discusses the strategies and motives of a relatively unrestrained creativity. One purpose of my book is to suggest that there are many kinds of performances and many kinds of selves enacted through performances. Charles Kinbote, as we will see in chapter 11, is Nabokov's parodic answer to celebrators of strong readings and autonomic performances.

35. Vladimir Nabokov, "The Creative Writer," *Bulletin of the New England Modern Language Association* 4, no. 1 (1942), p. 25, my emphasis; quoted by Vladimir Alexandrov in *Nabokov's Otherworld* (Princeton: Princeton University Press, 1991), p. 57. Here Nabokov states quite explicitly what I will argue for on the basis of internal literary evidence in chapter 11: that true artistic creativity takes its inspiration from *potustoronnost*, "the otherworld."

36. Alexandrov, *Nabokov's Otherworld*, p. 54.

37. Ibid., p. 228.

38. Steven Cassedy, *Flight from Eden: The Origins of Modern Literary Criticism and Theory* (Berkeley: University of California Press, 1990), p. 192.

39. John Macquarrie, *Principles of Christian Theology* (New York: Scribners, 1966), p. 105.

⊷— 8

"Nature's Riches": Parabolic Strategies

In *Sincerity and Authenticity*, a 1972 discussion of our moral and cultural economy, Trilling identifies authenticity as the distinguishing feature of our time. Twenty years later Charles Taylor takes Trilling's assertion as an axiom that has been confirmed by the intervening decades. But the anxiety about authenticity, about being our true selves, is not a late twentieth-century phenomenon. Trilling traces the concern at least as far as the eighteenth century, to Edward Young and Rousseau. "Born originals," Young asks, "how comes it to pass we die Copies?"[1] *Society* was Rousseau's answer to Young's question, and even the contentious Romantics could agree on the grave threat posed by the civilization within whose purview we are thrown. It is a threat that dominates American literature as well, at least from the time of the Transcendentalists. Society's appropriating strategies lie primarily in common myths, received opinions, social expectations, and aesthetic traditions, but *any* obligation that emanates from civilization eventually compromises the authenticity of the self. A kind of consensus—"authenticity through alienation"—can be found in thinkers as historically diverse as Rousseau, Nietzsche, Sartre, Heidegger, Foucault, Derrida, and

Lyotard. Authenticity, according to these alienistic strategies, demands an aggressive denial of the expectations of others. The virtue of *in*authenticity, however, is marked by enslavement to others—as Flaubert's Madame Bovary is enslaved to a series of men. Sartre's protégée Nathalie Sarraute decries Emma's subjection to the enslaving *regard* of others: even when she is indulging her fantasies, Sarraute says, Emma's concern about how she is "coming across" makes her the prototypical inauthentic character.[2] To those who aspire to authenticity, it may seem that Emma Bovarys are everywhere and that, as a consequence, a true artist or philosopher ought to resist the ways of the inhabited world with a "fresh" offensiveness.

By the midtwentieth century, anxiety about authenticity and its absence had spread from characteristically alienated artists and intellectuals to a more general public. David Riesman's influential *The Lonely Crowd*, a sociological study published in 1953, discusses inauthenticity under the rubric of the "other-directed" personality. In his own terms he describes T. S. Eliot's "dissociation of sensibility" theory: the "tradition-directed" personality of the Middle Ages (and of "primitive" civilizations of any period) gives way to the "inner-directed" personality of the Renaissance and Reformation. In turn this self-confident "type" disappears in the twentieth century, to be replaced by a hesitant, wary, self-conscious personality who merely conforms to cultural dictates by using highly developed "radar."[3] The other-directed personality's attentiveness to this radar is, for Riesman, a deplorable mark of inauthenticity. Organizing one's behavior in response to external signals was also condemned by social critics such as William Whyte (*The Organization Man*, 1956), Vance Packard (*The Status Seekers*, 1959), and C. Wright Mills (*White Collar*, 1951) in the 1950s. Some of the condescension, the "relentlessly censorious tone" that Trilling notes in Sarraute, can be discerned in these sociologists. The tone of Riesman's book, and even more the attitude implied by Mills's term "Little Man," is clearly disdainful of those whose very "adjustment" confirms their inauthenticity. The implied challenge issued by the authors of such books is to find a strategy for achieving an *autotelic* independence that has proven elusive for almost everyone these sociologists observe.[4]

Resisting homogenization does not come easy. Perhaps, as some cultural materialists insist, it does not come at all. Trilling sets forth the magnitude of the difficulty: "All other people, the whole community up and down the scale of sentience and of cultural development, make the Hell of recognized and experienced inauthenticity. They make the inhabited nothingness of the modern world. They speak to us of our own condition; we are members one of another. Certain exemptions are made: the poor, the oppressed, the violent, the primitive. But whoever occupies a place in the social order in which we ourselves are situated is known to share the doom."[5] The other-directed personality seems unavoidable and the inauthenticities of culture appear to be inescapable—a doleful situation that gives us all the more reason to practice strategies of alienation. Perhaps it may yet be possible to dissolve the intricate cultural valences that threaten to calcify the soul. Critics of adjustment and complacency, in the alienistic tradition of Sartre's character Roquentin, persist in their efforts to write parables of resistance that will be "beautiful and hard as steel and make people ashamed of their existence."[6] Parabolic strategies press the mendacity of our inauthenticity upon us and urge us to do what we can to avoid embracing it.

Parables of Resistance

Parables are the verbal form most preoccupied with the virtue of authenticity. Parabolic writers are suspicious of the givens of their culture, the familiar patterns of incident, belief, value, desire, and image with which they are expected to make do. Their work suggests that there is something else, something strange and not entirely expressible, something that is more true and fundamental than what passes for reality. Writers as diverse as Ernest Hemingway and Joseph Heller, Saul Bellow and Walker Percy, Ralph Ellison and Richard Wright are no less concerned than Sartre with the problem of writing in and for a culture that continuously threatens one's authenticity. Post–World War II fiction writers learned to depict inauthenticity with the aid of a characteristic protagonist whom critics later called the "anti-hero." As he is usually drawn and defined, the anti-hero (usually male) cannot succeed, cannot even function, except as an alien. He is essentially a resister, an antagonist, as James E. Miller Jr. says in describing what was then the "New American Novel" of the 1950s and 1960s. Whether Hemingway's Nick Adams or Bellow's dangling man, Wright's Bigger Thomas or Ellison's Invisible Man, the main character always seems to be in mortal conflict with a world that, as Miller says, "is out to crush or destroy him."[7] Thus *anti-hero* describes a lifelike character who is "anti" because he renounces the world: he will not abide the mendacity, cruelty, and oppression— the pernicious "adjustment" achieved by the world's complacent inhabitants. Ultimately suicide, the extreme gesture of renunciation, becomes a mark of a character's or even an author's authenticity.

Joseph Heller, with *Catch-22*, gives us a word that suggests the world's complacent response when confronted with charges of injustice, duplicity, or exploitation. When Yossarian, Heller's bemused but authentic resister, walks the streets of Rome after the "liberation," he recognizes the exploitation and cruelty not only of a time of war but also of the archetypal city, the *mater* of Western civilization. Here is Rome seen through parabolic eyes: "Yossarian strained helplessly not to see or hear. . . . [He] quickened his pace to get away, almost ran. The night was filled with horrors and he thought he knew how Christ must have felt as he walked through the world, like a psychiatrist through a ward full of nuts, like a victim through a prison full of thieves. What a welcome sight a leper must have been! At the next corner a man was beating a small boy brutally in the midst of an immobile crowd of adult spectators who made no effort to intervene. Yossarian recoiled with sickening recognition."[8] Yossarian is likened to a psychiatrist, to a rejected and unrecognized Christ, to a victim of a world in which adjustment and accommodation are synonymous with complicity and collaboration. As Trilling notes, only a few avoid inauthenticity: the poor, the oppressed, the misfits; in *Catch-22*, it is the lepers, the small boy, the wounded, and the insane. Yossarian, one of the "insane" victims in *Catch-22*, eventually abandons his world: he takes what critics in the fifties and sixties understood as the Huck Finn option and lights out for the territory. It has become a commonplace of social thought, at least since Michel Foucault and R. D. Laing, that the definition of sanity is culture specific: in an absurd and insane culture, those who are deemed insane by the world may actually be strange heroes who possess a charisma and a power that supersede authorized patterns and behaviors. Thus Yossarian's exit is presented as both authentic and courageous. Civilization as depicted in Heller's novel is not rational, not just, not sane, and finally not tolerable for those who value true justice and true sanity. Only the anti-heroes in and out of fiction recognize and face the absurd. They are the ones, paradoxically, who are labeled "mad" and who welcome their alienation, for only in alienation from an alienated culture can one discover authenticity. The rest, the comfortably encultured, are in denial, and their self-deception is the enabling, inauthentic adjustment that makes possible their worldly success. So when Yossarian recoils from the nightmare world of Rome, wised-up readers feel a "sickening recognition" while admiring his renunciation as a sign of authenticity.

Walker Percy's Binx Bolling also resists the claims of his encompassing culture. When *The Moviegoer* was selected by Lewis Gannett, Herbert Gold, and Jean Stafford to receive the 1962 National Book Award for fiction, the citation explained that Percy "examines the delusions and hallucinations and the daydreams and the dreads that afflict those who abstain from the customary ways of making do."[9] One of these is Binx, who, throughout most of the novel, re-fuses to *succeed* in the world into which he is thrown; he cannot use the con-ventional ways offered him to "make do." Making do, for Binx, means succumb-ing to "the malaise," the deadening of experience and dulling of one's authenticity. Most of the characters in *The Moviegoer* are good, civic-minded, other-directed personalities (with the important exception of Binx's aunt, who is from the old school and inner-directed). His characters are not unhappy, but Percy makes it clear to us that they *ought* to be. The alienated, neurotically self-conscious Binx and the intermittently suicidal Kate command our sympathy and allegiance. The others do not have the courage to recognize the malaise; beneath their conformity, their worldly success, and their self-satisfaction lies hidden a more intractable and poisonous alienation.

Stanley Kauffmann, Percy's editor at Knopf, asked him to consider an epi-graph that would capture the thematic coherence of what seemed at the time a rather unstructured, centrifugal fiction.[10] Percy selected an epigraph from Kierkegaard, a phrase that not only helps to unify *The Moviegoer* but also ex-presses succinctly the paradox of the post–World War II parabolic novel:

> . . . the specific character of despair is precisely this: it is unaware of being despair.
>
> Søren Kierkegaard,
> *The Sickness Unto Death*

Those who function smoothly in the world, according to Kierkegaard, are in despair precisely because they are unaware that their assimilation is a dissimu-lation. Kate voices this wisdom again near the end of the book: "Losing hope is not so bad. There's something worse: losing hope and hiding it from yourself."[11] Binx and Kate know their own despair and thus, in a paradoxical reversal of expectations, they are saved by being lost.

⊷— Parables: Fugitive and Cloistered Stories

Both Heller and Percy have created what narrative religionists call parabolic stories.[12] Sallie McFague, for instance, places *The Moviegoer* in the genre of parable and analyzes it as a characteristically *modern* parable. In the process she emphasizes the strangeness of all parables: they are indirect, deceptively sim-ple, and "about" something more or other than what they appear to be about. That "something more," the special matter of parable, can be identified as ex-istential authenticity. McFague calls it "the way to be in the world . . . essential reality, the really real."[13] It is available, she says, only through this rather humble genre, an extended metaphor called parable. J. Hillis Miller concurs, describing parable as "a language which is the indirect indication, at a distance, of something that cannot be described directly, in literal language."[14] Thus the parabolic writer achieves and offers (a temporary and oblique) access to "the really real" through indirection, extravagance, distortion, and riddles. The parabler's virtue, a "negative," Socratic wisdom, derives from the awareness that the access to wisdom is unstable, uncertain, and ephemeral. As Bernard Harrison says, "Parables defy precise doctrinal or moral interpretation; or, more infuriatingly still, admit it only on the level of moral commonplace, escaping all our attempts to articulate the more profound and numinous meanings which we feel to be obscurely present in them." The maker of parables is "a thorn in the side of theology," because "you cannot found a state religion, or a practical homiletic, on a collection of riddles."[15]

John Dominic Crossan, in a more extended examination of parable, borrows Sheldon Sacks's typology in Fiction and the Shape of Belief and extends the grid, as it were, on either end. Thus to Satire, Action, and Apologue, Crossan adds Myth on the right and Parable on the left as types of story. Myth, according to Crossan, "establishes world. Apologue defends world. Action investigates world. Satire attacks world. Parable subverts world."[16] Crossan's notion of parable emphasizes the element of surprise and the reversal of audience expectations. Parables affront. They are "limiting narratives about limits," and as such they keep us both honest and humble. But parables also stimulate frustration and anxiety—following Barthes, Crossan makes a distinction between the structure of expectation on the part of the hearer and the structure of expression on the part of the speaker. In parable, "these structures are in diametrical opposition, and this opposition is the heart of the parabolic event."[17] Parables offer the reader no clue as to the principle or moral that the reader is invited to seek, as Clayton Koelb says of Kafka's parables. The only principle they offer is "the principle that principles are not to be found."[18] For Crossan, too, parable is "intrinsically negative . . . the dark night of story" and functions as a contested site deliberately arranged "to show the limitations of myth, to shatter world so that its relativity becomes apparent."[19] As Burkean acts within cultural scenes, parables remind us that our seemingly settled ways are arbitrary and up for grabs.

J. Hillis Miller recognizes the destructive power of parable to "shatter world" but he is also interested in the power of parable to provoke a response and "make things happen." Referring to Burke's notion of symbolic action, he says that parables do not merely name something; instead, they evoke an otherness, and this unfamiliar "something" calls for a response, a reaction, a transition, or a transformation. Parables "want to get the reader from here to there. They want to make the reader cross over into the 'something' and dwell there. But the site to which parable would take the reader is something always other than itself, hence that experience of perpetual dissatisfaction. As Kafka puts this, 'There is a goal but no way. What we call the way is only wandering.' Nevertheless, this tropological, parabolic, performative dimension enables writing and reading to enter history and be effective there, for better or worse."[20] Understood in this way, parables are something more than a source of information, knowledge, or signification. They are not constative but performative utterances, to borrow J. L. Austin's distinction, and one of their virtues is the creation and maintenance of dissatisfaction.[21]

Though Crossan, like Miller, celebrates the parabolic mode, he notes that it is not possible to live exclusively in the counter-statements of parable. Similarly, insofar as writing itself is a mode of living, an entering into history, it is not possible to write with untrammeled authenticity. Hemingway's recollection of his occasional "writer's block" suggests well, I think, the problem faced by modern novelists who seek the purity of parable: "Sometimes when I was starting a new story and I could not get it going, I would stand and look out over the roofs of Paris and think, 'Do not worry. . . . All you have to do is write one true sentence. Write the truest sentence you know.' "[22] By "true" Hemingway surely means authentic, pure, uncompromising—*parabolic*. "If I started to write elaborately," he says, "like someone introducing or presenting something, I found I could cut that scrollwork or ornament out and throw it away."[23] Then, having cleansed his parable of baubles, he would begin again with the one true sentence, unencrusted and demythologized.

An authentic style worked for a while in Hemingway's fiction. But if authenticity is understood as a renunciation of other-directed manners and motives, then "authentic style" is a contradiction in terms. Eventually, Hemingway's wariness about mythmaking—about "presentation" and "scrollwork"—led to a stylistic reductio ad absurdum in his later work, a kind of parody of Hemingwayan parable. The failure of his project was predictable and, in its overweening insistence on authenticity, tragic. Hemingway was adamant in his unwillingness to grant Twain (a writer who battled his own authenticist demons) his elaborate ornament—the "escapement" section of *Huckleberry Finn*. Hemingway's unyielding and puritanical high-mindedness doomed him to the impossible burden of absolute honesty and truth-telling. Paring down as a means of producing the one true sentence eventually becomes its own compulsive formula. In the end, it does not work. Hemingway might have anticipated the stylistic and existential problem: Twain himself, who wrote the flawed and fugitive book that Hemingway said "all American literature" came from, foreshadowed Hemingway's vicious cycle of doomed authenticity when he self-righteously denounced James Fenimore Cooper's romantic adornments in the Leatherstocking tales.

Herbert N. Schneidau traces this preoccupation with unadorned truth and uncompromising authenticity to the puritan element in American culture and, indeed, to the prophetic Yahwist tradition in the Judeo-Christian West. Lear's prophetic unmasking of human exploitation and hypocrisy is in this tradition: "Thou hotly lust'st to use her in that kind / For which thou whip'st her," Schneidau says, "might have been said by Jeremiah."[24] He identifies powerful strains of "Yahwism," the uncompromising demand for authenticity, in various Western ideologies. And the result is inevitably a fatal emphasis on purity that leads to cultural cannibalism: "If latent Yahwism is present," Schneidau says, "naturally they eat themselves up sooner or later, no matter how ambitiously mythological they become."[25] Myth and epic—any establishing or foundational "grand narrative"—will be blatantly and manifestly intertwined with the larger society and culture to which and within which it speaks. Puritan and Yahwist imaginations are unlikely to adopt such imperial strategies because they corrupt the prophet's purity and make his or her effort to utter the "one true sentence" self-defeating. Milton may want to withhold his praise of fugitive and cloistered virtues, but the virtue of alienation may find its most durable form in the fugitive and cloistered stories we call parables.

►←   Beckett's Parabolic Comedy: *Krapp's Last Tape*

If parable benefits culture through provocation, one reluctant benefactor is surely Samuel Beckett. In one apology for his work Beckett as much as accepts the role of redeeming parabler: "I didn't invent this buzzing confusion . . . the only chance of renewal is to open our eyes and see the mess."[26] Beckett opens our eyes as thoroughly and painfully as any major writer of our time. He reminds us of the mess and shows us that our familiar and habitual ways of knowing, ordering, and rendering are part of a collective deceit. As Schneidau says, "*Waiting for Godot* stands as a rebuke to the adventure story" and other formulaic and traditional strategies to which we as a culture remain addicted. But even more to the parabolic point, Beckett's work rebukes "our tendency to assert that we can easily or habitually measure the significance of events," a tendency that Schneidau characterizes as "far more important and insidious."[27] Like other parablers, Beckett presses upon us the knowledge that we are missing it, blowing it, losing it, where *it* is "the way to be in the world . . . the really real." [28] As impertinent reminders, such disruptive, extravagant, alienistic performances may, like prophecy, bring freshness and renewal.

We could do a parabolic reading of almost any of Beckett's works, but *Krapp's Last Tape* is particularly germane because Krapp himself is an artist of sorts, a mythmaker *manqué* who creates "spools as equipment for living." [29] Thus *Krapp's Last Tape* is a good exemplar of parable, for it pits the world-maker and -defender, Krapp, against the world-attacker and -subverter, Beckett. Krapp's art differs significantly from Beckett's, for Krapp tries to record and historicize in order to understand himself and his function in the world. Krapp's taping, by now familiar and representative, was used in a classic gerontological article to exemplify the "life review" or reminiscence that many psychiatrists and gerontologists see as the principal work of old age. [30] The "piece"—Beckett's label suggesting the fragmented rendering of one man's alienation—is a critique of Krapp's life review, his mythologizing attempts to measure an intelligible world and to place himself within it. [31] Krapp tries to make his life meaningful by recording his personal assessments and private narrations on tape; his recordings are made to signify and celebrate milestones, usually birthdays. As such they are rituals, and as rituals they are connected to myth. The myth of Krapp, as it spools out, is a crappy myth.

To get himself in the proper state of mind for a retrospective analysis, Krapp guiltily eats bananas—Beckett makes sure that we do not miss the obsessive-compulsive dimension of Krapp's banana eating—and drinks an unknown inebriant offstage. He also listens to old tapes that were made on "significant" dates years earlier. On the ritual occasion of his sixty-ninth birthday Krapp plays a reel, or spool, made on his thirty-ninth birthday. On the tape, we hear Krapp's younger voice making a vain attempt to explain his feelings on the day his mother died and, at another point, his emotional response to separation from a lover. As he listens, Krapp impatiently skips the philosophical passages, for in his old age he has become cynical about the value of contemplation and analysis. He has given up, it would seem, his hope for a sense of purpose in his life. Nonetheless, Krapp gamely and perhaps courageously takes up the microphone once again, painstakingly locates the notes he scribbled on the back of an envelope, and tries to begin another "retrospect."

Harry R. Moody explains such an attempt at a life review as an effort "to sum up an entire life history, to sift its meaning, and ultimately to come to terms with that history at the horizon of death." [32] In other words, the life review is an essay in mythmaking. The successful resolution of a life review will signify, according to Moody, that "(1) my life is intelligible; (2) my life has a purpose; and (3) my hopes and desires ultimately can be satisfied."[33] Moody draws on the philosophy of Kurt Baier to suggest that what the life review seeks is what we call "meaning" itself, which derives from these three distinct but related concerns: intelligibility or causality, purposefulness or teleology, and self-actualization or happiness.

Krapp's last tape, his last life review, suggests that all meaning has been lost, stolen, or somehow forfeited. Finally, it seems, Krapp has given up on myth. He is interested only in playing and replaying a plain tale of passive lovemaking: "We lay there without moving. But under us all moved, and moved us, gently, up and down, and from side to side."[34] Some critics have argued that this little tale is the crux of Krapp's life, that his replaying of this story privileges it not only for Krapp but also for us. Yet in such interpretations, I would argue, we learn more about the nostalgia of readers for myth than about Beckett's parabolic performance.[35] Krapp's story has not been given shape or meaning by the scene of lovemaking; rather, a vision he had one "memorable night in March, at the end of the jetty, in the howling wind, never to be forgotten" served at least for a while as the ordering epiphany of his life. Yet the "memorable equinox" has been long forgotten, forgotten and even renounced, for just as Krapp's younger voice is about to explain the epiphany—"What I suddenly saw then was this, that the belief I had been going on all my life, namely—" Beckett has him impatiently advance the tape.[36] By his sixty-ninth birthday, and apparently for some time before, this conversion experience has seemed a cruel hoax; Krapp is left alone and mythless, his lifelines in tatters.

Thus the countless tapes, dusty and scattered, have scarcely helped him achieve intelligibility. Whatever life purpose Krapp may have felt at one time has been eroded by the paltry sales of his magnum opus—only seventeen copies in three years. And his "den," as he calls it, is a place of physical, emotional, and spiritual privation and squalor. As Kathleen Woodward says, Krapp "does not possess a past. . . . There is no continuity of the self, only fragments of stories, virtually empty words."[37] Beckett's dramatic piece offers us a few amusements and a brief romantic sketch, but these devices are subservient to his purpose: the presentation of an estranged figure whose attempts at personal mythmaking only intensify his alienation. As Moody says, "If my life lacks intelligibility, lacks a purpose, and is miserable, then it seems unavoidable to say that it is meaningless."[38]

How has Krapp's life come to such a pass? Again, some discover in the repeated scene of lovemaking a hint that Krapp has simply made a wrong turn, that the meaninglessness of his life might have been avoided: "I bent over her to get them in the shadow and they opened. (Pause. Low.) Let me in. (Pause.) We drifted in among the flags and stuck. The way they went down, sighing, before the stem! (Pause.) I lay down across her with my face in her breasts and my hand on her. We lay there without moving. But it under us all moved, and moved us, gently, up and down, and from side to side."[39] The obsessive replaying of this scene represents Krapp's stubborn hope for a mythic reconciliation, a simultaneous recapturing and redemption of a patterned past. But Krapp's romantic myth is still, when all is said and done, just a section of magnetic tape sliding through a machine; it is a bit of artificial, mimetic fantasy that represents an addiction as surely as his drinking does. One "epiphany" is as false as another, and Krapp's replaying of the old fantasy is ultimately as onanistic as his stroking of the bananas.

Krapp has been using this story for years to construct what he has missed in life, to pretend that love and happiness were once possibilities: in sum, to identify himself by locating himself in the world. For Krapp it is clearly a gratifying story—perhaps we could say that it is central to his life—and he is obviously trying to use this particular recording as strategic equipment for living. Yet his technique of resorting to a central "identity story" does not save him. When the play ends, a creaturely Krapp is alone in his den staring out in silence at nothing. Having imbibed his alcohol, consumed his bananas, and listened to his tape, Krapp is as alone as ever; and the tape of lovemaking, the glorious story that Krapp tries to make his salvation, instead renders the precise nature of Krapp's despair: "Past midnight," the voice on the tape says after describing the moment of passion. "Never knew such silence. The earth might be uninhabited."[40] Neither the act of love nor the repeated story of that remembered moment seem to provide any means for him to construct a meaningful, intelligible world and find his place within it. Thus does Beckett's "piece" fulfill one of the functions of parable identified by Crossan: "to create contradiction within a given situation of complacent security [and], even more unnervingly, to challenge the fundamental principle of reconciliation by making us aware of the fact that we made up the reconciliation."[41]

As parabolic world-subverter, Beckett debunks more than one myth. He undermines more than one instance of Krapp, more than one old man's quaint reminiscence. Our more sophisticated ways of knowing are also implicated in Beckett's thoroughgoing subversion. As readers or theatergoers we may initially scoff at poor Krapp, but without a firm vantage point we eventually lose our secure sense of superiority, and our derisive laughter trails off uncertainly just as Krapp's tape runs on in silence. *Krapp's Last Tape* undermines *any* assertions of integration, reconciliation, and the continuity of the self. What Ben Belitt says of the parables of Kafka and Jorge Luis Borges could also be said of Beckett's: as insights they constitute "an epistemology of *loss.*"[42] Beckett's little drama is a parable attacking the myth of individuality and self-creation; it is an alienistic strategy responding to our excessive faith in contemporary self-fashioning. As such, it deletes without replacing and can be judged an ethically destructive, alienating, enervating performance.

As parable, however, Beckett's play does have benefits to offer. Parables are specially designed, it seems, to serve those in an unredeemed condition. Though he eschews the well-made play, Beckett is not afraid to use *techniques* to create a character whose thoughts and actions make him intelligible and amusing to an audience. He decides to repeat an enchanting romantic story and goes for laughs with slapstick bits borrowed from vaudeville. The conscientious and fastidious playwright joins in the dance, and he is not above using rhetorical appeals to quicken complacent imaginations. In this act of compromise Beckett is not unlike Shakespeare, who was, according to Carlyle, a victim of convention and a servant of his culture: "Alas, Shakespeare had to write for the Globe Playhouse: his great soul had to crush itself, as it could, into that and no other mould. It was with him, then, as it is with us all. No man works save under conditions. The sculptor cannot set his own free Thought before us; but his Thought as he could translate it into the stone that was given, with the tools that were given. *Disjecta membra* are all that we find of any Poet, or of any man."[43] Without his appeals, his *disjecta membra*, Beckett's parabolic vision would lack the power to hurt. A dramatic piece like *Krapp's Last Tape* is made to be performed. Even Beckett beckons.

Along with Martin Luther, Montaigne, Blaise Pascal, Kierkegaard, and Baudelaire, Beckett can be listed as a contributing alienist, a "psychiatrist" in the sense recently revived by Caleb Carr's novels: Beckett and other parablers diagnose the soul sickness of the culture. Almost as if by design, the authorial desire for authenticity serves culture's need for the demythologizing function of parable. By figuring forth alienation, parablers become teachers and educators *malgré lui.* "Parable," Frye says, "is the *appropriate* way of educating a free man."[44] What Zweig says about other subversive writers can be aptly applied to those we are calling parablers: they overcome their isolation and help us to overcome our own by making alienation "work," and making "work out of it, creating thereby a new 'cultural' link with a world clarified by their ordeal." Thus their writing becomes an act of courage and their exposition of alienation a kind of heroism. Zweig hears "the tone of urgency in their work," a tone that makes it clear that, as flesh-and-blood persons, "they were . . . fighting for their lives, or, at the very least, for their sanity."[45] Excluded from common life by their strange and uncompromising perspective, they find in parable a way to include themselves again, and at the greatest possible risk.

Parabolic Tricksters and alien troublemakers provide the culture a demythol-ogized standpoint, an authentic grounding without which, Wadlington says, "no genuinely humane choice can be made concerning how, in what form, and with what order we wish to survive."[46] So by standing on the margins of culture, in its "conceptual crevices and perceptual blind-spots," in "the repulsive but strangely fertile realm of silence, of darkness," the parabler freshens the life of his or her culture.[47] Strategies of alienation do indeed make their contributions: paraphrasing another parabler tempted by worldly wealth and wonder, we do not live by myth alone.[48]

Notes

1. Edward Young quoted by Lionel Trilling in *Sincerity and Authenticity* (Cambridge, Mass.: Harvard University Press, 1972), p. 93.

2. Nathalie Sarraute, "Flaubert," trans. M. Jolas, *Partisan Review* 33, no. 2 (1966), p. 203.

3. David Riesman, with Nathan Glazer and Reuel Denney, *The Lonely Crowd: A Study of the Changing American Character* (1961; rpt., New Haven: Yale University Press, 1969), pp. 3–162.

4. R. J. Kaufman introduced me to the term *autotelic* and I employed it in an undergraduate thesis. The term is meant to suggest a character whose purpose, or *telos*, is self-defined. Nietzsche's *The Genealogy of Morals* suggests by a kind of indirect proof the value of the autotelic.

5. Trilling, *Sincerity and Authenticity*, p. 102.

6. Jean-Paul Sartre, *Nausea* (New York: New Directions, 1964), p. 203.

7. James E. Miller Jr., *Quests Surd and Absurd* (Chicago: University of Chicago Press, 1967), p. 13.

8. Joseph Heller, *Catch-22* (1961; rpt., New York: Dell-Laurel, 1994), p. 416.

9. Walker Percy, *The Moviegoer* (1961; rpt., New York: Noonday-Farrar, 1968), p. ii.

10. For the fascinating story of collaboration, creative prodding, and resistance between Kauffmann and Percy, see Heather Moore, "Walker Percy's *The Moviegoer*: A Publishing History," *Library Chronicle* 22, no. 4 (1992), pp. 123–43.

11. Percy, *The Moviegoer*, p. 193.

12. See Dan Otto Via, *The Parables: Their Literary and Existential Dimensions* (Phila-

delphia: Fortress Press, 1967); James Breech, *The Silence of Jesus: The Authentic Voice of the Historical Man* (Philadelphia: Fortress Press, 1983); Robert Funk, *Parables and Presence: Forms of the New Testament Tradition* (Philadelphia: Fortress Press, 1982); and various essays in the collection edited by Bernard Brandon Scott, *Parable Interpretation in America: The Shift to Language* (Sonoma, Calif.: Polebridge Press, 1988).

13. Sallie McFague, "The Parabolic in Faulkner, O'Connor, and Percy," *Religion and Literature* 15, no. 2 (1983), pp. 49–51.

14. J. Hillis Miller, *Tropes, Parables, Performatives: Essays on Twentieth-Century Literature* (Durham: Duke University Press, 1991), p. 135. Miller says that a parabolic narrative is "in some way governed, at its origin and at its end, by the infinitely distant and invisible, by something that transcends altogether direct presentation" (p. 136).

15. Bernard Harrison, *Inconvenient Fictions: Literature and the Limits of Theory* (New Haven: Yale University Press, 1991), p. 219.

16. John Dominic Crossan, *The Dark Interval: Towards a Theology of Story* (Sonoma, Calif.: Eagle Books, 1988), p. 42. See also Sheldon Sacks, *Fiction and the Shape of Belief* (Berkeley: University of California Press, 1964).

17. Ibid., p. 50.

18. Clayton Koelb, "The Kafkan Parable as Antithetical Hypersign," in *Semiotics 1984*, ed. John Deely (Lanham, Md.: University Press of America, 1985), p. 85.

19. Crossan, *The Dark Interval*, p. 43.

20. Miller, *Tropes, Parables, Performatives*, p. ix.

21. J. L. Austin, *How to Do Things with Words*, 2d ed., ed. J. O. Urmson and Marina Sbisa (Cambridge, Mass.: Harvard University Press, 1975).

22. Ernest Hemingway, *A Moveable Feast* (New York: Scribners, 1964), p. 12.

23. Ibid.

24. Herbert N. Schneidau, *Sacred Discontent: The Bible and Western Tradition* (Berkeley: University of California Press, 1976), p. 283.

25. Ibid., p. 36.

26. Beckett quoted by William A. Henry III in "Giving Birth 'Astride of a Grave,'" *Time*, 8 Jan. 1990, p. 69.

27. Schneidau, *Sacred Discontent*, p. 283.

28. McFague, "The Parabolic," p. 49.

29. One way to distinguish parabolic works is to say that they inherently resist, more or less tenaciously, being used as equipment for living.

30. Robert N. Butler introduced the term "life review" and considered *Krapp's Last Tape* in some depth in "The Life Review: An Interpretation of Reminiscence in the Aged," *Psychiatry* 26, no. 1 (1963), pp. 65–76. For a bibliography of gerontological publications dealing with the life review, see Harry R. Moody, "Bibliography on Life-Review," in *The Uses of Reminiscence*, ed. Marc Kaminsky (New York: Haworth Press, 1984), pp. 231–36.

31. Samuel Beckett, *"Krapp's Last Tape" and Other Dramatic Pieces* (1958; rpt., New York: Evergreen-Grove, 1960).

32. Harry R. Moody, "The Meaning of Life and Old Age," in *What Does It Mean to Grow Old: Reflections from the Humanities*, ed. Thomas R. Cole and Sally Gadow (Durham, N.C.: Duke University Press, 1986), p. 24.

33. Ibid., pp. 25–26.

34. Beckett, *"Krapp's Last Tape,"* p. 27.

35. I do not mean to use *nostalgia* in the pejorative sense currently in fashion. Many have argued, and I would agree, that the need for myth has not diminished in the late twentieth century. See, for example, Rollo May, *The Cry for Myth* (New York: Norton, 1991).

36. Beckett, *"Krapp's Last Tape,"* p. 21.

37. Kathleen Woodward, "Reminiscence and the Life Review," in *What Does It Mean to Grow Old*, p. 158.

38. Moody, "The Meaning of Life and Old Age," p. 27.

39. Beckett, *"Krapp's Last Tape,"* p. 27.

40. Ibid., p. 28.

41. Crossan, *The Dark Interval*, p. 40.

42. Ben Belitt, "The Enigmatic Predicament: Some Parables of Kafka and Borges," *TriQuarterly* 25 (Fall 1972), p. 273.

43. Thomas Carlyle, *On Heroes and Hero Worship*, in *The Works of Thomas Carlyle*, ed. H. D. Traill (New York: Scribner's, 1896–1901), vol. 5, pp. 110–11.

44. Northrop Frye, *The Critical Path: An Essay on the Social Context of Literary Criticism* (Bloomington: Indiana University Press, 1971), p. 124.

45. Paul Zweig, *The Heresy of Self-Love: A Study of Subversive Individualism* (1968; rpt., Princeton: Princeton University Press, 1980), p. 257.

46. Warwick Wadlington, *The Confidence Game in American Literature* (Princeton: Princeton University Press, 1975), p. 23.

47. Ibid., p. 17.

48. "Human beings live not on bread alone but on every word that comes from the mouth of God" (Matt. 4.4). Jesus is quoting Deuteronomy 8.3: "Human beings live not on bread alone but on every word that comes from the mouth of Yahweh." If Schneidau is right about the Yahwist tradition, then these caveats could be interpreted as explicit declarations of the value, even the necessity, of the parabolic.

All right, then, I'll go to hell.
    Huck Finn

"What's the use?" Beckett said. . . . "Even writing is not the
solution. The whole thing is absurd. Not a dialogue with
absurdity but a monologue in absurdity."
    "But Samuel Beckett, you should know one thing. . . .
A tale about absurdity is a tale against absurdity."
    Elie Wiesel, "The Modern Storyteller and the
    Ancient Dialogue"

PART 3
Performances
of Alienation

Man is born a coward (L'homme est né poltron). *It is a*
difficulty—parbleu! *It would be too easy otherwise. But habit*—
habit—*necessity*—*do you see?*—*the eye of others*—voilà."
Joseph Conrad, *Lord Jim*

 9

Reluctant Performers

Stories like *Lord Jim* explore and interrogate our personal and communal virtues. Conrad's narrative scrutinies led him to a Nietzschean understanding of
the genealogy of morals: they arise within social contexts, the unexamined traditions and habituations of a culture. When a person's culture is weakened or
absent, as it is for Kurtz in *Heart of Darkness*, the virtues themselves—those
habits of mind and act that define us—are thrown, as it were, "up for grabs."
Life plots are modified, subverted, or perversely fulfilled; narratives are truncated, forgotten, or stitched together. Conversions occur. One man jumps,
another takes an unwonted turn. Conrad's stories, like the metaphor of America-
as-melting-pot, contradict the old saw about taking "the boy out of the country." You *can* take the country out of the boy, and in our postcolonial world the
empirical evidence is never far to seek—perhaps it never was. The one who
would become Tuan Jim, heretofore a stalwart, reliable British sea officer, abandons his post and the helpless pilgrims adrift on the *Patna*.

Conrad provides a character whose tenacity in this situation exemplifies the
virtue of courage. The duty-bound French gunboat officer is the one who stays

with the ship those thirty treacherous hours as it is being towed back to port. A foil for Jim's cowardice, the enculturated sailor is likened to "one of those snuffy, quiet village priests, into whose ears are poured the sins, sufferings, the remorse of peasant generations, on whose faces the placid and simple expression is like a veil thrown over the mystery of pain and distress."[1] A naive, unassuming functionary, this Frenchman is not by a long shot the Achillean image of a hero. His action and his taciturn explanation belie the notion that a courageous man merely answers an inner call or fulfills a predestined entelechy. Courage is a virtue that has to be put there by the audience rather than by the actor, and even then "it is always to be seen."[2]

The pernicious effects of being seen, of being entrapped by the Gaze, have been extensively developed by cultural critics and Foucauldian theorists. Yet virtues are arguably "to be seen"—both in the sense of "yet to come," as in "we shall see" what virtues this character has, but also in the sense of taking place before an audience, real or imagined. The power of virtues is "proofed" and realized through actions, just as the energy latent in language is mobilized through speech. Audiences make virtues possible, just as meaning is made possible by the existence of conventions, *parole* made sensible by the presence of *langue*. Conrad's seaman endangers himself for the sake of foreign pilgrims, thereby performing the virtue of courage, because he is "held" by the scripts and opinions of others. He explains his action with a terse and simple observation, "It was judged proper."[3] Yet his sense of duty, "other-directed" to be sure, is not presented by Conrad as a materialist product of social pressures. Someone has to realize the virtue: someone has to stay with the ship. Like other virtues, courage is made possible, not provided, by the audience. The control of cowardice is ongoing. Fear is managed, not conquered. Those actions that prove virtues and define characters can never be taken for granted, the officer explains, because that "point when you let go everything (*vous lachez tout*)" is ever close at hand.[4] There are no permanently courageous characters; there are only courageous actions and kept promises. Even the best of us would prove to be cowards, the sailor says—like Jim we would jump clear, abandon our fellow pilgrims to save our own hides—were it not for habit, necessity, the eyes of others. Virtues require an other, an audience, a Gaze.

In that look of the other, *le regard*, Sartre discovers the source not of courage but of shame, the "bad faith" of being-seen-by-the-other, of performing for the other. The courageous ones for Sartre are the Kierkegaardian Single Ones—authentic men and women who act only in response to their interior, private calls.[5] Kierkegaard is, in fact, a beacon of authenticity in the twentieth century. His mode of uncompromising resistance provides a tempting strategy of alienation for those who cannot abide the mendacities of groups and institutions. In *Either/Or* he explains two modes of renewal: compensatory strategies that he deems *rotation* and *repetition*. The most commonly practiced method is rotation, the method of novelty and escape from the too-familiar: one travels, one reads diverting books, one acquires a new house, a new lover, a new child. Rotations temporarily satisfy the desire for the fresh, the new, the interesting, the unprecedented. But the rotation method, like every strategy, is subject to bureaucratization. What was special in midnineteenth-century Denmark has become dominant, some say universal, in the late twentieth century; the rotation method has been skillfully and relentlessly cultivated by the interests and institutions of the "white economy"—those empty, colorless, seemingly neutral exchange processes of market capitalism.[6]

But Kierkegaard discusses another strategy of renewal, a method he calls repetition. Repetition aims for a different kind of freshness, one more Nietzschean than Wagnerian. Unlike experiences of rotation, experiences of repetition trouble rather than divert. Repetition turns back on the alienating processes of culture and repeats them, fighting fire with fire. Alienistic performers "front" what is predictable and comfortable about culture (to borrow from American street idiom)[7] by confronting and affronting readers who may feel touched in ways that make them uncomfortable. The performers of alienation are usually "in your face," and the reversing aspect of their work often has the virtue of impropriety about it. Not infrequently, then, their freshness will be experienced as harassment. Harassment can be verbal, even literary, even canonical. Flannery O'Connor makes it clear that she intends to be "shouting" at the "hard of hearing" and drawing "large and startling figures" for the almost blind.[8] Her strategies of alienation help her fulfill a vocational obligation to scandalize and provoke. She imagines her complacent reader in a see-no-evil, hear-no-evil posture, saying, "I don't get it, I don't see it, I don't want it." Freshness of this kind, like other unwanted advances, may justly provoke a slap.[9]

There are many strategies of alienation and many ways of being fresh. We are concerned with refreshening by means of what Kierkegaard calls repetition—not escape from alienation by rotation but cancellation by re-presentation. By depicting the self-conscious otherness of estranged, sometimes suicidal or homicidal protagonists, alienists *repeat* it. Like their European mentors—Flaubert, Dostoyevski, Kafka, Sartre, Camus—American writers such as Nathanael West, Wright, Heller, Ellison, Burroughs, William H. Gass, Pynchon, J. D. Salinger, John Barth, and Barthelme figure forth despair to and for the culture that harbors it. Even Beckett, as we have seen, performs within the cultural context. The cooperation inherent in a literary performance leads Percy to assert that "there is no such thing, strictly speaking, as a literature of alienation."[10] Translating Percy's somewhat cryptic statement, we could say that alienistic writers compromise authenticity by writing it. The writing itself is a solicitation, a "Come be with me, come be like me" invitation. Absolute alienation from culture, the mark of a writer's authenticity as much as a fictional character's, is subverted by the performance, which is the poem, the drama, the fiction itself.

To contribute to culture is for some a pernicious act of collaboration. No matter how antimythic, corrosive, and authentic, parables and other alienistic works are yet recuperable and naturalizable. In *Roman et societé*, Michel Zeraffa makes this very charge against Beckett and Alain Robbe-Grillet. Zeraffa argues that the narratives (and presumably the dramas as well) of Beckett and Robbe-Grillet remain "acts of sociability" despite their alienistic strategies. Leon Roudiez affirms Zeraffa's critique: "In spite of themselves," he says, writers such as Beckett and Robbe-Grillet become "accomplices to a given social order."[11] They create fictions in which the characters and social order are readily recognizable. Seen as performances, the works of Beckett and Robbe-Grillet are indeed acts of sociability. But then, so are the critical performances of Zeraffa and Roudiez.

Burke's dramatistic model of symbolic action is also essentially social, based as it is on "cooperation, participation, man in society, man in drama"—all modes of performance. Even the individual's identity, according to Burke, "is formed by reference to his membership in a group." And membership in a group depends on a performance in that group's social order. "One's identification as a member of a group is a *role*," he says, realizing that the word often carries pejorative connotations. "Yet," he adds, "it is the only active mode of identification possible." Because people are neither animals nor machines, they must be those who act and those who are acted for and acted on, "actors and acters." Like *authentic style, authentic performance* is a contradiction in terms if authenticity is understood as a renunciation of other-directed motives. Burke suggests, moreover, that even the notion of authentic identity is a paradox, for "*individualistic* concepts of identity dissolve into the nothingness of mysticism and the absolute."[12] By reaching out through language, a writer places himself or herself in the social order, acknowledges the eyes of others, and perforce gives up the badge of authenticity. Thus Kafka's *The Castle*, for instance, is a parable of alienation *from* a repressive culture that yet remains a cultural performance *for* a repressive culture.

The action here is not a sell out: Ellison does not become a Zelig (Woody Allen's "human chameleon") and Eliot is not a latter-day Robert Southey. Their complicity with the world is more subtle and more therapeutic. The experience of alienistic literature should not create or intensify alienation, but repeat it symbolically, artistically. By calling on common understandings, the performing writer and reader join in a reversal of alienation. One of Percy's favorite accounts of such reversals is an anecdote about Kafka's reading his alienistic stories aloud to his friends, while they all laugh together until tears come to their eyes.[13] For Percy, a literary work is an act of "symbolization" that necessitates empathic identification: "Every symbolic formulation, whether it be language, art, or even thought, requires a real or posited someone else for whom the symbol is intended as meaningful."[14] "I am not only conscious *of* something," Percy asserts. "I am conscious of it as being what it is for you and me. If there is a wisdom in etymologies, the word consciousness is surely a case in point; for consciousness, one suddenly realizes, means a knowing-with!"[15] Thus an alienistic text, performed, becomes an instrument of the adoption of virtues. Regardless of the strategy, then, performative reading and writing are actions of adoption and Burkean identification, and hence functions of sociality.[16]

In *The Message in the Bottle*, Percy explains how the repetition of alienation results in identification:

> In the re-presenting of alienation the category is reversed and becomes something entirely different. There is a great deal of difference between an alienated commuter riding a train and this same commuter reading a book about an alienated commuter riding a train. . . . The nonreading commuter exists in true alienation, which is unspeakable; the reading commuter rejoices in the speakability of his alienation and in the new triple alliance of himself, the alienated character, and the author. His mood is affirmatory and glad: Yes! that is how it is![17]

The recognition "Yes! that is how it is," when shared between author and reader, achieves an aesthetic reversal of existential alienation. By performing her suspicions and disaffections, the novelist reaches out to potential "friends." When reader joins author in condemning a world that is more or less like the reader's own, he imagines, willy-nilly, a world of better, more honest, and therefore more authentic persons such as Yossarian, Binx Bolling, the Invisible Man, and, of course, other readers of *Catch-22*, *The Moviegoer*, and *Invisible Man*. He accepts the author's gift of reversed alienation.

Yet alienistic writers, as Zweig, Schneidau, and Jonas have shown, remain reluctant performers, uneasy with the social matrix, and maintain a wary suspicion of language and consciousness itself. Even Percy, who shares Burke's and Mead's appreciation for the virtues of sociality, has repeatedly articulated the banality of ordinary life and the difficulty of escaping it. Thus, in discussing a television soap opera, Percy asserts that "life in Elmwood with Linda and Father and Mother Young achieves a degree of alienation such as was never dreamed of by Joseph K. in Mitteleuropa; the difference between them is nothing less than the difference between the despair that knows itself and the despair that does not know itself." Percy occasionally approaches an almost Sartrean aversion for bourgeois family life: "The true smell of everydayness," he says, "is the smell of Sunday dinner in the living room."[18]

In *City of Words*, his survey of American writers from 1950 to 1970, Tony Tanner sees among the more serious writers "a dread of all conditioning forces," a dread that manifests itself through repudiation of conventional novelistic devices.[19] "Fictionists" practice certain techniques that are intended to signal their rejection of conventional expectations, their return of the reader's appropriating gaze. Tanner notes that the technique known as foregrounding is a favorite way of "demonstrating one's resistance to, and liberation from, other people's notions as to how one should use language to organize reality."[20] With Victor Schlovsky and the Russian formalists, this technique was originally understood as the author's attempt to "make strange" the language to startle the reader into fresh and beneficially disturbing recognitions. But since World War II, according to Tanner, authors have used foregrounding more as a *defense*, a way of manifesting their rejection of the common tongue and demonstrating their "power to resist and perhaps disturb the particular 'rubricizing' tendency of the [inherited] language." The alienistic writer wants to leave "the visible marks of his idiosyncrasies on every formulation" as evidence of his resistance to "recruiting assaults on his own consciousness."[21] We might say that these idiosyncrasies are the ways alienistic writers "mark their territory," letting the reader and other representatives of the larger culture know that they are ready to fight for sovereignty over their own consciousnesses. Thus foregrounding and other calculated idiosyncrasies are there to proclaim the freedom and authenticity of alienistic writers and to put the world on notice: No Trespassing.

Yet Tanner is well aware of the dependence of oppositionist writers on a larger culture that serves as a holding environment for their deviations and resistances. This is the point made by Charles Taylor: to be performed and recognized, authenticity requires general rules and rubrics, "horizons of significance" that keep authentic gestures visible and meaningful. David Lodge makes a similar observation in *The Modes of Modern Writing*: as a technique of fiction, foregrounding depends on a background to be perceived as a deviation.[22] The circle is a vicious one for the alienistic writer. It is essential that the performance be recognized as a deviation—otherwise it risks becoming just another cultural expression, another facile artifact, easily recuperable and replicable. Yet deviations must diverge from recognized standards or frustrate established expectations. Consequently, we sometimes encounter an alienistic writer beating the dead horse of a supposedly hegemonic and oppressive cultural tradition. She genuinely needs a powerful and pervasive environment so that her resistances can be seen and appreciated.

The problem is well illustrated by John Barth's celebrated and celebratory article of 1967 entitled "The Literature of Exhaustion." What we are calling alienistic performances are, according to Barth, conscious deviations from a bankrupt literary tradition that has "shot its bolt."[23] An author who is not deviating from cultural standards and expectations is not "technically up to date" according to Barth. If executed in the twentieth century, Beethoven's Sixth Symphony or the Chartres Cathedral "would be merely embarrassing."[24] Barth praises Joyce, Borges, and Beckett, because they deal with "ultimacies" both technically and thematically. The final ultimacy, the last exhaustion, yields only absence, darkness, silence. Thus Barth finds it appropriate and somehow satisfying that "Joyce was virtually blind at the end, Borges is literally so, and Beckett has become virtually mute, musewise, having progressed from marvelously constructed English sentences through terser and terser French ones to the unsyntactical, unpunctuated prose of *Comment C'est* and ultimately wordless mimes." The most thorough recognition of exhaustion and the most authentic "expression" of it would be literal silence: "for Beckett, at this point in his career, to cease to create altogether would be fairly meaningful."[25] The problem with extreme alienistic gestures such as silence is that they can be performed only once. Once the apocalypse arrives, once the death of the culture has been declared, there is scarcely anything left to say or do. So the tradition-bound, monolithic culture must be periodically resuscitated so that its threats can be heroically resisted. It must be said in fairness that Barth has since regretted the apocalyptic tone of this late-sixties essay.[26] But Barth's critical and fictional work served as an early and invigorating rallying cry for alienistic writers in the United States, just as the work of Barthes, Foucault, Derrida, and Maurice Blanchot inspired writers such as Luce Irigaray, Julia Kristeva, Gayatri Chakravorty Spivak, and Jean Baudrillard.

In a moment of exacerbated suspicion toward cultural forms, what techniques are available to an author who would continue to speak and perform? Several years before Anglo-American critics were reading Paul de Man, Barth was already extolling fictions that call attention to their own fictiveness and unreliability: Nabokov's *Pale Fire*, "a fine novel by a learned pedant, in the form of a pedantic commentary on a poem invented for the purpose"; and Borges's *Labyrinths*, "fictions by a learned librarian in the form of footnotes, as he describes them, to imaginary or hypothetical books."[27] The story-within-a-story, an alienistic technique used freely by Barth in his own fiction, proclaims its independence, disturbs its readers metaphysically, and involves them in an infinite regress. "We are reminded of the fictitious aspect of our own existence," Barth says.[28] He agrees with Borges that an infinite regress can refute many conceptual mainstays, such as the demand for valid logic, the expectation of cause and effect relations, and the linear passage of time. By denying or ignoring these axioms of the Western tradition, a fiction can foreground its suspicion of culture and press upon us the knowledge that "the world is our dream and that our creation is false or at least fictive."[29] But the purely authentic work would attempt to remain utterly unreliable, unrecuperable, and thus unperformable. It "would prefer not to" and would resist being made use of, even in a struggle against the mendacities of culture.

If extant works are any indication, it must be almost impossible to make a fiction that does not pretend or aspire to be a reliable and useful form of discourse: a first-person account, an "omniscient" report, a diary, an epistle, a confession, a lyrical address to the reader, an elliptical narrative, a riddle, a story. Fictions usually impersonate the cultural moments and artifacts that are typically used to get along in the world. They willingly become our "projects," to borrow Sartre's terminology; by taking a comprehensible form, they allow themselves to be co-opted by their readers. Some will scrupulously attempt to avoid the pretense "that the putative exactitude of words can ever measure up to the actual mystery of things," in Tanner's words; but every performance implies a "voice" behind the various masks of a literary work. The voice represents a person that we believe in, a person who promises us, in effect, that the imaginative experience being offered by the text will, all other things being equal, benefit us in some way: divert, entertain, distract, inform, confront, instruct, trouble, or whatever, but finally be worth our while.[30] As flesh-and-blood readers, we can use such literary works in our symbolic strategies and personal campaigns: in ad hoc life reviews, practical discussions, and the ubiquitous cultural criticism known as gossip. Barth describes *The Sot-Weed Factor* and *Giles Goat-Boy* as "novels which imitate the form of the Novel, by an author who imitates the role of the Author."[31] The imitating, the figuring forth, is not so unprecedented after all. It is what imaginative literature has always done, perhaps what it is somehow constrained to do.

In part 3 of this book, I want to examine several examples of writers pursuing authenticity through literary works, and in the process offering their audiences a benefit. A culture can ill afford to risk ignoring the insistent and compelling monitory voice of alienation, especially in a world where technology has made the brute march of power so efficient. We need ways to accommodate the antinomian energies and what Jonas calls the "acosmic negations of order" that we find in alienistic writing.[32] The question of how a culture can and does appropriate alienistic performances is clearly not a simple one. There are probably many ways. Teachers and critics, by taking their roles as public mediators seriously, will sometimes denature and domesticate such works in a well-meaning attempt to make them more available; or they may carelessly foist powerful, fully crafted, and profoundly disturbing works on unprepared readers — readers who have to get up in the morning and "make a day of it." Trilling, as we have seen, describes the evolution of an "adversary culture," an alienistic weed within the field of culture itself. But he does not explicitly suggest how or why we would welcome the "satanic," why we should find it invigorating, or why we literally canonize its works.

One possible explanation is suggested by the heuristic metaphor unifying this chapter. If alienistic texts are figured as performances, then we can use the work of anthropologists such as Mary Douglas and Victor Turner to understand their potential function as rituals, specifically liminal rituals.[33] Douglas describes periodic ceremonies of the Lele tribe, for example, in which certain initiates ritually confront ambiguity: the goal of the Lele is "to turn round and confront the categories on which their whole surrounding culture had been built and to recognize them for the fictive, man-made, arbitrary conventions that they are."[34] Such a recognition is a staple of critical theory and cultural criticism, the most prominent alienistic strategies in the academy. In S/Z, for example, Barthes calls our attention to the ubiquitous "dividing lines" of culture that allow it to perpetuate itself: "the paradigmatic slash mark which permits meaning to function (the wall of Antithesis), life to reproduce (the opposition of the sexes), property to be protected (rule of contract)."[35] Foucault asserts that "all behavior falls in the field between good and bad marks, good and bad points. . . . The disciplinary apparatuses hierarchize the 'good' and 'bad' subjects in relation to one another."[36] These binaries and hierarchies provide discipline and thereby allow culture to maintain its (oppressive) sovereignty and control. Baudrillard "turns round" on culture in a similar way when he suggests that the differential categories that comprise our reality are constructed so that the system can survive: "Any unitary system, if it wishes to survive, must acquire a *binary regulation*. . . . This goes for brands of soap-suds as well as peaceful co-existence. You need two superpowers to keep the universe under control: a single empire would crumble of itself."[37] Even Joyce Carol Oates, who utilizes the hierarchies of language as readily as anyone, had occasion in 1972 to condemn our cultural categories as arbitrary and feckless: "We are tired," she says, "of the old dichotomies: Sane/Insane, Normal/Sick, Black/White, Man/Nature, Victor/Vanquished, and above all this Cartesian dualism I/It. . . . They are no longer useful or pragmatic. They are no longer *true*."[38]

Disruptive performances, whether we label them as theory, criticism, or literature, can be understood as simulating boundary experiences—countercultural statements with designs akin to those of the liminal rituals of other cultures. The alienistic rituals of the Lele tribe described by Douglas momentarily exalt the "undesirable" side of structuralist distinctions: the evil over the good, the unclean over the clean, the ugly over the beautiful, the false over the true. Douglas defines such liminal moments as "dirt-affirming." The Nyakyusa, a highly pollution-conscious culture, ordinarily "avoid faeces and filth and reckon it a sign of madness not to do so." But in their death ritual "they give up everything, they even claim to have eaten filth as madmen do, in order to keep their reason. Madness will come if they neglect the ritual of freely accepting the corruption of the body; sanity is assured if they perform the ritual."[39] The culture is made stronger and more durable by *taking in* the proscribed material. Many alienistic strategies brought to performance function similarly—as dirt-affirming experiences.

For Nemoianu, we recall, the untidy secondary is a source of renewal and strength similar to the dirt-affirming liminal moments described by Douglas. With its disorder and waste, the secondary serves as "a gentle and persistent source of relaxation and defeat" of the earnest, overvigorous, conformity-seeking mechanisms of culture. Alienistic performances, as manifestations of the secondary, may similarly serve the principal by making "the vital gift of ever-renewed, ever-temporary defeat . . . one of the most charitable and precious endowments of the human creature, the faithful spring of gallantries and hopes."[40] Wadlington discovers in anthropology, especially in Victor Turner's work on liminal experiences, another analogy to suggest the capacity of the alienistic performer to renew and refresh. By transcending strict rules and categories of perception and behavior, an alienistic performance, like a liminal experience, may prepare performer and cultural audience for change and growth. For the duration of the liminal event, the dirt—that which is ordinarily rejected by the dominant patterns, scripts, and strategies of a culture—is temporarily affirmed. Turner explains using language borrowed from the alienated, unraveling world of *King Lear*: "In the liminal period we see naked, unaccommodated man, whose nonlogical character issues in various modes of behavior: destructive, creative, farcical, ironic, energetic, suffering, lecherous, submissive, defiant, but always unpredictable."[41] Turner's discussion could almost be read as an apologia for alienistic performances rather than an explanation of liminal experiences: "To be outside of a particularized social position, to cease to have a specific perspective, is in a sense to become (at least potentially) aware of all positions and arrangements and to have a total perspective."[42] The reveler in the liminal can gain access to the "primordial powers of the cosmos" through acts that question and transcend the norms of society. As beneficially refreshing as they are, however, Turner scrupulously notes that liminal experiences "are not to be treated as models of secular behavior." "These relatively short instants," he tells us, "counterbalance the long days of utilitarian and culture-bound experience."[43] Thus alienistic works can and probably do function liminally to support larger social and cultural patterns. It is not that as subversive strategies they are "contained" by being transformed, denatured, or domesticated; rather, as performances they are simply liminal *moments*. Strategies, as theoretical constructs, are out of time and can be revisited for their subversive virtues. But performances, whether constructive or subversive, are in time and thus temporally circumscribed experiments. These liminal performances apparently make a culture stronger, more resilient, and less efficiently coercive, by acknowledging the irrational, the unintelligible, the parabolic, the gnostic, the *Entfremdung*, the *Unheimlich*.

If the specific character of despair is to be unaware of despair, if the nature of true, intractable alienation is to be unaware of alienation, then those who confront us with our malaise, whether teachers or writers, minister to our collective disease. They confer a singularly valuable, albeit troublesome, gift. If we accept the gift, their alienistic performances may serve to dissipate our more profound alienation by re-presenting and repeating it. In any case, their parabolic effort implies, even if it does not overtly express, a dialogic hope. At the very beginning of *Catch-22*, there is a temporary reprieve from alienation through love, "love at first sight. The first time Yossarian saw the chaplain he fell madly in love with him." At the end of the book, the chaplain returns with a fresh promise: "I'll stay here and persevere," he says, "and we'll meet again when the fighting stops."[44] The fighting continues, of course, struggle and violence remain, but the hope for a fresh meeting abides, even in *Catch-22*. There is a similarly veiled promise held out by Percy in the last sentence of *The Moviegoer*: "I watch [Kate] walk toward St. Charles, cape jasmine held against her cheek, until my brothers and sisters call out behind me."[45] Binx has tentatively found a wife and a family. Even Riesman's *The Lonely Crowd* carries the implication that one can, if only through reading the book, become a more autonomous, authentic individual. Because they recognize that "the whole thing is absurd," in Beckett's words to Wiesel, alienistic performers offer readers hope: Yossarian's hope of "meeting again," Binx's hope of a life with "brothers and sisters," Riesman's hope of affiliation with those who "distort or reinterpret their culture" in an effort to revitalize it.[46]

In describing the functions of virtue criticism, I assume that we are similarly engaged in a process of revitalizing, of speaking *to* and *for* as well as *of*. If virtue criticism is a practice of making literary works intelligible and puissant through performance, then the presentation and evaluation of a resisting, alienistic text resembles interpretive anthropology: the foreign is translated, framed, and contextualized for the sake of understanding. Such a process of recovery (or recuperation, borrowing Culler's term) is, like anthropology, fraught with the colonizer's propensity for appropriation and violence. Yet the ambitious and important work of recovering the virtues of texts is, I believe, worth the danger and the trouble. A suggestion, then, for Trilling's teacher of "modern" literature—for those of us who profess and promote alienistic writing in the classroom: If an alienistic text can be presented as a liminal performance of the secondary, then perhaps the cultural renewal and freshening described by anthropologists such as Douglas and Turner and by diverse critics such as Burke, Zweig, Nemoianu, and Wadlington can be achieved. Liminal performances, like the formal rites and communal rituals of other societies, reveal and celebrate what would otherwise become paralyzing ambiguity. Brought to life, alienistic fictions can function like dirt-affirming rituals, making possible a return to the ordered and practical *res publica*. In such ways the Dionysian serves the culture by temporarily usurping the Apollonian. Thus subversive performances find their *appropriate* place on the margins of culture; it is there, in the seams and spaces and eddies of dissolution, that readers and writers can be revitalized by alien energies.

NOTES

1. Joseph Conrad, *Lord Jim* (1899; rpt., New York: Norton, 1968), p. 85.
2. Ibid., p. 89.
3. Ibid., p. 86.

4. Ibid., p. 89.

5. One of the central tenets of Sartre's existentialism is his assertion that a person who performs in response to the demands or expectations of others is a contemptible pretender, a hypocrite. Similarly, if a man blames an unsatisfying condition on others, as Sartre's infamous waiter blames his long working hours on his employer, he deceives himself in an act of *mauvaise foi*. When he places responsibility in one other than himself he becomes an imposter, a coward, and a stranger to himself. Even the conventional hero, if he acts out of a sense of habit or in response to the desires or expectations of others, is simply going through the motions of socially significant action; a habituated hero, like Conrad's sea officer, would be considered by Sartre a coward because he lives an inauthentic life. The authentic self recognizes its total freedom, according to Sartre, and "those who hide their complete freedom from themselves out of a spirit of seriousness or by means of deterministic excuses," he says, "I shall call cowards." *Existentialism and Human Emotions*, trans. Hazel E. Barnes (New York: Philosophical Library, 1957), p. 46.

6. Søren Kierkegaard, *Either/Or*, trans. David Swenson and Lillian Swenson, rev. by Howard A. Johnson (Princeton: Princeton University Press, 1959), pp. 279–96.

7. As in, "Ain't no wild boar gonna *front* Big Dog's bass," where "bass" refers to the lower frequencies of a music source, usually a car stereo's subwoofer played at high volume.

8. Flannery O'Connor, "The Fiction Writer and His Country," *Mystery and Manners*, ed. Sally and Robert Fitzgerald (New York: Farrar, Straus, and Giroux, 1969), p. 34.

9. "When I sit down to write, a monstrous reader looms up who sits down beside me and continually mutters, 'I don't get it, I don't see it, I don't want it.'" O'Connor made these remarks in a lecture given at Georgia State College for Women, January 7, 1960. The original manuscript is located in Folder 245, Flannery O'Connor Collection, Ina Dillard Russell Library, Georgia College and State University, Milledgeville, Ga. In our enthusiasm for personifying we do well to remember that reading performances are volitional, that books can be put down. In the literary classroom, however, books are officially placed in a power relationship vis-à-vis readers. It is there, perhaps, that true harassment may occur. See Lionel Trilling's "The Teacher of Modern Literature," *Beyond Culture: Essays on Literature and Learning* (New York: Viking, 1965), for an analysis of the literary classroom as a site where subversive texts are institutionalized.

10. Walker Percy, *The Message in the Bottle: How Queer Man Is, How Queer Language Is, and What One Has to Do with the Other* (New York: Farrar, Straus, and Giroux, 1975), p. 83.

11. Michel Zeraffa, *Roman et societé* (Paris: Presses Universitaires de France, 1971); Leon S. Roudiez, "In Dubious Battle: Literature vs. Ideology," *Semiotext(e)* 1, no. 1 (1974), p. 92.

12. Kenneth Burke, *The Philosophy of Literary Form: Studies in Symbolic Action*, 2d ed. (Baton Rouge: Louisiana State University Press, 1967), pp. 311, 306, Burke's emphasis.

13. Percy mentions the Kafka story in two different essays in *The Message in the Bottle* (pp. 5, 83). Percy may have read about the laughter of Kafka and his friends in Thomas

Mann's "Homage," included in the Modern Library edition (New York, 1969) of *The Castle*: "Kafka once read aloud to some friends the beginning of his novel *The Trial*. . . . His listeners laughed through their tears, and Kafka too had to laugh so hard that his reading was interrupted. . . . No doubt the same thing happened when he read *The Castle* aloud" (p. xvii).

14. Percy, *The Message in the Bottle*, p. 271.

15. Ibid., p. 274. In this chapter, "Symbol, Consciousness, Intersubjectivity," Percy extrapolates from Mead's assertion that the social matrix is the source of consciousness, communication, and identity. See esp. pp. 267–68.

16. Burke defines *identification* as *the function of sociality* in *Attitudes toward History*, rev. 2d ed. (Los Altos, Calif.: Hermes, 1959), p. 266.

17. Percy, *The Message in the Bottle*, p. 83.

18. Ibid., pp. 92, 93.

19. Tony Tanner, *City of Words: American Fiction, 1950–1970* (New York: Harper and Row, 1971), p. 16.

20. Ibid., pp. 20–21.

21. Ibid., pp. 16, 29.

22. Charles Taylor, *The Ethics of Authenticity* (Cambridge, Mass.: Harvard University Press, 1992), pp. 35–41; David Lodge, *The Modes of Modern Writing: Metaphor, Metonymy, and the Typology of Modern Literature* (Ithaca: Cornell University Press, 1977), p. 245.

23. John Barth, "The Literature of Exhaustion," in *Surfiction: Fiction Now and Tomorrow*, ed. Raymond Federman (Chicago: Swallow, 1975), p. 27.

24. Ibid., p. 21.

25. Ibid., p. 23.

26. See Barth's "The Literature of Replenishment," *Atlantic*, Jan. 1980, pp. 65–71.

27. Barth, "The Literature of Exhaustion," p. 28. Barth tells us that "Borges's favorite third-century heretical sect is the Histriones—I think and hope he invented them— who believe that repetition is impossible in history and therefore live viciously in order to purge the future of the vices they commit: in other words, to exhaust the possibilities of the world in order to bring its end nearer" (p. 31). Thus Barth and Borges have given us a ready-made association of alienism and the dualism of historical Gnosticism.

28. Ibid., p. 30.

29. Ibid., p. 31.

30. Tanner, *City of Words*, p. 27.

31. Barth, "The Literature of Exhaustion," p. 28.

32. Hans Jonas, "Gnosticism and Modern Nihilism," *Social Research* 19, no. 4 (1952), p. 444.

33. See, for example, Turner's *Dramas, Fields, and Metaphors: Symbolic Action in Human Society* (Ithaca: Cornell University Press, 1974) and *The Ritual Process: Structure and Anti-Structure* (Ithaca: Cornell University Press, 1977). For a brief summary of

Turner's notion of liminality, see Kathleen M. Ashley, ed., *Victor Turner and the Construction of Cultural Criticism: Between Literature and Anthropology* (Bloomington: Indiana University Press 1990), pp. xviii–xix.

34. Mary Douglas, *Purity and Danger* (1966; rpt., Baltimore: Penguin/Pelican, 1970), p. 200. In the chapter "The System Shattered and Renewed" Douglas considers in detail the regenerative power of liminal experiences.

35. Roland Barthes, *S/Z*, trans. Richard Miller (New York: Hill and Wang, 1974), p. 215.

36. Michel Foucault, *Discipline and Punish: The Birth of the Prison*, trans. Alan Sheridan (New York: Pantheon, 1977), pp. 180–81.

37. Jean Baudrillard, *Simulations*, trans. Paul Foss, Paul Patton, and Philip Beitchman (New York: Semiotext(e), 1983), p. 134. Baudrillard's wry observation about the need for a binary regulation in the world order may prove eerily prophetic as the millennium—bereft of the capitalism/communism, United States/Soviet Union binaries—comes to an increasingly violent close.

38. Joyce Carol Oates, "New Heaven and Earth," *Saturday Review of the Arts*, Nov. 1972, p. 53.

39. Douglas, *Purity and Danger*, p. 208.

40. Virgil Nemoianu, *A Theory of the Secondary: Literature, Progress, and Reaction* (Baltimore: Johns Hopkins University Press, 1989), p. 203.

41. Victor Turner, "Myth and Symbol," *International Encyclopedia of the Social Sciences* (1968), vol. 7, p. 580. *Liminoid* is the term that Turner gives to modern civilization's nonritualized counterparts to the "liminal rites" of ancient or "primitive" societies. I will, however, retain *liminal* to designate both formal rituals and informal, imaginative "events."

42. Ibid., p. 577.

43. Ibid., p. 581.

44. Joseph Heller, *Catch-22* (1961; rpt., New York: Dell-Laurel, 1994), p. 455.

45. Walker Percy, *The Moviegoer* (1961; rpt., New York: Noonday-Farrar, 1968), p. 242.

46. David Riesman, with Nathan Glazer and Reuel Denney, *The Lonely Crowd: A Study of the Changing American Character* (1961; rpt., New Haven: Yale University Press, 1969), p. 260.

⊷— 10

"Others but Stewards":
T. S. Eliot's Gnostic Impulse

To take up *The Waste Land* once again may seem feckless, even banal. "So many, . . . so many": Eliot might have been anticipating the superfluity of bustling critics.[1] Yet we do well to see again (to re-spect) those instigative texts that we blithely take for granted. The task of virtue criticism in taking up or taking on *The Waste Land* is not to find new information to communicate; the challenge is rather that faced by any performer of the familiar: to turn a text that has been disposed of back into a lament, a song that speaks the power to hurt. The attempt, then, is not to codify or enlist *The Waste Land* in an argument, and certainly not to say something about the poem that has never been said before, but to hear and feel again the alienistic voices "done" by one of our century's great gnostic poets.

Despite the slipperiness of the term and the treacherousness of the gnostic terrain, we should be encouraged because Eliot himself, though the darling of the New Criticism, invites his readers to employ whatever languages may prove useful—even those that are not native to, familiar with, or technically designed for the task. His own allusive, omnivorous poetic practice encourages cross-cultural and multidisciplinary responses. And in "Religion and Literature" Eliot invites us to bring to our experience of poems not only literary and aesthetic sensibilities and languages but also broader cultural habits and allegiances, social practices and affiliations, cultural strategies and commitments: "The author of a work of imagination is trying to affect us wholly, as human beings, whether we intend to be or not."[2] Thus Eliot sanctions a coductive, pragmatic, and even confessional criticism.

Calvin Bedient's declaration (in *He Do the Police in Different Voices*) that "insofar as Eliot is 'Christian,' he is Gnostically so, at least in *The Waste Land*," provides an explicit precedent for the tracing, or retracing, of Eliot's "blistered and blistering antihumanism." His disenchantment with civilization impelled him to seek what Bedient calls a purifying, antinomian "passage to India."[3] The pessimism-cum-transcendence strategy characteristic of gnosticism can be found in Eliot's most significant preconversion poem by following the testimony of the Thunder and the final "benediction" to their common source in the *Brihadaran-yaka* Upanishad. And, while a gnostic spirit of asceticism predominates, *The Waste Land* also evinces a strategy of exhausting the world and the flesh through anti-nomian license—another essential element of historical Gnosticism.

Wadlington describes *Huckleberry Finn* as a ritual of purification for its author—an attempt to create something that is authentic, uncompromised, and morally blameless. Eliot's poem is also a ritual of purification, his gnostic compulsions making him even more fastidious than Twain. Like other mystic and prophetic utterances, *The Waste Land* favors and fosters "what is essential or unmodified by circumstance"—the motive Wadlington ascribes to Huckleberry Finn. Like Twain, Eliot is ashamed of the world's arbitrary and punitive arrangements. His elusive method, which places fragments of culture "under erasure" in the very act of citing them, is part of a vatic poet's effort "to enact and disguise, to say and unsay his motive with the bland demeanor that is also blandishment."[4]

Eliot's blandishment, however, is not without cost. Whereas reform is presumably the satirist's and the prophet's nominal objective, worldly renewal or rebirth in any guise is seen as a delusion by the true Gnostic, or by the impermanent yet acute gnostic attitude that we all sometimes adopt. For the poet who has had a gnostic vision, the concomitant lyric impulse may never find a tolerable and pertinent form. Eliot, of course, does make a poem; he does act to make his gnostic strategy public. Even his laconic and cryptic notes, a bristling compromise with critics and book publishers, serve to flesh out his alienistic performance.[5] Nonetheless, in an effort to disclose and disguise simultaneously, Eliot more often sounds the hermit's raspy whisper of alienation than the prophet's public shout of reformation.

"The miseries that people suffer through their particular abnormalities of temperament are visible on the surface: the deeper design is that of the human misery and bondage which is universal."[6] Thus did Eliot introduce Djuna Barnes's *Nightwood*, which he saw as a tragedy of Everyman, though the book is populated by outcasts, misfits, and aliens. Eliot's introduction follows Kierkegaard's intuition that bondage, misery, and alienation are universals. In Barnes, Eliot had found yet another alienist imagination, another writer who, in Trilling's words, thought of the prison as "the ineluctable condition of life in society."[7] Rebelling against this general condition of misery and bondage, the knowing ones become questers and exiles; the rest remain denizens of vast yet confining polities. Thus it is appropriate that Eliot's sophisticated, multiplicitous, and belated poem should have an alien protagonist, deracinated and wandering. The poet uses hermits and prophets—Ezekiel, Ecclesiastes, Augustine, the Buddha, and Tiresias—and blends their voices into an otherworldly lament, a gnostic chorus that proclaims our common homelessness in a world of things and senses.

Abnegation of the World and the Flesh

The protagonist in *The Waste Land* often speaks with a gnostic voice that is disdainful of the earth and "hylic," or "earthly," stuff. In "The Burial of the Dead," for example, the voice asks, "What are the roots that clutch, what branches grow / Out of this stony rubbish?" (ll. 19–20). Ecclesiastes, the Preacher, proclaims the earth a desiccated, soulless place,

> A heap of broken images, where the sun beats,
> And the dead tree gives no shelter, the cricket no relief,
> And the dry stone no sound of water.
>   (ll. 22–24)

The "Isaiah" voice says, "I will show you fear in a handful of dust" (l. 30). In "The Fire Sermon" St. Augustine, a representative of Western asceticism according to Eliot's note, renounces his youthful life of lust in Carthage and proclaims, "O Lord Thou pluckest me out" (l. 309). Carthage represents the temptations of the flesh, the claims of the world and its individual counterpart, the human body; Augustine is rejoicing in his escape not from a particular place but from humanity itself—certainly his is a gnostic prayer.

In fact, the entire of Eliot's "Fire Sermon" section recalls the abnegation of the senses and the body urged by the Buddha in his Fire Sermon. Eliot's note to this section directs the reader to *Buddhism in Translation* by Henry Clarke Warren. As Warren records it, the Buddha's sermon to his priests is an ascetic renunciation of the eye, the organ that most intimately connects us with the external world: "The eye is on fire; forms are on fire; eye-consciousness is on fire; impressions received by the eye are on fire; and whatever sensation, pleasant, unpleasant, or indifferent, originates in dependence on impressions received by the eye, that also is on fire. And with what are these on fire? With the fire of passion, say I, with the fire of hatred, with the fire of infatuation; with birth, old age, death, sorrow, lamentation, misery, grief, and despair are they on fire."[8] "Perceiving this," according to the Buddha, "the learned and noble disciple conceives an aversion for the eye"—and not just for the eye, but for all the senses: for the mind, for ideas, for everything outside of the self. "And in conceiving this aversion, he becomes divested of passion, and by the absence of passion he becomes free." More importantly for us, "he knows that rebirth is exhausted . . . and that he is no more for this world."[9]

Being blind, Tiresias's eyes are, of course, not on fire; the sightless seer, who first appears in "The Fire Sermon" and whom Eliot calls in his note "the most important personage in the poem," possesses a purer consciousness and a higher mode of knowing. He is the gnostic one in the midst of the unknowing, wooden, and spiritless inhabitants of the world. Like the Gnostics who do not fit into the world's arrangements, Tiresias's anomalous status grants him a paradoxical superiority. Having lived life as both a woman and a man, he embodies sexual and physiological ambiguity, a mixing of memory and desire that further distances him from the world's hierarchies, arrangements, and categories of identification.

"A Game of Chess" presents us with a woman of leisure and opulence, a sort of *luxuria* figure whose profound boredom suggests that the sensuous life leads to the worst kind of unknowing alienation. The "synthetic perfumes" only "troubled, confused / And drowned the sense in odours" (ll. 88–89). The insipid exchange between husband and wife that follows also evokes a world-weary boredom. Dr. Johnson's curt observation that one who tires of London tires of life can be discovered in Eliot's darker poetic suggestion of neurasthenia:

"What shall I do now? What shall I do?"
"I shall rush out as I am, and walk the street
With my hair down, so. What shall we do to-morrow?
What shall we ever do?"
　　(ll. 131–34)

The final scene in this section is yet another depiction of "the hylic ones," the wooden proletariat, by one who sees them hopelessly imbedded in the "Unreal City." Hollow and spiritless, "unreal" like their city, even their sins are paltry.[10] "Lil," with her rotting teeth and chemically induced abortion, represents at the lower-class level the decline and infertility of Western culture. Eliot seems at pains to implicate not just the capitalists and the bourgeoisie but every social class and every worldly creature.

The interlude between the typist, "bored and tired," and "the young man carbuncular" is Eliot's most famous depreciation of modernity's passionless sexuality:

> [He] Endeavours to engage her in caresses
> Which still are unreproved, if undesired.
> Flushed and decided, he assaults at once;
> Exploring hands encounter no defence;
> His vanity requires no response,
> And makes a welcome of indifference.
>   (ll. 237–42)

In this central section of the poem, immediately preceding Augustine's gnostic prayer, the Thames Daughters, inhabitants of a river that "sweats / Oil and tar" (ll. 266–67) provide one last image of sex as sordid, dispirited, and common:

> "By Richmond I raised my knees
> Supine on the floor of a narrow canoe."
> . . . .
> "After the event
> He wept. He promised 'a new start.'
> I made no comment. What should I resent?"
>   (ll. 294–95, 297–99)

With no spirit, no *pneuma* to violate, the "people humble people who expect / Nothing" (ll. 304–5) are simply and irrevocably part of the world. They cannot be violated or besmirched because they are made of hylic, sublunary stuff.

The penultimate section of the poem is the very brief "Death by Water." Some interpreters have seen this section as symbolizing a death that precedes rebirth, but others see it as a real death that, because it is a death to this world, represents an escape from death-in-life and the cruel cycle of death and rebirth. Regardless of the interpretation, however, I would argue that the section continues to pursue the primary strategy of alienation—that is to say, the poet's rhetorical devices and admonishments describe a ritual of purification designed to diminish attachments to earthly life. Indeed, the final lines, with their implicit reproof of vanity, could have been spoken by the reproachful voice of Ecclesiastes:

Gentile or Jew
O you who turn the wheel and look to windward,
Consider Phlebas, who was once handsome and tall as you.
    (ll. 319–21)

"What the Thunder Said," the final section, begins with the possibility of salvation more remote than ever:

Here is no water but only rock
Rock and no water and the sandy road

. . . .
There is not even silence in the mountains
But dry sterile thunder without rain
There is not even solitude in the mountains
But red sullen faces sneer and snarl
From doors of mudcracked houses.
    (ll. 331–32, 341–45)

The isolation sought by the poet in the mountains is spoiled by "red sullen faces" that "sneer and snarl" from "mudcracked houses"—these are surely the earthen creatures so despised by Gnostic hermits. The "journey to Emmaus" then gives way to a nightmare vision of the demise of Eastern Europe, as the poet asks, "Who are those hooded hordes swarming / Over endless plains, stumbling in cracked earth" (ll. 369–70). The great cities of the West, "Jerusalem Athens Alexandria / Vienna London" have become, or always were, "Unreal" (ll. 375–77). Finally, the questing poet comes to the "Chapel Perilous":

There is the empty chapel, only the wind's home.
It has no windows, and the door swings,
Dry bones can harm no one.
    (ll. 389–91)

Yet at this darkest, most remote moment the cock crows, bringing rain and the sound of thunder. For an instant it seems that the water will stir the dull roots of civilization, but the Eastern directive to give alms, sympathize, and practice self-control will never be enacted: we are too reserved to give, too prideful to sympathize, too meek and demoralized to control. Instead, our hearts respond readily to the gestures of others, "beating obedient / To controlling hands" (ll. 422–23).

The poet is still "fishing" for some form of salvation at the end of the poem, a method of seeking transcendence that was introduced in "The Fire Sermon":

> A rat crept softly through the vegetation
> Dragging its slimy belly on the bank
> While I was fishing in the dull canal.
>   (ll. 187–89)

Thus the final posture of the fisher protagonist, having come to the end of his questing and heard what the thunder said, has not changed from this early impotence:

> I sat upon the shore
> Fishing, with the arid plain behind me.
>   (ll. 424–25)

He has turned his back on the arid plains and creeping rodents of the earth. The only worldly directive or administrative action left to him is that which precedes an imminent death: "Shall I at least set my lands in order?" the protagonist asks (l. 426). The poem then concludes with a series of fragmentary lamentations acknowledging the futility of enculturated efforts: "These fragments I have shored against my ruins" (l. 431). Ultimately, even this tenuous connectedness gives way to schizophrenic withdrawal: "Why then Ile fit you. Hieronymo's mad againe" (l. 432). The Kydian echoes here mark the protagonist's isolation from the world's modes of order and evidence a resisting insanity, an *alienation*.

Schizophrenia, "the malady of isolation" as Zweig describes it, may be willingly embraced by a gnostic seeking the separation of madness. Eliot's gnostic impulse impels him toward the dysfunction of Hieronymo because it represents an affront to conformity and an escape from the prison-house of the public sphere. Indeed, the distinction between an acute or extreme gnosticism and psychotic madness is "blurred and undependable," according to Zweig. Quoting Laing's description of schizophrenia, he explains that for both the gnostic and the madman, the world has become "a prison without bars [or] a concentration camp without barbed wire." We live our lives much closer to the danger than we are comfortable to admit, he says, and "we try, with all our resources of character and conformity, to forget" the potential imminence of a psychotic break.[11] Instead of attempting to forget, Eliot confronts the possibility of utter gnostic isolation. By making a poem, he performs his gnostic impulse and by means of that performance is able to win recognition from his culture. By exposing his alienation and giving it literary form, he practices the power to hurt, *repeats* Hieronymo's madness, and avoids a more clinical isolation.

◀── The Virtue of Transformative Damnation

As we have seen in chapter 6, gnostic alienation often includes the negation of earthly things through violence, overindulgence, and modes of transgression that are often explicitly sexual. Some early Gnostics were libertines, members of sperm or menstrual cults whose practices, according to Jonas and Zweig, constitute a more flagrant form of alienation than strategies of ascesis. Despite his priggish demeanor and punctilious image, it is clear that Eliot was drawn to both forms of renunciation. In "The Three Faces of Poetry," he says that an author can put into a character "some tendency to violence . . . that he has found in himself. Something perhaps never realized in his own life, something of which those who knew him best may be unaware."[12] To Paul Elmer More, a humanist confident that moderation could repair civilization, he wrote: "I am one whom this sense of the void tends to drive towards asceticism or sensuality."[13] Eliot thus recognizes in himself a bipolar strategy of alienation. The world as waste land cannot be reformed by "business as usual"; it must be withered by ascesis or exploded by transgression.

The strongest and best evidence of Eliot's admiration of transgressive, sexualized force comes not from *The Waste Land* but from other sources, such as "The Hollow Men," with its abbreviated Faustian theme, and his 1930 essay on Baudelaire. In a similar vein, Zweig devotes an entire chapter to Baudelaire, an exemplar of subversive transgression for him as well. Baudelaire's most striking poems, Zweig says, are "those in which the violence is unmistakably sadistic or masochistic."[14] Just as Orpheus must be torn to pieces by the women of Thrace, so the Baudelairean poet must rend and tear the world and himself, mentally and emotionally, in a destructive consummation that holds the only promise of transformation. It is Baudelaire's explication and valuation of what Eliot calls "evil"—the license, disruption, and violence of transgressive sexuality—that fascinates the gnostic poet. Baudelaire "was at least able to understand," Eliot says, "that the sexual act as evil is more dignified, less boring, than as the natural, 'life-giving,' cheery automatism of the modern world."[15] During the years when *The Waste Land* was gestating, Eliot was refining his admiration for transgressive gnostics such as Baudelaire and was, as F. O. Matthiessen points out, "stirred more deeply by *Les Fleurs du Mal* than by any other poetry written in the nineteenth century."[16] In this section I want to test the hypothesis that

The Waste Land includes intimations of a Baudelairean strategy of alienation: namely, that moral evil in the form of sexual transgression is superior to "cheery" conformity.

Before he came to grips with it—and *The Waste Land* must have been a significant step in this purgatorial process[17]—Eliot's generalized revulsion from humanity, what Gordon calls his apprehension of "the void in the middle of all human happiness and all human relations," made his life a living nightmare.[18] In his essays, Gordon says, he emerges as a writer who dallies with the possibility that "a mind becomes moral by becoming damned."[19] In his imagination and his imaginative works, Eliot periodically experimented with sadomasochistic situations: apparently he was intrigued by the transformative power of violence. In the unpublished "The Love Song of Saint Sebastian," completed in 1914, he portrays a desperate man who in the first stanza fantasizes about flogging himself to death in front of his lover to gain her attention and succor. In the second stanza the relation is reversed and the man becomes what Gordon calls "a sexual menace." In his fantasy, he uses "brute power over the white-clad body he loves," bending her beautiful neck beneath his knees. Eventually, he strangles her. Her response? "She loves him more."[20] This patently misogynistic fantasy would have titillated the Kurtz within the clerical Mr. Eliot: doing evil is better than doing nothing. Here and in *The Waste Land*—if only by implication and indirection—the poet suggests that the special virtue of brutality is its capacity to disturb and disrupt the stasis of conventionality.[21]

Eliot's correlate for the static, spiritually dead world is Dante's Limbo, the region of hell reserved for those who had lived without significant transgression but "are lost, afflicted only this one way: / That having no hope, we live in longing."[22] In the "Unreal City" stanza at the end of part 1, the poet brings together Baudelaire's preface to *Les Fleurs du Mal* ("hypocrite lecteur!") and Dante's "so many . . . so many." Matthiessen says that Eliot links Dante and Baudelaire to signal a disgust for those "who had not been strong enough in will or passion either to do good or evil, and so were condemned for ever to wander aimlessly, in feverish, useless motion."[23] Baudelaire's "swarming city, city full of dreams, / Where the ghost in broad daylight accosts the passerby" is the nineteenth-century version of Dante's Limbo, a tepid place of "sorrow without torment."[24] Eliot's "Unreal City" is twentieth-century modernism's version of the same vapidity, and his dualism cannot abide this homogenous, unchanging oblivion.

In this sublunary world the song of the nightingale, an icon of intensity and sexual passion, has become mechanical and vacant, nothing more than "'Jug Jug' to dirty ears" (l. 103). Yet according to Eliot's treatment, the nightingale's song did not become mundane until it was domesticated and safely packaged. Philomel, as Eliot reperforms Ovid's story, was raped—"So rudely forced"—by the barbarous king (l. 100). Although Philomel is the victim of a rape, for the gnostic poet this morally reprehensible act is at least an act of passion, and thus "more dignified, less boring," than a merely functional "weekend at the Metropole" or the tepid release of "the young man carbuncular" (ll. 214, 231). This sexual violation, with its transgressive intensity, is indirectly responsible for the nightingale's song: "there the nightingale / Filled all the desert with inviolable voice / And still she cried, and still the world pursues" (ll. 100–102). As in Ovid, so in Eliot: without the rape, Philomel would not have been transformed. The poet seems to suggest that the violent sexual transgression initiates a process that culminates in a glorious and powerful metamorphosis.

In the modern waste land, however, the terrible beauty of Philomel has been safely packaged as part of a modern decor. The story is told on a tapestry hung "above the antique mantel" (l. 97), possessed but unnoticed by the bored woman of leisure and luxury. The poet clearly regrets this degeneration of passion to ornament. His association of the beauty of the nightingale's song with the antinomian violation of Philomel suggests that sexual violence is preferable, perhaps an antidote, to the bland oblivion of the unreal city. Eliot's treatment here closely parallels the chilling claim of Robinson Jeffers, another poet with gnostic propensities, in "The Bloody Sire": "Violence has been the sire of all the world's values." "Who would remember Helen's face," the poet asks, "Lacking the terrible halo of spears? / Who formed Christ but Herod and Caesar / The cruel and bloody victories of Caesar? / Violence, the bloody sire of all the world's values."[25] In Eliot's performance of Ovid, an act that radically affronts our moral sensibility becomes the sine qua non of the nightingale's "inviolable voice." With Lil and the typist, an example of the conventional sexuality of modernity, there is no passion, no resistance, no violence, no retribution, no consequences; with Philomel there is "barbarous" desire, transgression, and, most importantly for a strategy of alienation, transformation.[26] Transformation goes the way of transgression, however: modernity, represented by the bored woman of leisure, "captures" the story, and Eliot evokes this domestication by having the rape appear as a grotesque tapestry.

Even in "The Fire Sermon," the most ascetic section of the poem, Eliot sympathetically and nostalgically includes a brief exploration of transgressive sexuality. The poet alludes to Andrew Marvell by using a line from "To His Coy Mistress," a line whose context again suggests the banality of modern sexual behavior when compared to disruptive, overweening desire:

> But at my back in a cold blast I hear
> The rattle of the bones, and chuckle spread from ear to ear.
> . . . .
> But at my back from time to time I hear
> The sound of horns and motors, which shall bring
> Sweeney to Mrs. Porter in the spring.
>   (ll. 185–86, 196–98)

Merely efficient encounters such as Sweeney's and Mrs. Porter's—discreet sexual behavior that serves the socially constructive function of "release"—are worldly in a way quite repugnant to the gnostic sensibility. Hence Eliot is driven to Marvell's articulation of dangerous liaisons. In "To His Coy Mistress" Marvell expresses a refined but passionate disregard for the mutable world and its moral laws, as if he would willingly destroy himself and his flesh-and-blood mistress in one final act of consummation. The final stanza of Marvell's poem, with its "amorous birds of prey" and its pleasures torn "with rough strife," recalls the violence of Philomel's rape. The act of love is evoked with the image of a siege gun's assault on the "iron gates of life"—arguably another celebration of transgressive force, perhaps even of sexual assault. Though readers disagree about Eliot's somewhat paradoxical appropriation of Marvell, it seems clear that even in the midst of "The Fire Sermon's" dominant asceticism, the speaker evokes the carpe diem theme of Catullus: this gnostic poet prefers either the regimen of abstention or the transgressive power of erotic abandon to the "safe sex" of Sweeney and Mrs. Porter.

To the same end Eliot implies the superiority of the Phoenician and Syrian merchants of the ancient world to the modern merchant, the "demotic" Mr. Eugenides. For centuries, "Smyrna merchant[s]" were formidable enemies of the Israelites who lived to the south in Samaria and Judea. They were also purveyors of wanton sexuality in the form of Phoenician fertility cults. "Eugenides"—the name suggests that he descends from a noble race—is in Eliot's treatment obviously inferior to his Phoenician ancestors. Like Sweeney and Mrs. Porter, Mr. Eugenides participates in the habituated peccadillos and calculated misdemeanors that are the hallmarks of a meek and routinized existence. Eliot's fascination with the Phoenicians, underscored by the fact that the "Phlebas" who dies "by water" in part 4 is also a Phoenician, parallels his preference for sexual abandon to the discreet indiscretions of modernity. For the sanguine appetites of Marvell's poet are far surpassed by the blood lust of the Phoenicians: they were worshippers of Baal, a Canaanite deity whose cults practiced holy prostitution and child sacrifice. However debased and "functional," the sexuality represented by Mr. Eugenides would seem preferable to the wanton slaughter of innocents. So it must have seemed to the Hebrew prophets who represent for Eliot, as they did for Matthew Arnold, the idea of moral law. The Phoenician cults were so abhorrent to them that they adapted the name of the Phoenician deity to signify the devil: "Baal-zebub" or "Beelzebub."

Yet the alienistic maker of *The Waste Land* must have felt a perverse and guilty attraction for these cults, as "The Hollow Men" suggests he did for Kurtz. The rape of Philomel as depicted by Ovid, the lust of the courtier as expressed by Marvell, the cults of fertility as represented by the Phoenician sailors—Eliot's ironic juxtapositions make their excesses seem more attractive than social conventions and collective morality. The intensity of the overreachers engenders a "terrible beauty," in Yeats's memorable phrase; their wantonness proves at least worthy of damnation. For Eliot, like Jeffers and even Yeats in the "Crazy Jane" poems, Baudelairean "evil" and damnation are superior to a tepid death-in-life.

If one manifestation of the gnostic impulse is to mortify the flesh by committing great evil—to repudiate the world by exhausting or "using it up"—then the possibility of significant transgression—the capacity to sin—must be maintained. Some years after *The Waste Land*, Eliot laments the disappearance of cultural restraints and embraces a higher, more traditional culture. Such a conversion might have been anticipated: traditional restraints provide a context for rebellion and "damnation," thus making strategies of alienation plausible. As Charles Taylor says in explaining the peculiar double bind of authenticity, "inwardly derived, personal, original identity" must win recognition of its resistance "through exchange" with society. In the modern age, generalized incoherence and an absence of norms mean that the "knowing ones" may fail to gain recognition as outsiders. I must negotiate my identity in dialogue with others, Taylor says, *especially* if I would develop an oppositionist role or identity.[27] The modern waste land has lost the contextual background that makes possible Luther's imperative, "Sin mightily." Baudelaire, forced to endure a "humiliating traffic with other beings," pursued what Eliot considered the "high vocation" of sinning mightily: he was "capable of a damnation denied to the politicians and the newspaper editors of Paris."[28] This gnostic attraction to overreachers is not limited to Baudelaire, and shards of Eliot's fragmented poem reveal a grim fascination with antinomian strategies and sexual transgression.

If we are offended by these bitter innuendos, then so be it. Like Camus's Merseault at the height of his alienation and his despair, the gnostic poet welcomes our cries of execration. "The poet's inner world of nightmare," Eliot says, is actually "a triumph; for hatred of life is an important phase — even, if you like, a mystical experience."[29]

◄— The Upanishads and Gnosticism

Many readers, seeking a more constructive vision, point to the resolution of the poem, to the Hindu Upanishads, which seem to offer a gesture and tonality of repose:

> Datta. Dayadhvam. Damyata.
> Shantih   shantih   shantih.
>   (ll. 433–34)

"Give, Sympathize, Control" — the testimony of the Thunder, as Eliot's notes tell us, is derived from the *Brihadaranyaka* Upanishad; "Shantih" is a formal ending to an Upanishad and is translated by Eliot as "the Peace which passeth understanding." These cues have been enough to convince many that the poet holds out a hope for the protagonist and the reader at the very end of his poem — that the modern waste land might finally be redeemed by the sacred words of Eastern scripture: "The Peace which passeth understanding," a benediction from *The Book of Common Prayer*, "is our equivalent to [shantih]," Eliot's note says. But the phrase is significantly elided (Eliot drops the reference to "Jesus Christ") and, given the nature of the experience that Eliot has brought us through, it is reasonable to question these "good words" rather closely. What kind of *earthly* peace might still be possible after the contempt, the renunciation, and the gnostic dualism of parts 1–4? As Eliot asks in *Gerontion*, "After such knowledge, what forgiveness?"

It is my intuition that the peace of "What the Thunder Said" "passeth understanding" because it is mystical, not of this world, and hence ineffable. It is not useful knowledge that can be put into action but an otherworldly, esoteric secret. "The word *Upanishad*," as A. C. Bouquet explains, means "secret or confidential teaching."[30] What the initiate eventually learns from the study of the Upanishads is *vidya*, or mystical knowledge. By means of this knowledge, this gnosis, he or she is raised above the world of the senses with its moral distinctions; through *vidya* he or she escapes fortune's wheel of death and rebirth.

Robert E. Hume, one of the first authoritative translators of the Upanishads, confirms the importance of knowledge in Upanishadic soteriology. Faith and

works are less important than "knowledge—not 'much learning' but the understanding of metaphysical truths." Acquiring this knowledge was, according to
Hume, "the impelling motive of the thinkers of the Upanishads."[31] The nature
of *vidya* varies somewhat within the Upanishads, but usually the knower is characterized as possessing the realization that the individual soul is one with the
great Soul, Atman. "That Thou Art"—the knowing one *is* Atman—has become
the most famous phrase of the Upanishads. Those initiates who seek Atman are
sometimes counseled to look into a mirror or pool of water to find him. For a
Westerner such as Eliot, the comparison to Narcissus would be inescapable.

Vidya, as appropriated by Western Transcendentalists, Symbolists, and theo-
sophical poets, might well admit equation with *gnosis*: not conscious or rational thought, not practical wisdom, but mystical knowledge—secret, ineffable,
and absolute. According to Jonas, the possession of knowledge distinguishes the
Gnostic from his or her environment and requires alienation from the world.
And the entreaty to abandon the political world and abnegate the social self can
be discovered throughout the Upanishads. The practical way of knowing Brahma, the world producer and controller, is by means of renunciation. The *Brihadaranyaka* is Eliot's source for "Datta. Dayadhvam. Damyata"; but there he
would also have read that the knower of Brahma is "He who passes beyond
hunger and thirst, beyond sorrow and delusion, beyond old age and death." The
body and its desires must be overcome, and the knowing ones must eventually
pass beyond the mind and the desiring parts of the contaminated psyche. The
knower of Brahma is urged to "become disgusted with learning"; he is to "desire to live as a child. When he has become disgusted both with the state of
childhood and with learning, then he becomes an ascetic (*muni*). When he has
become disgusted both with the non-ascetic state and with the ascetic state, then
he becomes a Brahman."[32] One becomes a Brahman, then, when the desire
for children and wealth and worlds is extinguished, when both innocence and
experience are sources of disgust, and when everything other than the mystical, unearthly soul is renounced.

This emphasis on otherworldly knowledge, however, is not culturally dominant, even in the land of the Upanishads. In *From Ritual to Romance*, Eliot
would have read Jessie L. Weston's description of the Eastern "Life-Cult": "the
sense of Life, the need for Life, the essential Sanctity of the Life-giving faculty," she says, "exercised an overpowering influence on primitive religions."[33] Yet
this Eastern Life-Cult apparently did not capture or quicken Eliot's imagination, at least at the juncture of *The Waste Land*. His poem serves as a counter-
statement, in Burke's sense, to the contemporary life-cults that he observed in
popular culture: "O O O O that Shakespeherian Rag— / It's so elegant / So

intelligent" (ll. 128–30) bitterly mocks the "upbeat" music of Eliot's time. Weston describes "a strong opposition to [the] cult in Indian literature, beginning with the *Rig-Veda*, and ripening to fruition in the *Upanishads*."[34] This literary opposition, with its ties to Buddhism and the Upanishads, clearly fascinated Eliot, and he articulates his rejection of the Life-Cult and his allegiance to the way of opposition and renunciation throughout the poem. The final Upanishadic benediction, far from offering hope for the world or humanity, opposes the "essential vitality" of the Life-Cult as common, popular, and sullied—not unlike the sexuality of Sweeney and Mrs. Porter, the Thames daughters, and the young man carbuncular. April, the Easter month of rebirth and life, belongs to the demotic polity.

Rebirth/reincarnation is undesirable because it means being trapped again in this world of bondage to senses and desires. In some of the Upanishads, the one who is attached to this world and successful in it is depreciated as a "doer of deeds":

> Whatever he does in this world,
> He comes again from that world
> To this world of action.
> —So the man who desires.
>   (*Brihadaranyaka*, book 4, canto 4, stanza 6)

The one who eschews action in the world, however, can hope for freedom from this prison-house. He who is without desire may be "released" from the world and the painful cycle of rebirth. He who is freed from desire, "Being the very Brahma, he goes to Brahma. / . . . Then a mortal becomes immortal! / Therein he reaches Brahma!" (*Brihadaranyaka* book 4, canto 4, stanzas 6–7): That Thou art—Atman is Brahman. The equation is found in Western Gnosticism as well: the soul or spark in the few was not merely a signal or reflection of the true Deity but literally a fragment of God. In both Gnosticism and the Upanishads, the rejection of the world of getting and spending comes with an apotheosis of this contra-mundane, spiritual self. Eliot seems to have imitated the thematic pattern found in the Upanishads when he contrasts his questing, gnostic protagonist with the secular "dead"—the doers of deeds and the accountants of "profit and loss" in the Unreal City.

Indeed, the structure of the *The Waste Land* reflects the transference from the world of Becoming to the Nirvana of Being; it is an escape from the memory of "the cry of gulls, and the deep sea swell / And the profit and loss" (ll. 313–14) to the undifferentiated, inviolable peace of "DA"—the cessation of the strenuous worldly quest in the gnostic quietude of "Shantih   shantih   shantih." *The*

Waste Land, like the Gnostic prophecies, seems to be working to intensify estrangement and renunciation. Eliot's note to line 308 ("Burning burning burning burning") directs the reader to the work of Henry Clarke Warren, who writes that "the minds of the thousand priests became free from attachment and delivered from the depravities" while the Buddha delivered his Fire Sermon.[35] Such a detachment seems to be the attitude pressed upon us by "The Burial of the Dead," "The Fire Sermon," and in fact by the entire poem. The reader who can make the abnegation of social identifications part of his or her performance of the poem may experience a liberating alienation like that enjoyed by the thousand priests who join the Buddha's eloquent performance of renunciation. Like the auditor/initiate who knows, according to Warren, "that he is no more for this world," the reader of *The Waste Land* may conceive an aversion for the created, sensuous world and, thus divested of passion, experience a kind of alienated freedom.[36] If so, then a consideration of Eliot's final benediction and the testimony of the Thunder, both adapted from the *Brihadaranyaka*, leads us back to "The Fire Sermon," the stony, ascetic heart of the poem. As Emerson had almost a century before, Eliot discovers in the Upanishads an ancient source of teachings and attitudes sympathetic to his own. These sacred texts provide an authoritative Eastern aversion to nature and culture, an aversion that Eliot's reading would have allowed him to recognize as similar to Neoplatonism, Augustine's early Manicheanism, and other salient theosophies and mysticisms—perhaps even historical Gnosticism itself.[37]

The authority of alien prophets, the banality of modern sexuality, the futility of action within this worldly prison-house—these thematic elements, together with the final benediction in *The Waste Land*, can be read as the elaboration of a gnostic impulse. At the beginning of the poem we hear the sybil cry, "I want to die"; and by the end of the poem—the end of the quest—a kind of death has been achieved. April, then, is the cruelest month because it initiates yet another rebirth into this world of memory and desire. The final extinction of the memory of earthly discriminations and of human attachments, the Upanishads tell us, can come only in *sushupti*, dreamless sleep, or better still, through a death that brings release from *samsara*, the chain of births, deaths, and rebirths. The eternal, dreamless sleep that is sought by the sybil is the Nirvana of both Buddhism and Hinduism: a transcendence of the desiccations and impurities of this world, a devoutly to be wished dissolution that signals the end of earthly rebirth and the final victory of the divine, alien spark.

It may be worth recalling that Augustine himself embraced two dualistic traditions, Manicheanism and Neoplatonism, before turning finally to orthodox Christianity. Eliot's celebrated conversion and his more orthodox poems came several years after his composition of *The Waste Land*. If the poem is, as I have argued, a lyric articulation of a gnostic impulse, then a spiritual progression similar to Augustine's would be evidenced in Eliot's own life. Whereas "The Journey of the Magi" and *Four Quartets* may figure forth a specifically Christian sensibility, *The Waste Land* moves toward the Silence of the One, not the Incarnation of the Word manifested in the abundance of the world.

Such exclusivity and isolation, central as they are to gnostic strategies, are often recognized as problematic. Even Rosemary Radford Ruether, who suggests that we look to Gnosticism for a usable feminist theology, regrets its dualistic depreciation of nature, embodiment, and creation as a whole.[38] Sallie McFague, writing in a similar vein, suggests that the necessary "otherness" of God is manifest and present to the Christian through a "*worldly* transcendence."[39] Incarnational theology, as opposed to Gnosticism, retains the fleshliness, the "hylic stuff" of God. Indeed, Renaissance artists often emphasized Christ's humanity by depicting him as a hungry infant—with prominent, naturalistic genitalia—eagerly nursing at the breast of his mother.[40] And in contemporary art we may be witnessing a return to "historic subject matter and transcendence *through* the human body," qualities discerned by Doug Adams in the work of George Segal and other postmodernists.[41] The reaffirmations of the body that Adams discerns in recent art, philosophy, and theology bespeak an appreciation not only of bodies but of wider communities and the earth itself. Later perhaps, after his second marriage, Eliot came to such an appreciation.[42] But we should not look to the words of the Thunder or to the Upanishadic benediction for earthly comfort and consolation. At the juncture of *The Waste Land*, the poet offers a bodiless ritual of purification. Eliot's alienistic impulse, as Bedient asserts, leads him to "the less indulgently anthropomorphic theology of the East"—leads him, we might say, not to incarnation but to gnosis, not to liturgical song but to abstract chant, not to Isaiah's "For unto us a child is born" but to the *Brihadaranyaka*'s "Shantih shantih shantih."[43]

And yet the poem continues to speak to "us," calling us—to what? Calling us to join, it seems, a coterie of knowing ones who look for a world perfected through art and religion . . . or want no part of it at all. Thus Eliot's gnostic strategy can be performed only gingerly. The poet continually and overtly alienates himself from his audience, slipping in and out of recognizable personas, interrupting, dislocating, fragmenting his lines, and "doing" disembodied voices. If, as many argue, the poet celebrates culture, it is an exclusively high culture manifesting the power of the true God and his true followers to achieve *vidya* and leave the demotic world behind. *The Waste Land* is a religious poem that does not rejoice in God's plenty; it is a purifying ritual that does not cleanse society. The poet "smuggles in," to borrow Burke's metaphor, a divine identification; he tells the story of an alien self's purgation of the mundane and the many.

We can admire Eliot's extensive range of cultural references and his omnivorous appetite for allusions without extolling his blistered and blistering hermeticism; we can decipher and take to heart his chastening voices without succumbing to his "ontological difficulty."[44] We can take comfort, as Albany might say, in what remains after gnosticism has done its worst. The poem does develop as a collaborative performance—not only between Eliot and Pound but also between Eliot and us. The flesh-and-blood Eliot relies on the multifarious constructions of culture, and this necessary reliance belies his otherworldliness. Even the gnostic poet, in order to be a poet, makes use of the artifacts of culture, the forms and functions of social discourse. Like Twain, whose countervailing motives are described by Wadlington, Eliot wants to both say and unsay; indeed, he must say in order to unsay. *The Waste Land* is a still-potent Jeremiad; like other great prophecies, its very artifice compromises its purity. Only by doing his work in culture's prison-house can the alienist practice the power to hurt.

NOTES

1. T. S. Eliot, "The Waste Land," *The Waste Land and Other Poems* (New York: Harcourt Brace Jovanovich, 1934), ll. 62–63.

2. T. S. Eliot, "Religion and Literature," *Selected Essays* (New York: Harcourt, Brace, 1950), p. 348.

3. Calvin Bedient, *He Do the Police in Different Voices: "The Waste Land" and Its Protagonist* (Chicago: University of Chicago Press, 1986), pp. 41–42.

4. I am applying Wadlington's observation about Twain to Eliot. See *The Confidence Game in American Literature* (Princeton: Princeton University Press, 1975), p. 243.

5. As James E. Miller notes, "Eliot's notorious footnotes that now accompany the poem were added only for the book publication. . . . Eliot was to remark on them later: 'I had at first intended only to put down all the references for my quotations with a view to spiking the guns of critics of my earlier poems who had accused me of plagiarism. Then, when it came to print *The Waste Land* as a little book . . . it was discovered that the poem was inconveniently short, so I set to work to expand the notes, in order to pro-

vide a few more pages of printed matter.'" James E. Miller Jr., *Heritage of American Literature: Civil War to the Present* (San Diego: Harcourt Brace Jovanovich, 1991), vol. 2, pp. 833–34.

6. Eliot quoted by Kenneth Burke in *Language as Symbolic Action: Essays on Life, Literature, and Method* (Berkeley: University of California Press, 1966), p. 245.

7. Lionel Trilling, *The Opposing Self* (New York: Viking, 1955), p. 53.

8. Henry Clarke Warren, *Buddhism in Translation* (1896; rpt., New York: Atheneum, 1973), pp. 352–53.

9. Ibid., p. 353.

10. "Sinning mightily," as I will suggest below, is an activity that Eliot reserves for transgressors and world-surpassing gnostics.

11. Paul Zweig, *The Heresy of Self-Love: A Study of Subversive Individualism* (1968; rpt., Princeton: Princeton University Press, 1980), pp. 259–60.

12. T. S. Eliot, "The Three Faces of Poetry," quoted by Lyndall Gordon in *Eliot's New Life* (Oxford: Oxford University Press, 1988), p. 63.

13. T. S. Eliot to Paul Elmer More, quoted by Lyndall Gordon in *Eliot's Early Years* (New York: Oxford University Press, 1977), p. 62.

14. Zweig, *The Heresy of Self-Love*, p. 232.

15. Gordon, *Eliot's New Life*, p. 236.

16. F. O. Matthiessen, *The Achievement of T. S. Eliot: An Essay on the Nature of Poetry*, 3d ed. (New York: Oxford University Press, 1959), p. 18. This fascination with Baudelaire persisted despite Eliot's concentration on the later Symbolists.

17. Reading *The Waste Land* as personally strategic acknowledges Eliot's own confession that the poem was "the relief of a personal . . . grouse against life." For an extended reading of the poem as a personal strategy of purgation, see James E. Miller Jr., *T. S. Eliot's Personal Waste Land: Exorcising the Demons* (University Park: Pennsylvania State University Press, 1977).

18. Gordon, *Eliot's Early Years*, p. 62.

19. Gordon, *Eliot's New Life*, p. 63.

20. Gordon, *Eliot's Early Years*, p. 28. According to Gordon, the part of Eliot's imagination that articulated the sexualized violence of St. Sebastian made possible "Eliot's later characters, the brute Sweeney, playful with his razor in the brothel, and Harry, Lord Monchensey, with his murderous heart" (p. 62).

21. Perri al-Rahim, in her senior honors thesis, has speculated on the psyche's attraction to "thanatos flow," an "optimal experience" superior to mundane existence but associated with suicide, sado-masochism, addiction, and violence rather than productivity. "Flow: An Inquiry into the Psychology of Optimal Experience," University of Houston, 1997. In so doing she extends and complicates the research of Mihaly Csikszentmihalyi, who describes the subjective phenomenon of "flow" in exclusively healthy and positive terms. See *Beyond Boredom and Anxiety* (San Francisco: Jossey-Bass, 1975), *Creativity: Flow and the Psychology of Discovery and Invention* (New York: Harper, 1996), and *Flow: The Psychology of Optimal Experience* (New York: Harper, 1990).

22. Dante, *The Inferno of Dante: A New Verse Translation*, trans. Robert Pinsky (New York: Noonday Press, 1996), book 4, ll. 31–32.

23. Matthiessen, *The Achievement of T. S. Eliot*, p. 22.

24. Eliot's note to line 60 refers readers to these opening lines of Baudelaire's "Les Sept Viellards" ("The Seven Old Men").

25. Robinson Jeffers, "The Bloody Sire," *Selected Poems* (New York: Vintage, 1965), p. 76.

26. Some readers may suggest that the sex between Lil and the young clerk is not consensual and therefore an instance of "date rape." Eliot, however, takes great care (in my view) to distinguish what he calls the "automatism" of such mundane sexuality and the "barbarous," Baudelairean violence of gnostic license.

27. Charles Taylor, *The Ethics of Authenticity* (Cambridge, Mass.: Harvard University Press, 1992), pp. 47–48.

28. Eliot, "Cyril Tourneur," *Selected Essays*, p. 236.

29. Eliot, "Baudelaire," *Selected Essays*, p. 142.

30. A. C. Bouquet, *Comparative Religions: A Short Outline*, rev. 3d ed. (Hammondsworth: Pelican-Penguin, 1950), p. 119.

31. Robert E. Hume, *The Thirteen Principal Upanishads*, 2d ed. (New York: Oxford University Press, 1962), p. 58.

32. Ibid., p. 112; *Brihadaranyaka*, book 3, canto 5, stanza 1.

33. Jessie L. Weston, *From Ritual to Romance* (1919; rpt., Garden City, New York: Anchor-Doubleday, 1957), p. 44.

34. Ibid., p. 45.

35. Warren, *Buddhism in Translation*, p. 353.

36. Ibid.

37. Though contemporary scholars of comparative religion must be more technical and discriminating, William James posits the existence of a single "mystical tradition," encompassing both Eastern and Western teachings, "hardly altered by differences of clime or creed." "The mystical classics have," according to James, "neither birthday nor native land." *The Varieties of Religious Experience* (1901; rpt., New York: New American Library–Mentor, 1958), p. 321. Eliot read *The Varieties of Religious Experience* at Harvard and took copious notes from the chapter devoted to Mysticism. Gordon provides a list of books on mysticism that Eliot read from 1908 to 1914, the formative years preceding his composition of *The Waste Land. Eliot's Early Years*, pp. 141–42.

38. Rosemary Radford Ruether, *Sexism and God-Talk: Toward a Feminist Theology* (Boston: Beacon, 1983), pp. 21–36.

39. Sallie McFague, *Models of God: Theology for an Ecological, Nuclear Age* (Philadelphia: Fortress Press, 1987), pp. 184–87.

40. Leo Steinberg, *The Sexuality of Christ in Renaissance Art and in Modern Oblivion* (New York: Pantheon-October, 1983). See, for example, figures 17, 18, 59, and 84–86.

41. Doug Adams, *Transcendence with the Human Body in Art: Segal, DeStaebler, Johns, and Christo* (New York: Crossroad, 1991), p. 13, my emphasis.

42. Eliot's "second wife, Valerie Fletcher, had sense and humour, and cared for him with all the generous love that he could have desired. His married happiness restored the self-confidence his turbulent years with Vivienne had undermined. 'Without the satisfaction of this happy marriage,' he wrote . . . 'no achievement or honour could give me satisfaction at all.'" Gordon, *Eliot's Early Years*, p. 81.

43. Bedient, *He Do the Police*, p. 42.

44. George Steiner, "On Difficulty," *On Difficulty and Other Essays* (New York: Oxford University Press, 1978), pp. 40–47.

"Lords and Owners": Vladimir Nabokov's Sequestered Imagination

We are told that both the self and the literary work are imprisoned constructs whose cognitive and imaginative functions are delimited by relations of power. Delimited, yes, the alienistic resister might say, but not defined, not articulated, not yet performed. Nabokov experienced firsthand the oppression of institutional power and control, both statist and capitalist.[1] He knew well that revolutions tend to produce campaigns that are monistic and relentlessly thorough. Régimes both nouveau and ancien are alike in this: they take no prisoners. Or, rather, they take only prisoners, for encompassing systems make the entire world a vast confinement.

Nabokov's reaction to the authoritarian control of language, like his personal response to the totalitarian control of the Red Army and the Leninists, was that of the underground rebel. His career made him a respected member of the establishment, but through his fiction he led the double life of a resister. Like Eliot, Nabokov was influenced by the syncretic mysticism and theosophy that swept through Europe in the late nineteenth century.[2] Though he was no fan of Eliot,[3] he too was influenced early by Symbolist strategies and remained sympathetic to their renunciation of utilitarian agendas.[4] Forced by circumstance to become a "Smyrna merchant" of the imagination, Nabokov's alienistic artifices are tricky, "sparkling," and subtle. Never attracted by asceticism or apocalyptic strategies, Nabokov practices a strategy of smiling alienation: he does not allow ascesis or transgression to overburden his performances, preferring to leaven them with magic, invention, and transcendent design.

Nabokov's *"Non Servium,"* then, is not so much openly defiant as savvy and circumspect. It is pragmatic in its dogged impracticality: to avoid defeat by the world's gross machinations, Nabokov departs from the agora of politics and secretly aligns with the aesthetic underground. In "Good Readers and Good Writers" he presses his claim that the artist is not a product of economic and political forces, but is a powerful "magician," "enchanter," and "inventor"— claims reminiscent of Simon the Magus.[5] Elsewhere Nabokov celebrates the apolitical, ahistorical "gleam" of true creativity as part of his lifelong effort to resist the gloomy news that art and artist are entrapped by the encompassing political world. "There is nothing dictators hate," Nabokov says in "The Art of Literature and Common Sense," "so much as that unassailable, eternally elusive, eternally provoking gleam. One of the main reasons why the very gallant Russian poet Gumilev was put to death by Lenin's ruffians thirty odd years ago was that during the whole ordeal, in the prosecutor's dim office, in the torture house, in the winding corridors that led to the truck, in the truck that took him to the place of execution, and at that place itself, full of the shuffling feet of the clumsy and gloomy shooting squad, the poet kept smiling."[6] By telling this story Nabokov suggests that writers and texts are not wholly inscribed within culture; the realm of art need not be a manifestation of institutional patterns of control and containment. *Pale Fire* is probably Nabokov's most ludic and liberated Gumilevian performance: a hare's nest of formal patterns, mock-scholarly apparatus, and shifting motives, *Pale Fire* is a cryptic, secretive text designed to disrupt and confound totalizing systems. It is a provocative gauntlet thrown down before systemizers of every stripe, an aesthetic performance put on with smiling fierceness.[7]

Nabokov specifically addresses the reductionist tendency of theory in the character of Charles Kinbote—literary critic, disenchanted intellectual, self-proclaimed political exile. Kinbote is Nabokov's parasitic processor of literary materials, criticism's answer to the Cuisinart. The appetitive and mechanical Kinbote has written an introduction and an extensive index to the lines of a poem ("Pale Fire") by the late John Shade. Kinbote reads into the poem his own preoccupations and disappointments, both personal and political, reducing Shade's poem to a gloss on the political affairs of Zembla, a "distant, northern land." A monarchist rather than a Marxist, Kinbote imagines himself to be King Charles of Zembla, who has been deposed by revolutionary forces and has barely escaped with his life. Gradus, a menacing fabrication of Kinbote's solipsistic, paranoid, and probably psychotic imagination, is hunting for the escaped King Charles in order to assassinate him. Such are the broad outlines of the "plot." But as readers we do not know, as Peter Rabinowitz says, whether we are supposed to believe that both Shade and Kinbote exist, whether one has invented the other, or whether a man named Botkin has invented them both.[8] We also do not know whether we are supposed to believe that Shade is a famous poet, whether Zembla is a real country (within the fiction), or whether Shade, or anyone, is actually shot and killed at the end of the "Commentary." The novel's unusual combination of modes of discourse—a foreword, commentary, and an index all enveloping a poem—makes *Pale Fire* an exercise in frame analysis and, for many readers, a hilariously complex aesthetic game.

Almost all commentators agree on the novel's complexity, but from the beginning there have also been persistent claims for *Pale Fire*'s morality and human significance, most notably from Mary McCarthy: "this centaur-work of Nabokov, half poem, half prose, this merman of the deep, is a creation of perfect beauty, symmetry, strangeness, originality, and moral truth. Pretending to be a curio, it cannot disguise the fact that it is one of the very great works of art of this century."[9] But the "moral truth" of *Pale Fire* remains artfully disguised, and we can only agree with Page Stegner that it would have been instructive if McCarthy had taken just a few sentences to expound the novel's human significance and ethical implications.[10] Germane to my purpose is that the novel raises questions—finally ethical questions—about the adequacy of any critique that confidently explains and systematically predicts the collaboration between text and culture. It is as if Nabokov set out, thirty years before the current critical fashion, to provide a text so aesthetically pure that it could not be reduced to an ideological product of extraliterary forces. Nabokov's declaration of independence from culture's containments, from power politics and institutional control, is part of his aesthetic strategy. Nominally discussing chess problems in his autobiography *Speak, Memory*, Nabokov says, "Deceit, to the point of diabolism, and originality, verging on the grotesque, were my notions of strategy."[11] Deceit and originality mark his artistic games as well and, to my mind, allow him to successfully free the artistic performance from the quotidian world. I am convinced that *Pale Fire*, like much of Gertrude Stein's work, offers us an alienistic performance of those virtues proper to the aesthetic imagination while at the same time daring and taunting materialist theories and their would-be reductions.

◄— The Critic's Unseemly Rush

Nabokov would agree with Carlyle that the heroic artist participates in something transcendent, that culture's *understanding*—its system of domination and control—cannot contain works of a sequestered *imagination*. And certainly Nabokov's ingenious literary performances are directed to "parts" of the mind, as the German Romantics would say, that are adamantly *un*concerned with the worldly tasks of predicting, calculating, accommodating, and negotiating. As a consequence, Nabokov's fiction, according to Dale E. Peterson, has the capacity to "liberate present and future victims from the drab prison houses of authoritarian language."[12] Ellen Pifer argues that *Pale Fire*'s "self-conscious design will have a liberating effect on the reader, as the patterns of artifice provide a perspective on reality that both reveals and transcends the narrow perception of a Kinbote."[13] If Peterson and Pifer are right, and I think they are, then that perspective is presumably made possible by the functioning of an independent aestheticist imagination. *Pale Fire* resists being incorporated into the political economy by discouraging us from apprehending the text with our culturally determined modes of interpretation; it retards Culler's "unseemly rush from word to world." To be sure, the novel reminds us that our *ordinary* methods of reading, our assimilative attempts at naturalization, are usually predatory instances of "overstanding"; but Nabokov's strange work also implies, by indirection, that there may be another way. *Pale Fire* appeals not to our capacity for calculation and appropriation, but to a more artistic and "final," less mediated and instrumental faculty.

The most deadening example of the wrong way to "apprehend" art is exemplified by Gradus, the killer of Nabokov's poet.[14] Gradus represents the material world: joyless, quotidian, grave. Like one of those "clumsy and gloomy" members of the political world's ubiquitous shooting squads, he is stubborn, relentless, and unleavened. As Tony Tanner says, "Gradus is representative of all that is utterly inimical and hostile to art and imagination."[15] He is guilty, as Kinbote's index to the poem tells us, of "lynching the wrong people."[16] But if Nabokov creates Gradus to be the nemesis of art's provocative "gleam," he might also be considered representative of Nabokov's professional opponents: Marxist and other historical-materialist critics who are motivated by partisan agendas. Gradus has numerous aliases and manifestations—"Jack Degree, de Grey, d'Argus, Vinogradus, Leningradus"—and he has been sent by the Shadows, a "regicidal organization" of bloody Zemblan revolutionaries (pp. 217, 223). In the index under "Sudarg of Bokay," Zemblan mirror maker, we are given the rather ominous news that this palindromic reflection of Jacob Gradus has a "life span not known" (p. 223). Gradus, then, is violent, jealous of power, polytropic, persistent, and ubiquitous: the oppressions of culture are everywhere.[17] He represents the common world, the "communal eye," and also, almost certainly, literature's social realists—contemporaries of Nabokov who harried him with their particular mode of materialist criticism.

It seems clear, then, that the greatest threat to the sequestered imagination is Gradus. Yet Nabokov also creates the parasitic critic, Kinbote—Sybil Shade calls him "King Bot"[18]—whose relentless scholarly apparatus and vested motives consume and assimilate John Shade's poem even as Gradus destroys the man. Kinbote, like institutionalized economic power, functions to take, to consume, to colonize, to own. Kinbote attempts to make Shade an implement of his own predatory consciousness and to use the poem as a means of fabricating structural preferments for his interests and fantasies. Kinbote's "use" of Shade and his poem thus serves as a negative model of culture's intellectually legitimated suppression and domination of the other.

Kinbote protests his personal devotion to his neighbor and "friend" repeatedly, but his affection for Shade, on examination, is nothing more than jealous possessiveness. When Shade is killed by a bullet meant for Kinbote (at least on one narrative level), his depiction of the incident in a "note" to line 1,000 of Shade's poem betrays Kinbote's egocentrism: "[Shade's] presence behind *me* abruptly failing *me* caused *me* to lose *my* balance. . . . *My* coccyx and right wrist hurt badly but the poem was safe. John, though, lay prone on the ground, with a red spot on his white shirt" (p. 208). To the envying and exploitive reader-critic, that the poet has died is of little consequence; the poem, the property, is safe. Kinbote has yet to take full possession of it, but he presently will by a blatant act of appropriation and commodification. Gradus kills the poet and Kinbote takes his poem. Both represent the machinations of culture.

The story of Zembla is the one Kinbote wants to see inscribed and perpetuated, and he has attempted during the period of composition to influence Shade to write an elaborate verse history of the Zemblan revolution and the escape and expatriation of its monarch, Charles the Beloved. Rightly or wrongly, Kinbote believes that he is in fact the exiled King Charles. (We cannot know from textual evidence whether Kinbote is right or wrong—Nabokov does not provide enough clues for us to decipher the direction of influence, thereby frustrating our inclination to neatly package, once and for all, his performance.) At any rate, Kinbote is incensed to find that Shade has not written the Zemblan saga, but a story of his own:

> I started to read the poem. I read faster and faster. I sped through it, snarling, as a furious young heir through an old deceiver's testament. Where was Zembla the Fair? Where her spine of mountains? Where her long thrill through the mist? And my lovely flower boys, and the spectrum of the stained windows, and the Black Rose Paladubs, and the whole marvelous tale? Nothing of it was there! The complex contribution I had been pressing upon him with a hypnotist's patience and a lover's urge was simply not there. Oh, but I cannot express the agony! (p. 209)

Nabokov casts the enculturated critic thus, as an acquisitive heir anxious to take the poet's treasure for his or her own. Like Joyce's Lynch who fervently wants to "take" woman and "the hypotenuse of the Venus of Praxiteles," Kinbote wants "Pale Fire" to serve his own desires. Kinbote is literally Shade's "executor," and he is already in the process of disposing of the poet's literary estate.

Nowhere is Kinbote, as the critic bent on making a text his or her own, more reflective of the process of cultural containment than when he likens Shade's poem to "a fickle young creature who has been stolen and brutally enjoyed by a black giant but now again is safe in our hall and park, whistling with the stableboys, swimming with the tame seal." The poem has become for Kinbote a helpless young catamite that has been free of his exploitation for a time but is now back under his dominating influence: "The spot still hurts, it must hurt, but with strange gratitude we kiss those heavy wet eyelids and caress that polluted flesh" (p. 210). Thus Nabokov likens Kinbote's "use" of the poem to an adult's sexual abuse of a helpless ward—conceived by Kinbote, revealingly, as a "creature."

Despite Kinbote's appetitive exploitation of poem and poet, Frank Kermode is right to salvage Nabokov's sympathy for him. After all, Nabokov himself had recently played Kinbote to Pushkin by translating, with the same parasitical apparatus of scholarly notes and commentary, the great Russian poet's *Eugene Onegin*.[19] And Nabokov realizes—perhaps he learned the lesson only too well from his Pushkin exercise—that scholarship unleashed on hapless texts is inevitably a process of domination and control. Like Derrida in his celebrated debate with Foucault, Nabokov acknowledges his own participation in those processes of culture that oppress and enslave.[20] Ultimately, however, Kinbote's similarity to Nabokov rests not on his literary scholarship but on his inventiveness, not on the crimes he commits against Shade's "Pale Fire" but on his ability to escape to *other* states of being . . . where art is the norm"—Nabokov's definition of aesthetic bliss. "For me," he says in an afterword to *Lolita*, "a work of fiction exists only insofar as it affords me what I shall bluntly call aesthetic bliss, that is a sense of being somehow, somewhere, connected with other states of being where art (curiosity, tenderness, kindness, ecstasy) is the norm."[21] Like many others, Kermode sees this passage as one of crucial Nabokovian self-definition, and he argues that Kinbote's obsession is actually a state of being where art is indeed the norm.[22] "One should not disregard . . . a person who deliberately peels off a drab and unhappy past and replaces it with a brilliant invention," Shade says, defending a minor character who thinks he has become God (p. 169). Shade's endorsement of creativity might well constitute a Nabokovian defense of Kinbote. "The author has to show us," Kermode says, "that Kinbote's activity is the model of his own."[23]

But what are the costs of such brilliant aesthetic contraptions, of stepping outside the world of power politics and marketplace repressions? Nabokov may succeed in demonizing Kinbote and then "resympathizing" him, but to do so he must enforce a distinction between the inventing imagination and the quotidian world. There have been various critical debates about whether Shade creates Kinbote or Kinbote Shade, but how do such puzzles reveal Nabokov's resistance to appropriation and the costs of that alienistic strategy? The question is, How far is Nabokov willing to go to ensure that the literary imagination will not be contaminated by the mundane?

---— Shade's Earnest Effort

In *Pale Fire* the world is divided into groups, and the principle of classification is aesthetic sensibility. Most readers agree that the poet rather than the critic occupies the apex in the novel's hierarchy. As the maker of "Pale Fire," Shade has the most highly developed capacity for achieving aesthetic bliss, reaching that place where art is the norm. To be sure, Kinbote has a capacity for creativity, but his art consists in colonizing the labor of others. And Gradus is wholly of the world, a grim functionary, recognizable to a gnostic as one of the *hylicoi*. Yet Shade, despite his relative distance from power politics, market economies, and erotic exploitation, is finally no Promethean of the imagination. He attempts in a rather clumsy way to integrate personal and universally human concerns into a poem that is essentially a life review, not unlike Krapp's. "Pale Fire," a poem complete with the real names, places, and dates that validate a personal narrative, is straightforward autobiography recounting the suicide of

Shade's only daughter and his quest for an assurance of life after death—his "faint hope" for her and for himself. Most commentators have presumed that Shade's poem, as a creative performance that successfully resists Kinbote and his motives, evinces Shade's success in escaping the prison-house in which criticism would incarcerate him. Yet Shade may not be as wildly inventive as many presume. There is a strong lexical connection between the poet and his killer: "shade" means "degree" as well as relative darkness (a gray color) and Gradus's aliases are Jack Degree and Jack de Grey—the color or "shade" of a shade. Kinbote's disappointed impression after removing the poem from Shade's dead body is accurate: "Instead of the wild glorious romance—what did I have? An autobiographical, eminently Appalachian, rather old-fashioned narrative in a neo-Popian prosodic style" (p. 209). It seems unlikely that Nabokov would ask such a shopworn poetic form to serve *his* aesthetic and subversive purposes. In my view, Shade is still too utilitarian about art's contribution to life, and his gross employment of poetry is not aesthetic, alienistic, or Nabokovian.

Kinbote claims that Shade's poem is "beautifully written of course" (p. 209); but an "of course" from Kinbote might be a clue that the implied author of the novel does not concur with his pathologically egocentric character. And the prosodic tricks played on Shade by Nabokov belie Kinbote's cavalier puffery. These tricks, what we might call the jester bells of "Pale Fire," are made possible by Shade's use of a highly traditional verse form, the rhymed pentameter couplet. The rhymed or heroic couplet has an established, broadly recognized function in traditional English prosody, conforming to the shared expectations of poets and audiences since at least the sixteenth century. Nabokov gives Shade the conventional couplet form that Dryden selected for the weighty and politically important theme of *Absalom and Achitophel*, the form that Keats used in *Endymion*, and the one that Pope chose for *An Essay on Man*. Moreover, since the seventeenth century, pentameter couplets have been associated with the elegy, a form characterized by gravity, seriousness, and consistency. Inherent, then, in the prosody of "Pale Fire" is a tradition of treating matters of solemn significance, including death, immortality, and the justification of the ways of God in the world. But Nabokov knows well that the most formal poetic devices lend themselves to subversive satire as well as solemnity: Pope used the same heroic couplet form for his great mock-epic *The Rape of the Lock*, and Byron achieved a sudden "balloon prick" deflation in *Don Juan*, usually by a polysyllabic rhyme at the end of a stanza. By having Shade work in heroic couplets on an elegiac theme, Nabokov sets him up for a series of bathetic falls.

Shade characteristically begins his stanzas with a candor and sincerity appropriate to themes of high seriousness. The first lines of many stanzas guilelessly address matters of general human concern. But Shade's typical stanza evidences a shift as it proceeds from sincere artlessness to device-encrusted versifying. The harmony between manner and elegiac matter disappears. Since his theme remains consistently lofty throughout the individual stanzas and the poem, Shade's self-parody must be unintentional: One does not joke about a daughter's suicide.[24] The collapse of artistic control by Shade, however, gives Nabokov the opportunity to practice his own virtuosity. He can parody Goldsmith and Wordsworth, show himself off as the equal of Pope and Byron, and at the same time distance himself from a this-worldly writer clumsily trying to mythologize his real-life experiences and heartfelt emotions.

Hence it is when Shade is most autobiographical, most concerned with transforming actual experiences into poetry, that Nabokov makes him most ludicrous. Describing his boyhood as a cripple, Shade writes:

> Then as now
> I walked at my own risk: whipped by the bough,
> Tripped by the stump. Asthmatic, lame and fat,
> I never bounced a ball or swung a bat.
>   (ll. 127–30)

Shade begins this self-revelation in a forthright, prosaic manner, thus signaling to the reader that he will be communicating with sincerity and artlessness. The enjambed line "Then as now / I walked at my own risk" has a proselike rhythm and includes a locution common to ordinary conversation as well as to quasi-official communications—"swim at your own risk," for example, is not poetic diction. The familiarity of this clause serves to enforce our confidence in the honesty of the speaker: he is going to say something important without seducing or beguiling. But then the sincerity breaks down in a deluge of artificiality as Shade gropes for a parallelism: "whipped by the bough, / Tripped by the stump" stands in sharp contrast to the conversational style that precedes it. Here, the exact repetition of the grammatical categories (participle + preposition + article + noun) is compounded by the internal rhyming of "whipped" and "tripped." This obtrusive artifice creates a suspicion that the speaker is not so much a struggling wayfarer as a playful maker of rhymes, perhaps even an artful deceiver like Humbert Humbert in *Lolita*. Our suspicions are confirmed when Shade closes off the stanza with "five marching iambs," a grammatical parallelism, and a too-neat rhyme:

> Asthmatic, lame and fat,
> I never bounced a ball or swung a bat.
>   (ll. 129–30)

Perceiving this, we have to wonder whether the poet's afflictions have been introduced solely to make "fat" rhyme with "bat." We know that Shade's theme is elegiac, so a descent into bathos like this one cannot be *his* plan. His poetic devices are laid bare, thereby spoiling, or at least radically changing, the effect.

The collapse of our confidence in Shade's self-revelation stanza is typical of other crucial moments in "Pale Fire." The most significant stanza thematically and autobiographically occurs at the close of "Canto Two" and concludes at the exact midpoint of the poem—line 500. Here Shade describes the suicide of his daughter, a personal tragedy that has naturally intensified his concern with the question of an afterlife. Hazel Shade's death is perhaps the poet's most important lyric impulse for the composition of "Pale Fire." The stanza begins with a general description of nature, a summing up that sets the general scene for a personal cataclysm:

> It was a night of thaw, a night of blow,
> With great excitement in the air. Black spring
> Stood just around the corner, shivering
> In the wet starlight and on the wet ground.
> (ll. 494–97)

As in the self-revelation stanza, Shade begins with heavily enjambed lines, uninverted syntax, and ordinary, unobtrusive diction. The phrase and sentence breaks fall irregularly, as we would expect in prose but not in formally patterned poetry. The poet has chosen to evoke the natural "cosmic" scene with monosyllabic words. Further, since repetition is common to oral patterns of speech, the repetition of "night" mitigates the effect of the parallelism and introduces a colloquial rhythm to the lines: the poet is "telling it like it is." Suddenly, however, the lines become end-stopped and the rhyme words, as a consequence, begin to chime obtrusively:

> In the wet starlight and on the wet ground.
> The lake lay in the mist, its ice half drowned.
> (ll. 497–98)

Shade's poetic devices are again displacing his narrative, and our attention is diverted from the human story to the artificial scaffolding. The stanza concludes with an almost slapstick depiction of Hazel's watery pratfall:

> A blurry shape stepped off the reedy bank
> Into a crackling, gulping swamp, and sank.
> (ll. 499–500)

First of all, referring to Hazel as "a blurry shape" that "sank" reminds us that Shade's daughter is obese, myopic, and physically unlovely: ships, not people, sink. Moreover, the artifice of the heroic couplet form intrudes again on the human story: "A blurry shape stepped off the reedy bank / Into a crackling, gulping swamp"—these words comprise a complete sentence and hence our grammatical expectations are satisfied. The formal expectations associated with the heroic couplet form, however, remain frustrated until we come to the final foot, "and sank." The addition of another clause and another image, in this case dehumanizing ones, dissipates the force of a serious story forthrightly told. The story could have ended with restraint and sincere pathos, but the poetry rambles on. Shade seems to be straining for a word to rhyme with "bank" as he previously did for "fat." Surely it is here that Shade most wants us to perform the poem empathically, to identify with Hazel and to feel with him the suffering that leads to her suicide. Yet in the midst of this performative identification we are distracted by the clanking machinery of Shade's inept prosody.

Our confusion about what we are supposed to feel is intensified by the unsatisfying noun/verb closure of the canto in its unbalanced final couplet. Shade's choice of a verb to end the line that precisely breaks the poem into halves, the line that concludes both the last couplet in the stanza and the last stanza in the canto, is difficult to justify. According to George Amis, couplets rhymed noun/verb sound to the ear "more independent, and the couplet seems indecisively closed."[25] The conventions of the form lead us to expect the stanza and the canto to achieve a dignified closure; in an elegy mourning the death of a child, we expect the poet to bring the child's life to a humane and dignified end. But in "Pale Fire" both expectations are disappointed. If we take pleasure in the verse as *Shade's* poetry, it is the patronizing pleasure of watching a man fail grandly in a noble undertaking. After appealing to our common humanity at the beginning of his stanzas, Shade falls prey to our wit as he closes them off, unintentionally evoking a smirking embarrassment rather than sympathy.

Nabokov himself calls attention to the humorous potential of rhyme in his *Notes on Prosody*, part of the scholarly apparatus originally attached to *Eugene Onegin*. His depreciation of "fancy rhymes" in English poetry is invaluable for an analysis of Shade's poem. "In English," Nabokov says, "fancy rhymes or split rhymes are merely the jester bells of facetious verselets, incompatible with serious poetry." Hinting at what he means by "fancy rhymes," Nabokov says that "the Englishman Byron cannot get away with 'gay dens'—'maidens.'"[26] And as the following selected rhymes indicate, Nabokov has undermined "Pale Fire's" elegiac seriousness by his exotic rhyme pairs:

stillicide / nether side (ll. 35–36)

always well / her niece Adele (ll. 83–84)

my Triassic; green / Upper Pleistocene (ll. 153–54)

Age of Stone / my funnybone (ll. 155–56)

would debate / Poetry on Channel 8 (ll. 411–12)

Maybe, Rabelais: / I.P.H., a lay (ll. 501–2)

the big G / peripheral debris (ll. 549–50)

in that state / hallucinate (ll. 723–24)

the gory mess / of prickliness (ll. 905–6)

does require / Will! *Pale Fire.* (ll. 961–62)

In all of these examples a monosyllable rhymes with a polysyllable—the very combination that Nabokov says "Byron cannot get away with." A couple of them even carry the rhyme to an extra syllable in an adjacent word: "Rabelais / a lay"; "gory mess / prickliness." Such examples are only a selection of the "jester bells" to be found throughout "Pale Fire," and it is certain that Nabokov meant them facetiously. To my mind, it is just as certain that Nabokov's Shade is unaware of their parodic jangling. His aesthetic limitations are also evinced by the obtrusiveness of the rhymes, for, as Leigh Hunt wrote in *Imagination and Fancy*, the mastery of rhyme "consists in never writing it for its own sake, or at least never appearing to do so."[27] Through his poetic practice, the creation of a traditional elegiac poem, Shade is earnestly trying to make sense of his own intimations of immortality and to reconcile himself to the death of his daughter. But such a frank, unsophisticated performance exposes the aesthetic imagination to culture's engines of power and consumption. Shade's versified candor commits the classic sin against Nabokov's aestheticism. To remain sequestered and uncorrupted, one's imagination must not be Lynched or Krapped. Art must not be slavishly put in the service of extraliterary enterprises—not by Kinbote, not by Shade, both of whom, in the end, are befooled by the author's jester bells.

◂— Nabokovian Virtues

Nabokov would agree with those materialist critics who assert that ordinary, conventional art cannot escape the determinations of its historical moment. Most examples of artistic practice are contaminated by intercourse with a world whose facticity is often brutal, corrupt, and infectious. So it is not a simple matter of art versus reality; the distinction that Nabokov presses is between that which is heavy, wooden, and glandular and that which is "worthwhile art." As Nabokov says in the introduction to *Poems and Problems*, "chess problems demand from the composer the same virtues that characterize all worthwhile art: originality, invention, conciseness, harmony, complexity, and splendid insincerity."[28] Tanner explains how Nabokov stylistically associates the quotidian world with a Gradus-like art: "It is worth noting that when Nabokov/Kinbote is describing the behaviour of Gradus he does so in a style which is minutely factual and detailed. . . . By itemizing his meals, his newspaper, his bowel movements, Nabokov emphasizes the utter physicality of the man—a thing among things— and it seems clear that Nabokov is at the same time offering a low parody of realism and naturalism, as though to demonstrate that such a style is only appropriate for creatures immersed so deeply and mindlessly in the realm of fact."[29] This enculturated world threatens the aesthetic bliss of the independent, alienistic imagination. Hence the need for complex, reflexive texts such as *Pale Fire*, decentering empuzzlements that invite the processing critic and the naturalizing reader to a heterogenous, exotic, and necessarily frustrating performance.

Even if his compositional style is a "grade" above naturalism and social realism, Shade too immerses himself in the material world, a world that is the "filthy" realm of politics and murder. The readerly virtues needed to perform Shade's poem are therefore distinct from those needed to perform Nabokov's novel. Shade's error, a crude "combinational" one, is suggested by the penultimate stanza of "Pale Fire":

> I feel I understand
> Existence, or at least a minute part
> Of my existence, only through my art,
> In terms of combinational delight.
>   (ll. 970–73)

So far, so good, but Shade's project, a Krapp-like attempt to understand the world by means of his art, is undermined in the next lines:

> And if my private universe scans right,
> So does the verse of galaxies divine
> Which I suspect is an iambic line.
>   (ll. 974–76)

While many critics point to these as quintessentially Nabokovian lines, they actually betray a flesh-and-blood poet who is solipsistic, anxious, controlling, impatient, and unreceptive. Nabokov's family history and emigration made him only too aware that one cannot squeeze evidence of a divine plan from the bloody events of private life. Perhaps Shade is only suggesting that art, a well-written iambic line, can somehow translate its orderliness to the universe. But if so, surely those divine galaxies are not to be reduced to heroic couplets or verse narratives in a neo-Popean style. Nabokov prefers an inventive, unconnected, blissfully independent aesthetic strategy to Shade's simplistic connection between a journeyman's scansion and the world's arrangements. "Pale Fire," Shade's aesthetic composition, is penetrated by not-art, and the result is a fatal confusion of realms. Being "reasonably sure that we survive / And that my darling somewhere is alive," Shade is also reasonably sure that he "shall wake at six tomorrow" (ll. 977–80), but he dies almost immediately after drafting the line. Thus does life, Nabokov seems to say, discomfit clumsy, ego-serving art. Shade's iambic lines are riddled with undisguised hopes and fears, manipulative cries for pity and attention, and even mundane hygienic preoccupations such as shaving, tender skin, and "Our Cream" (l. 922). Shade's personification and even deification of shaving cream is Nabokov's gentle satirical jab at the obsessively sacramental imagination. It may also be a swipe at Joyce's opening scene in *Ulysses*, in which Stephen's razor and mirror metamorphose into sacred instruments of transfiguration. Anxious and confused, Shade is trying too hard and reading transcendence into everything. Unlike Harold Bloom, Nabokov does not approve of "strong" readings and egotistical interpretations. His treatment of Shade's epiphanies *manqués* are gentler than Beckett's send-up of poor Krapp and his forgotten "life-transforming" realization, but the ethical mistakes of these two characters (presented within a few years of each other) are analogous. Shade debases his poem and his "splendidly insincere" imagination by trying to make "Pale Fire" *his* story, a utilitarian personal myth.

Nabokov does not make the same mistake. He has created a novel that ambushes routines and rubrics before they can settle in and take over. His multiplicitous patchwork prevents readers from appropriating *Pale Fire* for their worldly projects, Kinbote-style. In his foreword Kinbote suggests that we read his notations first "and then study the poem with their help," perhaps rereading the notes a third time "so as to complete the picture" (p. 18). Certainly Nabokov does not want us to take anything attributable to Kinbote at face value, but here as elsewhere Kinbote is right for the wrong reason: we might as well start with the notes. Or we could read only the poem without consulting the notes at all. Or we could even start with the index. Kinbote's suggestion that we buy two copies and shuffle the cut pages is another indication of his shameless self-promotion, but it aptly raises the question of how readers should proceed with their imaginative cutting and pasting. Perhaps the game has no objective or even any rules of play. *Pale Fire* is troubling but not, as Rabinowitz argues, because it "raises difficult philosophical questions, as *The Brothers Karamazov* does; it is rather that we can't tell precisely what issues the novel does address . . . [or] what questions it is asking, what solutions it is proposing."[30] These uncertainties, I am convinced, are designed to make it impossible for a sluggish reader, thick with cultural categories and preconceptions, to "get" the text in the same way Gradus gets Shade and Kinbote gets the poem. Nabokov uses discordant, competing genres and precomputer "hypertext" as part of his alienistic strategy to check the recruiting, "overstanding" assaults of the ordinary and the utilitarian.

How, then, should we as readers enact his aesthetic strategy of alienation? To what kind of performance does Nabokov call us? The author provides several models of imagination in *Pale Fire*: Kinbote, the critic who thinks that "Pale Fire" is about his psychotic imaginings; Shade, the poet who makes a versified spiritual autobiography; and Gradus, who is so immersed in the world of banal common sense that he has no imaginative life whatsoever. But there is at least one other model of the imagination—the one represented by Nabokov himself. Readers of the novel should use *Pale Fire* to achieve epiphanies like those Nabokov describes in *Speak, Memory*.[31] As Alexandrov says, Nabokov's "irrational standards," the virtues he would cultivate in the performing reader, "turn out to be a form of maximally enhanced consciousness."[32] One cannot help but recall Pater's celebration of the imagination burning with a "hard, gem-like flame."[33] Only in such intense and inventive states—"so different from commonsense and logic"—do we "know the world to be good," according to Nabokov.[34] Alexandrov underlines the point: for Nabokov, common sense "typifies all that is gray, tepid, and banal"; the aestheticist performer should avoid "accepted, conventional, and therefore stultifying literary prescriptions" in favor of the "freakish" and "irrational," while discovering "secret connections" within lexical patterns and figures of speech.[35] Imagination, that special quality extolled by Carlyle and Coleridge as well as the German Romantics, should have no truck with what Nabokov depreciates as "those farcical and fraudulent characters called Facts."[36]

If we don the mask, put on the Nabokovian ethos, it becomes more difficult to denounce Kinbote for the capriciousness of his glosses on Shade's poem. We must remember, however, that the virtues of Nabokov are not identical with the virtues of Kinbote. In addition to inventiveness, there are other virtues required for a Nabokovian performance: care, delicacy, patience, receptivity, in a word, *precision*. Precision is as important as creativity. Indeed, just as he equates artifice and nature, Nabokov would see precision and creativity not as different virtues but as alternative manifestations of the same virtue. "Precision in all things," as Alexandrov says, "is an essential virtue that Nabokov imposes on his readers"; and precision does not cohabitate with lazy estimations or indulgent theorizing.[37] For Nabokov, reading is fraught with care. His readers need to be patient and vigilant as well as playful and inventive—Kinbote is the latter but not the former. Access to Nabokov's *potustoronnost*, the otherworld, the underlying desire of Kinbote as well as Shade, demands artful precision as well as resplendent creativity.

Since no certainties are possible regarding this other realm, Nabokov would say that simple correspondences, autobiographical explanations, and materialistic formulas are all reductive and misleading. *Potustoronnost* literally means the "other side," according to Alexandrov, and its primary virtue is "irreducible alterity."[38] Hence for Nabokov the construction and reconstruction of aesthetic performances takes on the utmost ethical importance. Those enactions are the very exercise of otherworldly powers, the ephemeral and strenuous unconcealing of creativity itself at work. Those who read carefully, precisely, and vigilantly, whether reading events or texts, are saved; those who read stupidly, slothfully, and theoretically are damned. He often associates criminals and murderers with the "moronic," the lazy, and the imprecise. Inferior readers, or performers as we are calling them, depend on encompassing theories and convenient systems, common categories and "step-saving" clichés. Because the true aesthetic performance, at least for Nabokov, partakes of a realm that is persistently unassimilable, it cannot be captured by general categories and conventional modes—not by writers and not by readers: "The main favor I ask of a serious critic is sufficient perceptiveness to understand that whatever term or trope I use, my purpose is not to be facetiously flashy or grotesquely obscure but to express what I feel and think with the utmost truthfulness and [precision]."[39] In other words, performing Nabokovian strategies requires Nabokovian virtues: the combining of work with play, tough precision tempering high-spirited inventiveness, imagination continually checking predatory inclinations. These are the salient virtues of *Pale Fire*, and it calls for similarly complex and labor-intensive virtues in its performers.

—(—

Aesthetic strategies such as *Pale Fire* may inspire care, creativity, and precision; but we should not leave Nabokov's aestheticism without acknowledging its costs.

Calling Nabokov's view of reading "elitist and demanding," Alexandrov cites the 1937 lecture on Pushkin in which Nabokov insisted that "the only valid method of study is to read and ponder the work itself, to discuss it with yourself *but not with others*, for the best reader is still the egoist who savors his discovery unbeknownst to his neighbors. . . . The greater the number of readers, the less a book is understood, the essence of its truth, as it spreads, seems to evaporate."[40] These conversations with fictions and persons are, of course, the coductions that Booth recommends, and *Power to Hurt* is designed as just such a conversation with persons and stories. Nabokov, however, warns his readers away from each other. He approves of coductions with art and with oneself, but not with others. The fewer conversing about the truth of a book, the better.

In discussing books as friends, Booth decries the wary cultivator of a coterie who encourages us to join "a saved remnant looking down on the fools, slobs, and knaves."[41] But let us temporarily set aside our egalitarian anxieties and the demographic question "How many?" to focus on the virtues of those readers who do, at least temporarily, join the remnant.[42] Nabokov's high-handed caveat seems more comprehensible if we agree that the work of reading *Pale Fire* can be accomplished only by means of an alienistic performance, a purposeful "othering" of the imagination from the pragmatic and the political. Ordinary conversations with "neighbors," even about our "everyday epiphanies," can and do erode and degrade such experiences by domesticating them. Alexandrov's insights (and a rereading of Nabokov's autobiography *Speak, Memory*) have convinced me that *Pale Fire*'s particular aesthetic strategy does incorporate a conviction about the presence of a transcendent realm, a partially and only momentarily accessible otherworld. But with or without an otherworld, Nabokov's strategy, like other strategies of alienation, evokes the foreign, the secret, and the uncanny—as the Germans say, the *Unheimlich*.

No one can doubt the splendidness, the gleam of Nabokov's artistic craft. When we read Kinbote's commentary and Shade's verse, they become much more than irresponsible, self-aggrandizing scholarship and bad poetry. Insofar as the various elements of *Pale Fire* are the work of Nabokov, they are delightful and rewarding virtuoso performances of a certain kind. As long as we remain in the region of "Lex," the realm of words in which Gradus loses his way, we can enjoy the aesthetic pleasures of *Pale Fire*. If we expect Kinbote's discourse to be an explication of the poem, we are disappointed; but if we relinquish our demands for a gloss and abandon ourselves to the world of Zembla, we are gratified. If the metrical contract of Shade's poem leads us to expect a moving elegy, we may feel cheated; but if we join in the gentle mockery and listen for the jester bells, some of the best in the language, we enjoy what is in some sense Nabokov's poem rather than Shade's. Nabokov has earned, it seems, the praise that Booth reserves for extraordinary friends: "your company is superior to any company I can hope to discover among the ordinary folk with whom I live—including myself. . . . To dwell with you is to grow toward your quality."[43]

Nabokov's genius inspires a strategy that urges us toward his favored virtues and prods us out of our habituated torpor. (Often, perhaps a bit too much like Pozzo, the author seems to be calling to his reader, "On! On!") If we tire and object to Nabokov's demanding verbal genius, his ludic excesses, we risk reducing ourselves to the level of the Russians in Kinbote's Zemblan fantasy: stupid, totalitarian literalists who tear the palace apart looking for jewels that are fictional constructs, not real gems. If we ask, "Where would Nabokov have seen such gems?" or, "How do diamonds function in a late-capitalist consumer economy?" we "Kinbote" the novel and completely miss Nabokov's discrete performance. Nabokov's index is, among other things, a maze to discourage and frustrate the predatory virtues of a Kinbote or a Humbert. If we are foolish enough, for example, to search for the crown jewels by using the index's directions about the whereabouts of the *words* "crown jewels," we will be led on a fruitless, perplexing, page-turning quest. We can never find the actual faceted crystals, nor the power they represent, for we are in the bailiwick of the aesthetic imagination, the region of Lex. Nabokov sets about to gull the generalizing reader who does not catch on to the author's peculiar kind of inventiveness; he prevents, in the process, our materialist rush from word to world to word. Nabokov's fiction brings not information, in Percy's sense, but news—"radical, subversive, antirealistic news," as Dale E. Peterson says.[44] Nabokov, I think, takes great comfort in that news, and in knowing that his metaphorical patterns can never be put wholly in the service of repressive political patterns. He has taken care not to propose a counterideology—that is for pedestrian mythmakers such as John Shade—but, instead, he offers a sequestered performance with teasingly public enticements and invitations to participate. *Pale Fire* is a splendidly insincere reminder that all ideologies suppress the daemonic deceit proper to aesthetic strategies of alienation.

NOTES

1. Valdimir E. Alexandrov notes that Nabokov's life was "brushed by the worst horrors of the twentieth century. Nabokov and his family had to escape from the Bolshe-

viks in Russia, his father was murdered in Berlin by political assassins, one of his brothers perished in a Nazi concentration camp, and Nabokov and his wife (who is Jewish) risked the same by staying in Germany until 1937." *Nabokov's Otherworld* (Princeton: Princeton University Press, 1991), p. 53.

2. Ibid., p. 228.

3. John Burt Foster describes how Nabokov "reworks three words from *Four Quartets* so as to undermine Eliot's depersonalized, mythico-symbolic version of modernism" in "Nabokov and Proust," in *The Garland Companion to Vladimir Nabokov*, ed. Vladimir E. Alexandrov (New York: Garland, 1995), p. 479.

4. Brian Boyd documents Nabokov's fascination with Alexander Blok (1880–1921), the greatest of the Russian Symbolist poets. Nabokov was particularly sympathetic to several Symbolist strategies: a turning away from nineteenth-century positivism and civic-mindedness; the placement of the individual before society; the independence of art; and the capacity of art to evoke "a higher reality beyond the sensual world." According to Boyd, Nabokov was particularly drawn to the aesthetic refinements of Symbolism: "the increasing richness and subtlety of mental association, the greater acuteness and diversity of the senses and the emotions, the readiness to seek other architectures than logic, proportion, classical meter." See *Vladimir Nabokov: The Russian Years* (Princeton: Princeton University Press, 1990), p. 93.

5. Vladimir Nabokov, "Good Readers and Good Writers," *Lectures on Literature*, ed. Fredson Bowers (New York: Harcourt, 1980), pp. 5–6.

6. Vladimir Nabokov, "The Art of Literature and Common Sense," *Lectures on Literature*, pp. 377–78.

7. Vladimir Nabokov, *Pale Fire* (New York: Berkley, 1962). Nabokov challenges anti-volitional materialisms wherever he finds them. Freud and Marx, for example, are favorite targets of his fictional and nonfictional barbs.

8. Peter Rabinowitz, "Truth in Fiction: A Reexamination of Audiences," *Critical Inquiry* 4, no. 1 (1977), p. 137.

9. Mary McCarthy, "A Bolt from the Blue," *New Republic* 146 (11 June 1962), p. 27.

10. Page Stegner, *Escape into Aesthetics: The Art of Vladimir Nabokov* (New York: Dial, 1966), p. 134.

11. Vladimir Nabokov, *Speak, Memory: An Autobiography Revisited* (New York: Putnam, 1966), p. 289.

12. Dale E. Peterson, "Nabokov's *Invitation*: Literature as Execution," *PMLA* 96, no. 5 (1981), p. 834.

13. Ellen Pifer, *Nabokov and the Novel* (Cambridge, Mass.: Harvard University Press, 1980), p. 118.

14. At this point it might be worth reminding ourselves that virtue criticism, as described in part 1, posits literary characters not as flesh-and-blood human beings but as strategies that are manifested through the performance of particular characteristics and virtues. Thus to say that Gradus "is" relentless or quotidian is to ascribe those particular

virtues to the character of Gradus, whether he is considered a product of Kinbote's be-deviled imagination or Nabokov's ingenious one. For virtue criticism it does not matter whether an ethos is flesh-and-blood. Similarly, the "ethical value of the stories we tell each other," as Booth says, does *not* depend on "whether or not they in fact claim to depict actual events." *The Company We Keep: An Ethics of Fiction* (Berkeley: University of California Press, 1988), p. 15, see also pp. 3–22.

15. Tony Tanner, *City of Words: American Fiction, 1950–1970* (New York: Harper and Row, 1971), p. 37.

16. Nabokov, *Pale Fire*, p. 217. Subsequent references will be given in the text.

17. "Freudian faith has dangerous ethical consequences," Nabokov once said, "as when a filthy murderer with the brain of a tapeworm is given a lighter sentence because his mother spanked him too much or too little." *Strong Opinions* (New York: McGraw-Hill, 1973), p. 116.

18. A "bot" is the larval form of the parasitic botfly. In the following passage Richard Selzer narrates the encounter of a surgeon with Kinbote's namesake: "No explorer ever stared in wilder surmise than I into that crater from which there now emerges a narrow gray head whose sole distinguishing feature is a pair of black pincers. The head sits atop a longish flexible neck arching now this way, now that, testing the air. Alternately it folds back upon itself, then advances in new boldness. And all the while, with dreadful rhyth-micity, the unspeakable pincers open and close. . . . A Mayan devil, I think, that would soon burst free to fly about the room, with horrid blanket-wings and iridescent scales, raking, pinching, injecting God knows what acid juice." *Mortal Lessons: Notes on the Art of Surgery* (New York: Simon and Schuster/Touchstone, 1987), p. 20. Nabokov has chosen a particularly terrifying creature to signify the "critic as parasite."

19. Frank Kermode, "Zemblances," *New Statesman*, 9 Nov. 1962, p. 671.

20. For the debate, see Edward Said, "Criticism between Culture and System," *The World, the Text, and the Critic* (Cambridge, Mass.: Harvard University Press, 1983), pp. 178–225.

21. Vladimir Nabokov, *Lolita* (New York: G. P. Putnam's Sons, 1955), pp. 316–17.

22. Kermode, "Zemblances," p. 672.

23. Ibid., p. 671.

24. Shade's poetry is, of course, Nabokov's construction, and Nabokov uses it to par-ody what we might call the "low-Romantic" tendency to versify personal losses and "rec-ollect" emotional states of mind.

25. George Amis, "The Structure of the Augustan Couplet," *Genre* 9, no. 1 (1976), pp. 44–45. Based on an analysis of some 13,000 lines of Augustan poetry, Amis finds that couplets rhymed verb/noun occur much more often than couplets rhymed noun/verb. Amis also associates the use of verbs as second-line rhyme words with "artificial word order" (p. 45). Shade's "Pale Fire" is in the "neo-Popian" genre, as Kinbote rightly says, and is therefore part of the tradition analyzed by Amis.

26. Vladimir Nabokov, *Notes on Prosody* (London: Routledge and Kegan Paul, 1965), p. 93.

27. Leigh Hunt, *Imagination and Fancy* (London: Smith, Elder, 1944), quoted in "Rhyme," *The Princeton Encyclopedia of Poetry and Poetics* (Princeton: Princeton University Press, 1974), p. 707.

28. Vladimir Nabokov, *Poems and Problems* (New York: McGraw-Hill, 1970), p. 15.

29. Tanner, *City of Words*, p. 37.

30. Rabinowitz, "Truth in Fiction," p. 139.

31. See, for example, Nabokov's description of a sense of "timelessness" standing "among rare butterflies and their food plants. This is ecstasy, and behind the ecstasy is something else, which is hard to explain. It is like a momentary vacuum into which rushes all that I love. A sense of oneness with sun and stone. A thrill of gratitude to whom it may concern—to the contrapuntal genius of human fate or to tender ghosts humoring a lucky mortal." *Speak, Memory*, p. 139.

32. Alexandrov, *Nabokov's Otherworld*, p. 54.

33. Walter Pater, "The Renaissance," *Walter Pater: Three Major Texts (The Renaissance, Appreciations, and Imaginary Portraits)*, ed. William E. Buckler (New York: New York University Press, 1986), p. 219.

34. Nabokov, *Speak, Memory*, p. 374.

35. Alexandrov, *Nabokov's Otherworld*, p. 53.

36. Nabokov, "The Art of Literature and Commonsense," *Lectures on Literature*, pp. 372–73.

37. Alexandrov, *Nabokov's Otherworld*, p. 5.

38. Ibid., pp. 3, 5.

39. Nabokov, *Strong Opinions*, p. 179. Alexandrov quotes this passage and suggests in his note that its ending as published, "utmost truthfulness and perception," must have been a misprint. Obviously for my purposes, it is advantageous to accept Alexandrov's reconstruction over the published "misprint." Alexandrov, *Nabokov's Otherworld*, pp. 11, 236.

40. Vladimir Nabokov, "Pushkin; or, The Real and the Plausible (1937)," trans. Dmitri Nabokov, *New York Review of Books*, 31 Mar. 1988, p. 41, quoted by Alexandrov in *Nabokov's Otherworld*, p. 11, my emphasis.

41. Wayne Booth, "'The Way I Loved George Eliot': Friendship with Books, a Neglected Critical Metaphor," *Kenyon Review*, n.s. 2 (Spring 1980), p. 27.

42. We may well want to ask, Under what social arrangements might more people have the opportunity to enjoy the sort of companionship offered by Nabokov? What reformations in the realm of politics and education would allow more than an elite group of readers to practice "precision-and-creativity," the signature Nabokovian virtue? Such questions about political and social arrangements are timely and crucial. As a literary critic I do not feel qualified to address those questions here, except to say, If we value those virtues, we should do what we can to encourage persons to read Nabokovian works with care, empathy, and joy.

43. Booth, "'The Way I Loved George Eliot,'" p. 27.

44. Peterson, "Nabokov's *Invitation*," pp. 834.

12

"The Basest Weed":
Donald Barthelme's Parabolic Fairy Tale

Performances of alienation are usually directed at cultural myths that are perceived to be smug, triumphant, and simplistic. These myths are the repressive scripts and ideologies—the grand narratives—that generate and support the world's institutions and practices. For the authentic alienist, their pervasive circulation and general acceptance are as objectionable as their preferences and exploitations. Radical authenticists, as we saw in chapter 8, abhor civilization's "rubricizing" patterns of meaning and prepackaged versions of reality. True revelations are ineffable; authentic intuitions and genuine epiphanies cannot be communicated using the debased forms palatable to society. "Oh I wish there were some words in the world that were not the words I always hear!"[1] Thus does Barthelme's Snow White lament the banal repetition of the world's oppressive patterns and plots. Her lament could serve well as a refrain or slogan for alienistic writers generally, and, indeed, Barthelme's use of a cartoon character to embody a profound "desire to be elsewhere" is strategically similar to Eliot's gnostic adaptation of Augustine—"O Lord Thou pluckest me out."

The problem of the alienistic writer is that she remains "unplucked" and, try as she will, cannot effect her own apotheosis. She is obliged to stay, for there is nowhere else to go. When Snow White searches for words to explain her inability to abandon the dwarfs and their house, she says, *"I have not been able to imagine anything better"* (p. 59, Barthelme's emphasis). Some have seen her explanation as an admission of inadequacy, a signal from Barthelme that Snow White's enculturated imagination is not strong or supple enough. I would argue that it is rather a rueful acknowledgment that the imagination of any artist, of any person, is inescapably embedded in its cultural sensorium. This embedding is more than an abridgement of freedom; it is also a discursive interpenetration, dynamic and invasive. Snow White may be willing to remain with the dwarfs, however reluctantly, but Barthelme's Jane character, an obsessive, resentful "wicked-stepmother," constructs the situation in more agonistic terms. She has figured out that living in the world entails hurting and being hurt, and she is resolute to meet power with power, threat with threat. Determined to be the rock that strikes the pitcher, she transforms the hermeneutics of suspicion into ready malice. "Now it may have appeared to you," she writes to Mr. Quistgaard, a man whose name she randomly selects from the phone book, "that the universe of discourse in which you existed, and puttered about, was in all ways adequate and satisfactory. . . . People like you often do. That is certainly one way of regarding it, if fat self-satisfied complacency is your aim. But I say unto you, Mr. Quistgaard, that even a plenum can leak. Even a plenum, *cher maître,* can be penetrated" (pp. 44–45). For Jane, the arena of cultural exchange is the site of a zero-sum game in which she wants to be the winner. "You are correct, Mr. Quistgaard, in seeing this as a threatening situation," she says, confident that her "u. of d.," her universe of discourse, can dilute without becoming diluted: "The moment I inject discourse from my u. of d. into your u. of d., the yourness of yours is diluted. The more I inject, the more you dilute. . . . You are, essentially, in my power" (p. 46). Like Jane, some alienistic strategists would prefer authoritarian control. But it is hard to imagine how public discourse— a performance of the imagination—could function as a unilateral injection. Intercourse requires a partner, as Kubrick's General Jack Ripper knows all too well; the dilution and contamination are mutual and inevitable. Jane's advice to Mr. Quistgaard: cover your discourse and protect yourself from dilution and contamination by getting an unlisted number (p. 46).

Barthelme, however, does not want an unlisted number. His writing, to be sure, bears evidence that he was tempted by absence, negativity, and apocalypticism. In a scoring review of Graham Greene's *The Comedians,* Barthelme attacks Eliot as well as Greene, who, he says, "put themselves at the mercy of an unexamined assumption, that it is better to exist than not to exist." On the other hand, he praises Beckett, whose genius allows "his characters [to] act precisely in the area of the unexamined assumption: they yearn toward non-existence."[2] As an alienist, then, Barthelme is attracted to isolation and fascinated by silence; but as a parabler he wants to perform. His passion for play drives him to seek out grand narratives—myths that support the world's vapid and oppressive arrangements—so that he can "dis-play" their hollow solemnities with broken stories. But what's a parabler to do when there are no grand narratives left to debunk? If F. Scott Fitzgerald's generation had grown up to find "all Gods dead, all wars fought, all faiths in man shaken,"[3] what disruptive work could possibly be left for Barthelme and his peers, almost fifty years later?

Barthelme is conspicuously conscious that his is a belated strategy of alienation. To distance himself from naively impassioned resisters and subversives, he acknowledges, usually through mockery, a host of familiar alienistic strategies: there is Marxism ("We are getting pretty damned sick of the whole thing and our equanimity is leaking away and finding those tiny Chairman Mao poems in the baby food isn't helping one bit, I can tell you that"), spiritual hermitism ("Yet there is no denying it, something is pulling me toward that monastery located in a remote part of Western Nevada"), Kierkegaardian rotation ("If I had been born well prior to 1900, I could have ridden with Pershing against Pancho Villa"), discursive retrieval ("But retraction has a special allure for me. I would wish to retract everything, if I could . . ."), escape through intoxication ("Well my mind is blown now. Nine mantras and three bottles of insect repellent . . . sick tomorrow. But it is worth it to have a blown mind. To stop being a filthy bourgeois for a space, even a short space"), conspicuous consumption ("sitting inside an Eldorado, Starfire, Riviera or Mustang"), and the refusal to perform socially responsible roles ("be a man about whom nothing is known") (p. 18). In passing, Barthelme also alludes to subversive individualism, mysticism, aestheticism, and, perhaps most tellingly, Romanticism. With ambivalent irony, he elliptically defines three alienistic strategies perennially associated with Romanticism:

THE SECOND GENERATION OF ENGLISH ROMANTICS INHERITED THE PROBLEMS OF THE FIRST, BUT COMPLICATED BY THE EVILS OF INDUSTRIALISM AND POLITICAL REPRESSION. ULTIMATELY THEY FOUND AN ANSWER NOT IN SOCIETY BUT IN VARIOUS FORMS OF INDEPENDENCE FROM SOCIETY:

HEROISM

ART

SPIRITUAL TRANSCENDENCE. (p. 24)

"SPIRITUAL TRANSCENDENCE" most closely resembles what we have called a gnostic strategy, "ART" an aesthetic strategy, and "HEROISM" the cult of authenticity associated with Rousseau, Carlyle, Nietzsche, and the anti-heroes of the twentieth century. Though his short novel is marked by comedic excess, bathetic letdowns, and just plain silliness, Barthelme is on to something: insofar as strategies of alienation share a common essence, it is an attitude, or "anti-tude," of being *not satisfied.*[4] Like other alienistic strategies, Barthelme's parable is motivated by dissatisfaction, and of that there is no end. Mythmakers may work from sun to sun, but alienist work is never done.

⤙ Labor, Love, Language: Rounding up the Usual Suspects

The salient characteristic of the Barthelme ethos is dissatisfaction. He is unhappy with the way we work, the way we love, and the way we talk—or, stated more formally, with labor in a system of market capitalism, with sexuality in its sanctioned American modes, and with public communication, tainted as it is with innumerable deceits and inauthenticities. Alienists, by definition *not satisfied,* often trace their antipathy to its sources: the scripts and patterns that support the ways of the world. Working, loving, communicating: these are the primary engines of worldly arrangements, the objectionable practices that instigate alienistic performances. In traditional cultures, such practices are supported by communal myths and authorizing stories; as a consequence, parablers and other "fools" find ready employment. When grand narratives are scarce, however, a subversive parabler like Barthelme is forced to make do with the rather shabby, second-class myths that are available. When *Snow White* appeared in the *New Yorker* in the midsixties, "Heigh-ho, heigh-ho, it's off to work we go" and "Someday my prince will come" were still ringing in the ears of moviegoers; and in Walt Disney's optimistically Americanized version of the Grimm folk tale, Barthelme found a timely pop culture myth that cried out for parabolic correctives and corrosions. Moreover, as Disney's sanitized celebration continues to find new video audiences, the novella retains its timeliness as a parody of unreflective work, vapid sexuality, and debased, commercialized communication.

Barthelme's dwarfs are, for the most part, unreflective and routinized in their activities; but at one point he does have them consider the possibility that their devotion to their work—tending vats of Chinese baby food and washing buildings—may be fundamentally misguided, part of a comprehensive delusion or deceit: "Perhaps we should not be sitting here tending the vats and washing the buildings and carrying the money to the vault once a week, like everybody else.

Perhaps we should be doing something else entirely, with our lives. God knows what. We do what we do without thinking. One tends the vats and washes the buildings and carries the money to the vault and never stops for a moment to consider that the whole process may be despicable" (p. 87). The dwarfs momentarily worry that there may be someone, somewhere "despising us . . . a gouty thinker thinking, father forgive them" (p. 87). This flicker of self-doubt may be Barthelme's parabolic version of similar but more solemn reconsiderations and examinations of conscience, like those found in works such as Tolstoy's *The Death of Ivan Ilych*.[5] In any case, there is enough here to let us know that the dwarfs are troubled and their complacency is threatened. They are worried that there may be something or someone else—a Flaubert or a Sartre, a Mallarmé or a Barthelme—who, being other and alien, does not approve of their way of "doing business." They grow concerned because Bill, their erstwhile leader, withdraws and "doesn't want to be involved in human situations any more" (p. 4). Snow White, their erotic object, is bored, and she is writing a poem whose "theme is loss" (p. 59). They feel themselves and their bourgeois work judged. It becomes increasingly evident, even to the usually placid and phlegmatic dwarfs, that their habitual patterns are neither seamless nor sufficient.

Their reaction to this disturbance in the little commonwealth is, not surprisingly, an act of retribution and scapegoating. To restore their prized equanimity, the sine qua non of their functionality as laborers, they decide that they must eliminate Bill. Bill has become an alienated resister, and it is his withdrawal that reveals the emptiness of their mundane, workaday lives. His crime is boredom and nonparticipation—performances summed up by the term "not-liking," a childish but eloquent indicator (pp. 4–5).[6] The tribe is quick to cast out those whose alienation makes them "sick," unfit, or simply unsuccessful. Bill is guilty of alienation, and their resolution of the problem is extermination: though Bill "leaped about on the platform quite a bit," Hogo's quirt "expedited things. Now there is a certain degree of equanimity. . . . Things are going well" (p. 180). Earlier in the novel, as the dwarfs are "sitting around the breakfast table with its big cardboard boxes of 'Fear,' 'Chix,' and 'Rats,'" Howard, another "failure," is driven away violently but not lethally: "we took [his sleeping bag] away from him and took away his bowl too, and the Chix that were in it, and the milk on top of the Chix, and his spoon and napkin and chair, and began pelting him with boxes, to indicate that his welcome had been used up. We soon got rid of him" (p. 6). Civilization survives on fear, chicks, and rats—implicit threats, erotic diversion, and Hobbesian competition—and the group will kill, quickly and without remorse, when its equanimity is threatened. After the ritual sacrifice of Bill, the dwarfs (and by implication enculturated reader-laborers) are ready again to march off to work. By making "HEIGH-HO" the last word of the novel, Barthelme sardonically signals a return to the unreflective status quo.

Barthelme also uses the character of Bill to connect mundane work with banal sexuality. Bill is guilty of "vatricide and failure," violating the economic and sexual expectations of the tribe (p. 180). Not only is Bill dissatisfied with the food processing and the building cleaning but he is also "tired of Snow White now," the collective dwarf voice tells us. "He can't bear to be touched" (p. 4). He performs his alienation by no longer coming to the shower room to take his place in the queue of guys that forms to enjoy Snow White. The dwarfs themselves link labor and sexuality when they associate their work cleaning buildings ("Clean buildings fill your eyes with sunlight, and your heart with the idea that man is perfectible") with erotic diversion and desire ("Also [buildings] are good places to look at girls from.... Viewed from above they are like targets.... We are very much tempted to shoot our arrows into them, those targets. You know what that means") (p. 8). "Snow White's arse" has served them as a sustaining cultural principle; but now, like Bill whose "not-liking" alienation reveals the emptiness of their labor and their lust, Snow White begins to resist their routinized erotic visits to the shower room. Her withdrawal and resistance precipitate the same suspicion that the dwarfs direct at Bill, and murder is again their reconstituting "solution." Immediately after they hang Bill, they forcibly "revirginize" Snow White through an unspecified process that involves her "ris[ing] into the sky." The group then celebrates "THE APOTHEOSIS OF SNOW WHITE" (p. 181). By this point in the narrative, the menace of the threatened group is palpable, so we assume that Snow White, like Bill, has been disposed of. In a chilling conclusion, then, Barthelme renders both the motive and the cost of alienation.

Of most importance to Barthelme and to us is alienation from shared language. The dwarfs are aware that ordinary language can be oppressive and may therefore foster resistance. "You know," Dan (one of the dwarfs) muses, "Klipschorn was right I think when he spoke of the 'blanketing' effect of ordinary language, referring, as I recall, to ... (1) an 'endless' quality and (2) a 'sludge' quality" (p. 96). In spite or because of this sludge quality, language blankets the individual with the "filling," "stuffing," and "blague" of the group. Common language thereby functions as a means of group enslavement akin to other patterns of constraint and bondage and serves the needs of the dwarfs for control. It is appropriate that the group receives a first clue that Snow White may be hatching an alienation when she begins to write, an activity associated with the independence and privacy of the interior life at least since the time of Augustine. At some level they realize that the privacy of writing makes subversive resistance possible. Hence the dwarfs, who want to see all and to know all, are alarmed when they learn that Snow White is writing a letter: "'A letter?' we asked wondering if a letter then to whom and what about" (p. 10). Nothing is to be withheld from their gaze. "'Well,' we said, 'can we have a peek?'" (p. 11). They are further alarmed when they learn that Snow White has written a four-page poem about which they know nothing: "There it was," they say of the news about the mysterious poem, "the red meat on the rug" (pp. 10–11). They realize that the power and durability of group patterns depend on its lingo "getting inside." Only there can the prison-house of language do its work. So the dwarfs are anxious to control the discourse of Snow White's interior life as they control external behavior through coercion and the threat of violence.

The group is right to fear poetry. Snow White's poem is part of an alienistic strategy to differentiate herself by finding fresh language. Her poem is the performance of alienation that, according to the dwarfs, comes "between us like an immense, wrecked railroad car." She uses it to create some distance, some difference, to free herself from her oppressing companions. The dwarfs do not want to seem too eager and alarmed, but they cannot resist a few prying questions. First they want to know "'Is it rhymed or free?' 'Free,' Snow White said, 'free, free, free.'" Then they want to know the theme. "'One of the great themes,' she said, 'that is all I can reveal at this time.'" Beside themselves with curiosity, they ask, "'Could you tell us the first word?' 'The first word,' she said, 'is "bandaged and wounded."'" They object that this is not just one word. "'Run together,' she said." After "mentally review[ing] the great themes in light of the word or words, 'bandaged and wounded,'" they ask, "'How is it that bandage precedes wound?'" Snow White's reply summarizes the strategies and performances of alienation examined in this book: "['Bandaged and wounded' is] a metaphor of the self armoring itself against the gaze of The Other" (p. 59). As with other alienistic performances that we have examined, the bandage precedes the wound because the wound has been anticipated. Gnostic esoterics, asceticism, antinomianism, aesthetic escapes, artsy conundrums, typographical tricks—all these strategies can be understood as bandages that prepare for and perhaps mitigate the reciprocal hurt involved in transmission, communication, and exchange.

⊷ The Techniques of Postmodern Parable

To reiterate the point: Barthelme shares with other alienistic writers a pervasive dissatisfaction with culturally sanctioned labor, sexuality, and communication — the world's essential "ways." Of these, it is often language that is scrutinized most closely because it is language that supports alienating forms of work and love and makes them possible. By demonstrating Barthelme's dissatisfaction with the deceits and exploitations inherent in these practices, we identify *Snow White* as a strategy of alienation. As would-be practitioners of virtue criticism, however, we should do more than round up the usual suspects. Our evaluative co-performance with Barthelme ought to enunciate the how as well as the what and the why. So we want to distinguish the otherworldly gnosticism of an Eliot and the sequestered aestheticism of a Nabokov from Barthelme's parabolic strategies, those "base weeds" — pesky, sly, resilient — that surreptitiously thrive in the tended gardens of myth. The parabler does not want to replace myth, but to mess it and mess with it by means of passages and pieces that are often self-consciously absurd.[7] It seems that wherever there is a broad, totalizing elaboration, there will be little sprouts of parable to remind us that this is only one way to pattern things, that this particular mythic garden is a human construction with varying elements of what Charles Molesworth calls "self-delusion and self-aggrandizement."[8]

Thus John Dominic Crossan's observation that mythic works tend to be long and parabolic works short makes sense, and Barthelme, without consciously using the term, must have been a natural parabler, temperamentally suited for the "dis-perfecting" purposes and techniques of parable. The short pieces collected in *Sixty Stories* and *Forty Stories* are often, despite their titles, not stories at all but strange sketches, mock interviews, and quirky personal essays, and they frequently include graphics — etchings and woodprints that Barthelme "clips" from the public domain.[9] The Monty Pythonesque heterogeneity of the story collections functions parabolically insofar as it disrupts expectations and disappoints the reader's longing for unity and harmony. With such techniques Barthelme adapts the strategies of the dadaists, who, in the words of R. P. Blackmur, "prevented masterpieces at all costs."[10] Barthelme's parables are at pains to be truncated, fragmented, or generically "broken" in some way, and in *Snow White*, he takes a comforting, "blanketing," too-familiar story and tears it apart by dividing, extending, burlesquing, and estranging it. The effect is provocation to performance: the reader is called to participate, to resist, even to compete with the writer. Barthelme imposes a fresh distance between the participants by exposing the suppressed complexity, even suspicion, inherent in the reader-writer relationship. The imagination, his parables reminds us, is an instrument of alienation as well as identification.

Like other parablers, Barthelme wants to slow down the process of recuperative interpretation. Inveterate decoders, we anxious readers are uneasy and want to know, like the dwarfs, "Where is the figure in the carpet?"[11] We fear that it may be "just carpet" and want a mythic or at least a coherent narrative to present itself (p. 129). But Barthelme's techniques prevent us from hastily identifying his little works as instances of this or that convention, genre, or theme. For example, he avoids the label of satire by alternately inviting our condemnation of the world and then undermining the terms that we have available for practicing that condemnation—thereby preventing his parable from calcifying into yet another predictable myth of disaffection. Moreover, his parabolic tactics create something more (or less) than what Booth calls an unreliable narrator. Ordinarily, a reliable implied author lies behind an unreliable narrator. But it is my sense that *Snow White* implies not just an unreliable narrator but an unreliable author, a parabler who deftly resists cultural recuperation. To say this is simply to say, in different terms, that Barthelme is a postmodernist.

David Lodge's typology of literary techniques is helpful in understanding the peculiar *how* of an alienistic parabler like Barthelme. Among the principles of composition that Lodge identifies as postmodernist is *contradiction*. A good example from *Snow White* comes when a dwarf named Clem begins a discourse on cans of olive oil and the quality of life in America. "Why am I talking to myself about cans?" Clem asks. "Cans are not what is troubling me. What is troubling me is the quality of life in our great country, America. It seems to me to be deprived." Clem's focus has suddenly gone from "cans" to a more serious topic, "the [deprived] quality of life in our great country, America." But, just as suddenly, what was becoming an indignant, proactive concern for the body politic disappears, and Clem reverts to his imaginative lassitude: "I suppose one could say that they are all humpheads and let it go at that" (p. 140). Barthelme also utilizes what Lodge calls *permutation* to make the reader slow down the interpretive process. Jane (formerly the fairest of them all) has become the evil stepmother figure. She permutates her malice toward Snow White: "Now I cultivate my malice. It is a cultivated malice, not the pale natural malice we knew, when the world was young. I grow more witchlike as the hazy days imperceptibly meld into one another, and the musky months sink into memory as into a slough, sump, or slime. But I have malice. I have that. I have even invented new varieties of malice, that men have not seen before now" (p. 40). This kind of word play is designed to drain the word *malice* of its maliciousness. *Excess*, similar in its effects to permutation, is also used throughout the novel. The lengthy and painstaking description of Snow White's house cleaning is but one example (pp. 37–38). By depicting actions in unconventional ways and burdening categories with self-canceling techniques like contradiction, permutation, and excess, Barthelme prevents an alienistic impulse from becoming first co-opted, then enshrined, and finally mythologized.

The postmodernist technique that Lodge calls *short-circuiting* works in a similar way to discourage and disconcert the seeking of patterns that can calcify into ideologies. As Lodge explains the technique, short-circuiting is the self-conscious playing with concepts of transparency, illusion, authorship, and literary convention so that the reader is denied a complete, seamless, and organic experience. Instead we are offered a series of disjunctive experiences: sincere and passionate moments are juxtaposed with absurdities, conventional and rational episodes are followed by gratuitous and arbitrary fantasies. The overall effect is typically one of anxiety or uncertainty since the categories by which the reader orders, interprets, and "overstands" the text are undermined. As Lodge explains, the "process of interpretation assumes a gap between the text and the world, between art and life, which postmodernist writing characteristically tries to short-circuit in order to administer a shock to the reader and thus resist assimilation into conventional categories of the literary."[12] Lodge's short-circuiting is what could be more informally termed a bait-and-switch technique. The method might also be called bathetic, because it usually moves without warning from the sublime, or at least the serious, to the vulgar and the ridiculous.

Perhaps the best example of Barthelme calling forth serious sentiments just to short-circuit them is the reader-response questionnaire that he inserts midway through the book. Its existence and strategic placement are meant to disrupt whatever narrative pattern we have been constructing of this centrifugal fiction. In addition to asking how readers like the story "so far," the questionnaire asks whether we would like more or less emotion in the remainder of the story and more or less blague in the narration. But we are also asked, "Would you like a war? Yes ( ) No ( )" and "Has the work, for you, a metaphysical dimension? Yes ( ) No ( )." If at this point we begin to ruminate about the possibility of war and the philosophical import of a book like *Snow White*, those thoughts are undermined by the bathetic effect of the next question: "What is [the metaphysical dimension] (twenty-five words or less)?" which is followed by a few blank lines, presumably for writing in a response. The final question is also a "short-circuiter": "In your opinion, should human beings have more shoulders? ( ) Two sets of shoulders? ( ) Three? ( )." Betty Sue Flowers has rightly called Barthelme's a "studiedly innocent" or "mock-innocent" style, and the reader questionnaire does seem to maintain this mock-innocence, especially syntactically.[13] But Barthelme's commitment to parabolic disruption does not permit a consistent use of any style, no matter how devious. Hence the bait-and-switch even within the questionnaire. As Flowers says, "Every shift from mock-innocent to mock-heroic, to mock-poetic, to mock-patriotic, to mock-mythical, to self-mocking is timed to unbalance the reader."[14] This short-circuiting is part of Barthelme's alienistic performance and, like other postmodernist techniques, ensures that his parable remains vigilantly parabolic.[15]

This parabolic vigilance is also manifested in Barthelme's almost obsessive impatience with literary conventions.[16] Seen as rubrics, conventions signal an imprisonment within other people's systems. His need for authenticity and his suspicion of the recruiting assaults of culture are underscored by an impatience with the words *he* always hears. According to Barthelme's literary agent, his "central obsession is not to be boring, because he is so easily bored himself."[17] No doubt Barthelme's susceptibility to boredom is, like Flaubert's and Baudelaire's, "a highly moral matter," as John P. Sisk says, an authentic response to the processes of culture.[18] Sisk quotes Flaubert's enthusiastic reception of Baudelaire's *Les Fleurs du Mal*: "Ah! How well you understand the boredom of existence!"[19] Often a quick and impatient mind will anticipate the boredom that begins as a by-product but eventually degrades the exchange of ethical goods. Like a silver mine or a water well, strategies will "play out," regardless of their original freshness; alienistic writers are haunted by a sense that the common tongue does get tired, that culture does wear out its forms. Parablers such as Barthelme attempt to forestall cultural assimilation and keep the performance alive by means of surprise, disruption, and other techniques similar to those we have examined.

How far can a writer go before alienation is simply produced, awkwardly and inartistically, rather than mutually performed and thereby reversed? The answer will depend, of course, on the expectations, experience, and flexibility of co-performing readers. Over time, one can develop a tolerance and indeed a taste for postmodernist forms and techniques. In any case, it should be noted that Barthelme's alienistic performances by no means define the outer limit of parabolic writing. Other "disruptionists," so dubbed by Jerome Klinkowitz, include Ronald Sukenick, Raymond Federman, and Jerzy Kosinski. Klinkowitz praises Barthelme for a "comic disabuse [that] has made it uneasy for writers to write, or readers to read, in the insipid forms of the past." *Snow White* is a "tour de force," he says, and names Steve Katz (*The Exagggerations of Peter Prince*), Eugene Wildman (*Montezuma's Ball*), Gilbert Sorrentino (*Imaginative Qualities of Actual Things*), and William H. Gass (*Willie Master's Lonesome Wife*) as writers whose disruptionist work goes beyond theme and form to question "the entire premise of traditional fiction," which is that stories have plots and words have public meaning.[20] By not pretending to be anything else, disruptionist fiction avoids becoming a "sham illusory representation." Since it is not a version of realism, not a reflection of something, and not about anything else, Klinkowitz says "it is simply itself."[21] Disruptionist fiction is literature with an attitude, and its extreme examples flaunt their uncompromising authenticity and mimic the provocations and confrontations of so-called performance art.

It is not surprising, then, that Klinkowitz thinks parabolic works such as *Catch-22* and *Invisible Man* do not go far enough in their alienistic strategies. Richard Gilman comes to the same conclusion, finding too much "transparency" and "communication" in Heller and Ellison.[22] Gestures that merely mock commonplace values or express disaffection are not alienistic enough. "The trouble with much so-called black humor or absurd writing or neosurrealism," Gilman wrote in the late sixties, is that "it accomplishes little aesthetically. The proof of this is that it mostly stays within the formal structures of previous literature."[23] In the nineties, suspicions are directed toward "culture" rather than what Gilman and Klinkowitz call "actuality" or "reality," but the motives and the arguments have not changed in thirty years. Satirical works in the realist or naturalist tradition may be "superficially [and] *thematically* rebellious," but they remain, according to Gilman, "artistically tory, holding on to one or another conception of beauty, to tension and development, to character, story and plot, to moral or social or psychological 'significance.'"[24]

Snow White seems to be located, like liminal experiences, somewhere betwixt and between—and perhaps a place *between* is parable's proper topos. Alienistic strategies that maintain a consistent stance, employ publicly recognized forms, and offer themselves as metaphors to live by remain artistically tory in spite of themselves and calcify into "myth[s] for disaffiliation," in Gilman's words.[25] Like other postmodern parablers and discerners of the absurd, Barthelme's performances are structured to resist a reader's efforts to habituate them and transform them into myths, even myths of opposition and disaffiliation. Designed to call conventions of language and storytelling into question, they make use of techniques such as those identified by Lodge to simulate complete independence from the enveloping culture. Ultimately, those parables that approach nonbeing or absence will be more profoundly and doggedly alienistic than conventional, plotted, and representational writing can ever be. Highhanded and unaccommodating, parabolic performances occur in the gaps between a culture's dominant codes and interpretive categories.

◄— Unspeakable Bandages, Unhealable Wounds

Barthelme brandishes his parable in the space between himself and his enveloping, auditioning culture just as Snow White constructs her private poem as an anticipatory bandage against the wounding Sartrean gaze of the group. Like the dwarfs, readers are led to ask of the author's diffident text, "Why do you remain with us? here? in this house?" Snow White's answer is also the author's: "I have not been able to imagine anything better" (p. 59). Barthelme remains with us in the house of fiction, the world of story, perhaps only because he has not been able to imagine anything better. Yet he does remain; he does show up; he does perform. Perhaps we are to take some comfort in the failure of parablers to exclude us utterly. "We were pleased by this powerful statement of our essential mutuality," one of the dwarfs says, "which can never be sundered or torn, or broken apart, dissipated, diluted, corrupted or finally severed, not even by art in its manifold and dreadful guises" (p. 59). Forever joined by the imagination in essential mutuality—this is Barthelme's unsentimental burlesque of St. Paul's assurances to the Romans.[26] Yet even as burlesque the playful passage serves as a revealing postmodernist manifesto for parablers who grudgingly reside within and manipulate the world's sensorium. Insofar as it is an artful utterance that can be brought to performance, alienistic parable, despite its manifold and dreadful guises, cannot separate us, one from another.

If the rudiments of virtue criticism—mutual performance, empathy, identification, and adoption—are present for even the readers and writers of parable, then what question should the critic pose to the parabler? Let us borrow the metaphor with which Snow White begins her alienistic poem: bandaged and wounded, "run together." The question for virtue criticism is, "What kind of bandage for what kind of wound?" In the case of Snow White, we have proposed that culture's formulaic modes of love, labor, and language constitute the wound; moreover, that Barthelme's bandage consists of certain reflexive, "postmodernist" techniques. Other parables, of course, would develop different bandages for different wounds.

Run together: It is important to reiterate the wounding, transgressive motive of parable even as we acknowledge its homeopathic function. Barthelme's parabolic bandage has both the power to hurt and the power to heal because it calls attention to wounds that have been ignored or repressed. As we have seen, when values are transferred in other symbolic modes, the imagination is always an instrument of both alienation and identification; and so it is with parable. In fact, like Snow White's worrisome act of writing a poem, Barthelme's very construction of a parable signals his alienistic desire to use his imagination to disentangle himself. "My imagination is stirring," the parabler says. "Be warned." But the parabler knows that even an imagination bent on alienation draws from a reservoir or sensorium held in common. When Barthelme attacked Greene and Eliot for "put[ting] themselves at the mercy of an unexamined assumption, that it is better to exist than not to exist" and praised Beckett because "his characters act precisely in the area of the unexamined assumption: they yearn toward non-existence," he was obviously tempted by the apocalypticism of the cultural moment and the negativity inherent in parabolic forms. And yet he was able to recognize that Beckett's characters do act and, further, that their actions suggest motives, yearnings. In recognizing the symbolic action of Beckett and his characters, Barthelme locates himself in a dramatistic realm, based, as Burke says, on "cooperation, participation, man in society, man in drama"—all modes of identification and mutual performance.

During the fifties, Donald Barthelme founded and edited a periodical at the University of Houston called *Forum*. He was one of the first to identify and publish the nonfiction of Walker Percy, and the two shared a recognition of cultural belatedness and semantic contamination—what Steiner calls "the inauthentic situation of man in an environment of eroded speech."[27] We have inherited "a defunct vocabulary," Percy says; "a certain devaluation" of "the old words" has occurred. But the reader participates with the author in the "reversal of alienation through its representing," and the "literature of alienation" becomes "an aesthetic victory of comradeliness, a recognition of plight in common."[28] The imagination of alienation is the repetition and reversal of alienation. As an alienistic performance, reenacted in this chapter, Barthelme's novel plays a communal role. Like Nabokov's, his book contributes to culture by cultivating needed virtues: tolerance of stylistic diversity, suspicion of surfaces (but also appreciation of surfaces), intellectual suppleness, recognition of absurdity and exploitation in everyday life, and a lively and unsentimental sense of humor.

There is also an ironic heroism required of a performer such as Barthelme. The cultural work of alienism often entails a degree of self-sacrifice; when the sacrifice is for the sake of the offending culture, then the work of the parabler takes on heroic qualities. The nature of Barthelme's ironic heroism is clarified for me if I think of the character Bill as the author's alter ego. Bill dies at the hands of the group—a proper end for a prophet or parabler. Yet before his execution he does his best to carry a warning to them. "I cannot fall apart now," Bill says, perhaps speaking for Barthelme, who continued to write and to publish and to teach despite his acute awareness of the degradation of language and the exploitations of culture (p. 71). No doubt some kind of dysfunctional madness was always a tempting strategy for him. But when confronted with the option of giving up and falling apart, Bill/Barthelme says, "Not yet. I must hold the whole thing together. Everything depends on me. I must conceal my wounds, contrive to appear unwounded. They must not know." In a sense, Barthelme's professional life was a long attempt to appear unwounded, and his fiction worked as a "bloody handkerchief stuffed under the shirt," a bandage that both concealed and revealed the hidden hurt, allowing the writer to go on. Barthelme's parabolic techniques help to stop "the spiritual spoor" and bind the "invisible wounds" so that he can manage a recognizable and restorative performance. "Don't think about it," Bill tells himself, suppressing in classic hero fashion a preoccupation with his injuries—no doubt Donald Barthelme suppressed countless moments of enervating boredom and alienation in a similar fashion. Like other isms, though, even an alienistic heroism can settle into a formula. So before his parable degenerates into principle, Barthelme comically and at his own expense traces the hardening process: "Think about leadership," Bill says to himself, falling into a convenient cultural rut, as if leadership can take his mind off his alienation. Quickly, however, Bill extricates himself as he senses the deadening, blanketing "blague" of such formulations. Bill, Barthelme, and we as readers realize that leadership, like every other conventional category, has been evacuated of meaning by the relentless engines of the cultural economy: "No," Bill says, "don't think about leadership" (p. 71). Here again Barthelme has used the postmodernist technique of contradiction to keep his performance unpredictable and fresh and to avoid the heaviness of mythmaking. At the same time he practices a serious alienistic strategy designed to help us see our ways, and the errors of them. *Snow White* is Barthelme's gift to us: a parabolic bandage for an unhealable wound, a broken fairy tale about the imagination's power to hurt.

Notes

1. Donald Barthelme, *Snow White* (1967; rpt., New York: Atheneum, 1972), p. 6. Subsequent references will be given in the text.

2. Donald Barthelme, "The Tired Terror of Graham Greene," *Holiday* 39, no. 4 (1966), pp. 148–49.

3. A virtual battle cry for him and his disaffected contemporaries, the phrase comes from Fitzgerald's first novel, *This Side of Paradise* (New York: Charles Scribner's Sons, 1920), p. 255.

4. Armin Paul Frank analyzes Burke's *Counter-Statement* in a chapter entitled "Art as Anti-tude" in *Kenneth Burke* (New York: Twayne, 1969), pp. 44–71.

5. Barthelme's "At the Tolstoy Museum" is an amusing (and I think finally sympathetic) send-up of the Russian master's solemn themes, preoccupations, and personality. In the sketch a visitor at the museum confirms that Tolstoy "has been a lifelong source of inspiration to me." The narrator is less certain about Tolstoy's value: "I haven't made up my mind," the narrator muses, somewhat overwhelmed by the "640,086 pages (Jubilee Edition) of the author's published work." Nonetheless, the narrator decides that Tolstoy is worth a bit more of his attention and effort, and he decides to "march on" to the next room in the museum, hoping that "something vivifying will happen to me there." *Forty Stories* (New York: Penguin, 1987), p. 128.

6. Another measure of Barthelme's boredom, nonparticipation, and suspicions of prescribed labor is his failure to earn an undergraduate degree at the University of Houston: even though he accumulated over 160 semester credit hours in courses that *he* wanted to take, he never completed the coursework required for graduation.

7. An example is Snow White's exasperated outburst of discontent ("I just don't like your world . . . a world in which such things can happen"), which is prompted not by the vacuity of human work, the debasement of sexuality, or the commodification of language, but by a giant egg meringue that rises to the ceiling when she bakes it, trapping Snow White and the dwarfs inside. The renunciation and sense of entrapment are genuine, but the enveloping situation is, well, light and airy. The dwarfs try to mollify Snow White's disenchantment with their world and bring her back into the circle by (what else?) gifting. They present her the leftover egg yolks in an aluminum container, gamely adhering to the practice of using gifts as a means of reconciliation. But Snow White "still wasn't satisfied. That is the essential point here, that she wasn't satisfied" (p. 69). It is as if Barthelme had anticipated Nemoianu's insight about gifts creating their own alienation.

8. Charles Molesworth, *Donald Barthelme's Fiction: The Ironist Saved from Drowning* (Columbia: University of Missouri Press, 1982), p. 31.

9. Donald Barthelme, *Sixty Stories* (New York: Penguin Books, 1993). With his later works, *Paradise* and *The King*, Barthelme did construct narratives that are longer and

less parabolic; but *Snow White* was published in its entirety in a single issue of the *New Yorker*, and even when dealing with big questions and unwieldy topics, Barthelme prefers sharp brevity and economy.

10. R. P. Blackmur, *Anni Mirabiles, 1921–25: Reason in the Madness of Letters* (Washington, D.C.: Library of Congress, 1956), p. 15.

11. Barthelme parodically alludes to Henry James's conceit in "The Figure in the Carpet." In the introduction to the story written for the 1909 New York Edition of his works, James argues (in a characteristically bloated, late-James style) for the value of "analytic appreciation," which he calls "the Beautiful Gate itself of [literary] enjoyment." *Heritage of American Literature*, vol. 2, ed. James E. Miller Jr. (San Diego: Harcourt Brace, 1991), p. 342.

12. David Lodge, *The Modes of Modern Writing: Metaphor, Metonymy, and the Typology of Modern Literature* (Ithaca: Cornell University Press, 1977), pp. 239–40.

13. Betty Sue Flowers, "Barthelme's *Snow White*: The Reader-Patient Relationship," *Critique* 16, no. 3 (1975), p. 39.

14. Ibid., p. 39.

15. Taking a cue from Lodge, who concerns himself with local techniques, Molesworth offers a helpful typology that is oriented toward structure rather than texture. He offers five categories for classifying Barthelme's short fiction: total aleatory structure, the surreal place, the counterpointed plot, the extended conceit, and parodies of narrative structure (pp. 74–77). Even from this more structural typology we can see that Barthelme's parabolic strategies only gingerly partake of generic patterns, probably because even parodic structures gravitate toward myth.

16. Sensing the exhaustion of Anglo-American literary realism, Barthelme launched a denunciation of Graham Greene, who, he said, was persisting in using "tired" and tiresome narrative conventions. He writes that "the feeling of terror Mr. Greene could once produce from these materials has leaked away." "Tired Terror," pp. 146, 148–49. Barthelme's metaphor of leaking follows Percy's suggestion that language can be "worn out" or "used up" and anticipates Barth's metaphor of exhaustion or exhausted possibility.

17. Quoted by Jerome Klinkowitz in *Literary Disruptions: The Making of a Post-Contemporary American Fiction*, 2d ed. (Urbana: University of Illinois Press, 1980), p. 74.

18. According to Sisk, for modernism and postmodernism, disgust and boredom are positive moral virtues (p. 27). Sisk's insight provides additional impetus for attempting an ethics of alienation. "The End of Boredom," *Georgia Review* 39, no. 1 (1985), pp. 25–34.

19. Ibid., p. 28.

20. Jerome Klinkowitz, "Literary Disruptions; or, What's Become of American Fiction," *Partisan Review* 40, no. 3 (1973), pp. 433–44. See also Klinkowitz, *Literary Disruptions*.

21. Klinkowitz, "Literary Disruptions," pp. 441, 436.

22. Richard Gilman, *The Confusion of Realms* (New York: Random House, 1969). According to Paul Mann, the silent writer (who has taken disruption to the next level of

resistance) views all communication as part of an efficiently functioning economy that renders every meaning arbitrary. "Invisible Ink: Writing in the Margin," *Georgia Review* 39, no. 4 (1985), p. 809. Mann's provocative insights are discussed more fully in the conclusion.

23. Gilman, *The Confusion of Realms*, p. 44.

24. Ibid.

25. Ibid., p. 45. For a discussion of the role of metaphor in the construction of life-plots, see George Lakoff and Mark Johnson, *Metaphors We Live By* (Chicago: University of Chicago Press, 1980).

26. "For I am certain of this: neither death nor life, nor angels, nor principalities, nothing already in existence and nothing still to come, nor any power, nor the heights nor the depths, nor any created thing whatever, will be able to come between us and the love of God, known to us in Christ Jesus our Lord." Rom. 8:38–39. After drinking several bottles of Chablis, Dan, the dwarf who becomes the leader after Bill is hanged, expresses a lament that may be another parodic allusion to St. Paul's Epistles: "What is merely fashionable will fade away, and what is merely new will fade away, but what will not fade away, is the way I feel. . . . I feel abandoned" (p. 137). ("But if there are prophecies, they will be done away with; if tongues, they will fall silent; and if knowledge, it will be done away with. For we know only imperfectly, and we prophesy imperfectly . . . but then we shall be seeing face to face. Now, I can know only imperfectly; but then I shall know just as fully as I am myself known." 1 Cor. 13:8–9, 12.)

27. George Steiner, "On Difficulty," *On Difficulty and Other Essays* (New York: Oxford University Press, 1978), p. 44.

28. Walker Percy, *The Message in the Bottle: How Queer Man Is, How Queer Language Is, and What One Has to Do with the Other* (New York: Farrar, Straus, and Giroux, 1975), pp. 118, 93.

Conclusion: "Lilies That Fester"

It is clear that strategies of alienation are not limited to the realm of artists or creative writers. Cultural critics and theorists frequently engage in alienistic performances. Another book might be devoted to an ethical analysis of recurrent alienistic strategies manifested in the work of influential critics and theorists. Alienists are everywhere, performing their adversarialism and disaffiliation in various ways for various audiences. For this book, I have limited my evaluation to a few representative makers of imaginative literature in the twentieth century. The principal question about these writers has been not, Adversaries of what? but rather, What kind of adversaries? The performance of character has remained the central concern. We have been less interested in the culture resisted than in the character of the resisters themselves. Thus we have practiced a special kind of cultural criticism, a virtue criticism that uses close reading and analysis for evaluating clusters of virtues — texts, speakers, literary characters, implied authors, flesh-and-blood persons, and other "corporate we's."

Isolation, absence, silence, ultimately suicide and death — these are more efficacious strategies than gnosticism, aestheticism, and parable, if alienation is the sole or final objective. As symbolic patterns, literary texts require adoption and identification to do their work, even if their work is alienation. In an effort to protect his vital fluids from exposure and commingling, Kubrick's General Jack Ripper instigates a nuclear attack on "the Russkies"; his final, complementary gesture, committing suicide, protects his universe of discourse ("u. of d.," in Barthelme's abbreviated formulation) from the mixing and dilution inherent in capture and questioning. In a passage from "Friendship" that is eerily similar, Emerson explains: "I cannot afford to talk with [my friends] and study their visions, lest I lose my own."[1] Emerson's desire for independence and isolation, hardly an exception, is endemic to the American tradition. D. H. Lawrence sensed the importance of alienation in the culture when he characterized the classic American hero as "hard, stoic, isolate, and a killer."[2] It is what Barth and Barthelme admire so much in Beckett, what Melville embodied in Bartleby and, in a quite different way, in Ahab.

Despite his strategies of independence, even Emerson could recognize that his friend Thoreau's uncompromising virtues of alienation "sometimes ran to extremes" and thus became vices. Thoreau pressed an "inexorable demand on all for exact truth," Emerson writes, and this austere perfectionism "made this willing hermit more solitary even than he wished." Thoreau had a disgust for crime and an unrelenting scorn for paltering, as well as a well-developed knack for discovering it, especially among the dignified and prosperous. Though his younger friend was "himself of a perfect probity," Emerson eventually saw that Thoreau's severe *authenticism* became destructive, preventing his intercourse with others, and "depriv[ing] him of a healthy sufficiency of human society."[3]

Emerson implies that suspicion, isolation, and other strategies of staying away eventually become pathologically self-effacing. And yet something in the status quo does indeed seem to be rotten. Figures such as Thoreau have developed an acute sense of cultural smell. They are loathe to become a part of the festering sweetness they see around them and often develop authorial resistance to audience appropriation. William H. Gass, providing a candid and contemporary expression of writerly alienation, complains about the unusually large readership of his "In the Heart of the Heart of the Country":

> There's a whole world of people out there waiting like sharks to devour this sort of stuff. Our Town. How horrible. I don't get a lot of mail, but every once in a while somebody will write me from Texas or Iowa, places quite different from this little Indiana town, I should imagine, and they write to tell me that their town is the same, their lives are the same, their apprehensions are the same. I don't worry about readers when I'm writing, but it does annoy me, because apparently what they do when

they are reading the story—and what must move them—is to put themselves in the narrator's place. They say: "Gee whiz, this *is* what it's like to live in this shitty little town; this *is* the way my shitty little life is," and so forth, and on, and on, and on. . . . They are saying that the language of the work is theirs.[4]

Here Gass articulates the alienistic impulse without pulling any punches. His evident frustration with being unable to control the performance of his books may derive from the hard fact that even oppositional writers can never quite achieve absence, nonexistence, or total control by means of a proffered and recognizable text, however explosive and undermining.

The alienated writer often consciously or unconsciously functions as an *alienist* in the now rare sense of the word, meaning a psychiatrist, a shrink, a diagnostician. Percy explicitly identifies the novelist as a diagnostician who can disclose the culture's hidden but not asymptomatic malaise.[5] The more extreme the strategy of alienation, however, the less likely the writer is to function in a service capacity. More often, suspicion and a fear of being culturally appropriated lead to versions of resistance like the indignant Romanticism of Thoreau or the condescension of Gass.

Many alienistic writers turn to *difficulty* as a functional means of resistance. Difficulty, according to George Steiner, is an artistic strategy commonly enacted by writers who feel that language is "being cheapened, brutalized, emptied of numinous and exact force, by mass usage."[6] Steiner sets forth a useful typology of difficult texts. *Contingent* difficulties can be "looked up" and thereby resolved; *modal* difficulties arise because no one reader or community of readers can fully affirm and understand all possible instances of discourse; *tactical* difficulties are authorial efforts to produce a sense of "rich undecidability"; and *ontological* difficulties intentionally violate the agreement between writer and reader, between text and meaning. Of ontological difficulties, Steiner adds: "Difficulties of this category cannot be looked up; they cannot be resolved by genuine readjustment or artifice of sensibility; they are not an intentional technique of retardation and creative uncertainty (though these may be their immediate effect). Ontological difficulties confront us with blank questions about the nature of human speech, about the status of significance, about the necessity and purpose of the construct which we have, with more or less ready consensus, come to perceive as a poem."[7] Performances that enact this most intractable of difficulties constitute formidable disruptions, and Steiner is right to assign to them a formidable term. Hostility toward the audience and suspicion of conventional patterns of making, saying, and doing motivate this strategy of alienation. Unlike tactical difficulty (employed widely, but especially by metaphysicals such as John Donne and modernists such as Eliot and Stevens), ontological difficulty is not exclusively an artistic device. Encountering tactical difficulty, a reader senses the existence of an ambiguity constructed to heighten pleasure or refine meaning: the difficulty is part of the aesthetically pleasing performance. Confronted with ontological difficulty, however, the reader is discouraged from auditioning the performance and, put off, may simply stop reading. The ontologically difficult text is a serious disruption or dislocation, if not quite a cessation or dissolution, of the literary performance. Steiner suggests that it is too early to tell whether recent strategies of hermeticism, examples of what he calls a "movement toward darkness," are merely transient phenomena or "some ultimate break in the classic contract between word and world."[8] Logically, however, if the ultimate break that Steiner speaks of were to occur, *we would not know*. If the figure that we identify as writer, author, or performer were completely silent and inaccessible, the ethos would simply not exist for us.

The virtue of *silence* in literary works inspired a flurry of critical books and articles roughly thirty years ago. Among them were Ihab Hassan's *The Literature of Silence* (the preface is dated "July, 1966"); Susan Sontag's "The Aesthetics of Silence" (1966) as well as Barthelme's "The Tired Terror of Graham Greene" (1966) and *Snow White* (1967). Of these, Sontag's essay has been the most influential and has become a critical classic. In it she lays out most of the recurring issues and motives of artistic or aesthetic silence. She borrows a metaphor from gnosticism when she says that "the 'spirit' seeking embodiment in art clashes with the 'material' character of art itself." The problem is that the reader carries with him or her the demands of culture and thus becomes "the enemy of the artist": "The very presence of an audience" becomes "*unacceptable*" to the artist.[9] As a consequence, the serious artist "is continually tempted to sever the dialogue he has with an audience." Silence, then, "is the furthest extension of that reluctance to communicate, that ambivalence about making contact with the audience which is a leading motif of modern art, with its tireless commitment to the 'new' and/or the 'esoteric.' Silence is the artist's ultimate other-worldly gesture: by silence, he frees himself from servile bondage to the world, which appears as patron, client, consumer, antagonist, arbiter, and distorter of his work."[10] For the artist, the endpoints of the alien way are versions of absence: for Heinrich von Kleist and Lautréamont, suicide; for Friedrich Hölderlin and Antonin Artaud, madness; for Arthur Rimbaud and J. D. Salinger, silence. Fedor Tiutchev's nineteenth-century poem "Silentium" includes an endorsement of silence that was influential throughout Europe: "*Mysl' izrechennaia est' lozh*" (An uttered thought is a lie).[11] William Burroughs provides a similar denunciation of speech and one that has served as an American apologia for strategies of silence: "To speak is to lie—to live is to collaborate."[12] Extreme strategies of alienation may entail the conviction that communication of any kind is complicitous, that speaking and cultural interaction are evidence of what Paul Mann calls "incriminating sociability."[13]

Mann's article on the ethics and aesthetics of silent writing takes up again the issues that Sontag and Hassan were exploring in the sixties. Like gnosticism, aestheticism, and parable, the strategy of silence, Mann says, is the result of "a long and progressive disillusionment" with culture. But unlike the alienistic performers that we have examined, the silent writer has renounced *poetics*— the performative "making" of opposition and resistance—to become "locked in a *frozen* conflict with culture."[14] Avoiding the complicities of symbolic exchange, the silent writer practices the ultimate strategy of alienation. He or she realizes that when difference and critique are communicated, they disappear into the homogeneity of the cultural economy. Otherness is appropriated quickly and with scarcely a shudder. This almost instantaneous accommodation is the problem at the heart of any poetics of alterity and the frustration inherent in any alienistic expression. The monstrously efficient "white economy" of market capitalism circulates critical opposition as a commodity; with a "general indifference to difference," it finds "the dizzying plurality of texts nothing more than a well-balanced diet" and recognizes every performance as a solicitation, a come-on. "Every articulation, critical or affirmative," is recast at the site of cultural exchange and becomes nothing more than "goods for sale." "Once a critique is displayed," Mann writes, "once a margin becomes visible, it has already entered into circulation. In a sense the boundary between critique and advertising barely survives at all." The voracious appetite of the cultural economy means that the silent writer "can never retreat fast enough to blind himself from the vulnerability, the recuperability, inherent in every text." Once again, recuperation is cast as a fate or nemesis, a result of the imprisoning power of discourse and the artist's helplessness before the "total administration" of enculturated patterns. Mann endorses the authenticity of "a purer sort of defeatism," an alienism for which cultural assimilation is equivalent to death itself: "Perhaps to look at a work and think, *soon to be recuperated*, is no more (or less) dramatic than to look at a friend and think, *soon to die.*"[15]

The alienistic performer may take the role of Nathan or Jeremiah, but for the silent writer there can be "nothing prophetic about silence." Instead of feeling that "one must speak out against iniquity, we have now discovered the iniquity of speech itself." Alienation and alterity may remain the urgent dream, but effective opposition will not be found in ideology, "nor in aesthetics—neither in content nor in form—but in secrecy, seclusion, the refusal of any ideological or aesthetic display." Mallarmé's white page and W. S. Merwin's deserts and stones are not examples of silence because "these were always utterances," performances, "blankness *displayed*." Mann is not satisfied with those performers who absent themselves "only so far as to flaunt their presence." He would agree with Carlyle, who says that the poet is also "the Politician, the Thinker, Legislator, Philosopher"[16]—but for Mann such efficacious participation is precisely the rub. He has in mind a strategy of true silence, an alienism that is "ascetic, negative, rigorous, ludicrous, egomaniacal, ecstatic, sad. An art so absolutely for its own sake that it is no longer art." Thus silence is not a performance at all: "monkish," "a moral stance," "a negative witness," it has crossed the edge of the outer circle of culture "and disappeared."[17]

As a "total resistance to the total conscription of language," an alienistic strategy of silence is an "absolute refusal to submit to the law of recuperation and exchange." Mann is most concerned with the cultural economy of twentieth-century market capitalism, but his analysis draws on Foucault, Guy Debord, Theodor Adorno, Herbert Marcuse, the early Marx, and Plato's "media-critique" in the *Republic*. Even a brief catalog of examples suggests the likelihood that silence, like other strategies of alienation, is cross-cultural and panhistorical. Indeed, Mann sees in silence the twin regimens of ascesis and excess that we discovered in gnosticism. "We could conceive of silence as an interminable fast from discourse," he says; but the ascetic strategy has its gorge-purge dimension as well. The silent writer continues to indulge his or her compulsive habit in secret, "endlessly burning off the inexhaustible reserve of discursive toxins." Like a religious who prays continually in utter privacy, the silent writer could surpass even Thomas Wolfe's mountainous production of words—but we would not know. Unavailable strategies are not there for us to perform, and thus not *there* at all. One thinks of Mead's claim that food does not exist in nature, that it can be generated only through action and relationship. Food is not present until an ox eats the grass and draws sustenance from it. A strategy is not present until a reader performs the text.[18]

For the purposes of virtue criticism, we presume that even a "silent" text is or can be made present—that readers are offered enough and receive enough to make possible their performance of aesthetic patterns of abnegation and withdrawal. The questions then become, What personal or corporate attributes are enacted? What vices and virtues are implicit in a high-minded strategy of purification? Are not the qualities cultivated by a strategy of silence precisely those of Kafka's hunger artist: fastidious control, stultifying self-consciousness, and, borrowing again from sonnet 94, festering *ressentiment*?[19] If so, then strategies of alienation alter both the abnegating and the abnegated ethoi; they mark and perhaps damage the person who renounces, as well as the culture renounced. In literary-symbolic terms, alienistic writers risk the loss of artistic potency by practicing only fugitive and cloistered virtues. Remaining "as stone," their inscrutability may preclude their "moving others." In more generally human terms, alienated persons may risk losing other capacities. For the French, *alienation* is a diagnosis, a clinical term denoting emotional dysfunction and psychic isolation. Even in the United States, where alienation has for decades been understood as a synonym for *disaffected*, the primary technical meaning is still associated with psychic pathology.

Pathology and dysfunction are culturally specific terms, of course, and madness is often celebrated as a buffering or compensation strategy for certain enlightened ones who must perforce exist in an insane world. Norman O. Brown and R. D. Laing, for example, as well as Foucault, analyze insanity as an authentic and exemplary strategy of abnegation. "True sanity," in the words of Laing, entails "the dissolution of the normal ego, that false self completely adjusted to our alienated social reality."[20] Thus alienists such as Laing and Foucault, ironically practicing a kind of critical/clinical analysis, discern authenticity in that psychic state known vulgarly and misleadingly, they would say, as schizophrenia. An insight of Zweig's about Dostoyevski's *Dream of a Ridiculous Man* suggests the connection between psychic alienation and the refusal to perform. Driven by a desire for isolation, Dostoyevski's character fashions ever more extreme strategies of alienation. Finally, however, he saves himself from semantic privacy and insanity when he undertakes the public performance of his ridiculous vision. He makes a fool of himself before his audience and willingly becomes for them "a queer fellow," as one translator has it. "He finds a new way to do a new thing in his life," Zweig says. "To speak to people instead of to his fantasies." Each of us similarly constructs a sanity, an "adaptation to life." Dostoyevski's character makes his own peculiar adaptation by becoming, in their eyes, the ridiculous man. "By becoming 'ridiculous,'" Zweig says, "he becomes sane." The madman, on the other hand, adamantly refuses to play the fool. His unperformed alienation is so authentic that he will not or cannot collude with a crazy world.[21]

The progenitor of this influential paradigm—authenticity through alienation—is said to be Nietzsche. Nietzsche himself, oddly enough, recognizes the potential virulence of alienistic strategies. Cultural performance and the exchange of values may indeed generate alienation—Nietzsche is as aware of this "side effect" as Thoreau, Jesus, or the prophets. But Nietzsche reserves no pity for the "failures and victims who undermine our faith in life and our fellow men."[22] The self-identified victims of culture, Nietzsche says, "walk among us as warnings and reprimands incarnate, as though to say that health, soundness, strength, and pride are vicious things for which we shall one day pay dearly; and how eager they are, at bottom, to be the ones to make us pay!"[23] It is surprising to find Nietzsche, with his justly deserved reputation as the nemesis of conformity and the godfather of individualist authenticity, defending the virtue and value of "all who go cheerfully about their business." *"There is too much misery in the world!"* Nietzsche exclaims in exasperation, implying that much of this misery could be avoided. "The real danger," Nietzsche says, "lies in our loathing of man and our pity of him."[24] The loathing and pity of humankind— this phrase might well characterize, or "sloganize," as Burke would say, the vices of pathological alienation.

Yet Nietzsche has been followed by countless other resisters who, vaguely invoking the maker of *Zarathustra* and the *Genealogy*, champion instinct and sanction violence. These strategies of opposition are designed to undermine the "bourgeois" ethic of order and to dismantle the straitjacketing virtues that shore it up. Among twentieth-century writers and artists, Charles Taylor cites Georges Bataille, Filippo Emilio Marinetti and the futurists, and Antonin Artaud and the Theatre of Cruelty as influential examples of the cult of violence. Other examples dominate a recent collection called *Apocalypse Culture*, edited by Adam Parfrey.[25] Parfrey contributes an essay on "the Soul of Feral Man" for a section entitled "Apocalypse Theologies"; in it he celebrates the rapacious ways of the wolf and laments the instinct-killing control of Christianity, capitalism, and psychiatry.[26] The virtues that Parfrey celebrates are animalism, "becoming a monster" (as preparation for transcendent escape), and other modes of "calling up the wolf." (Feral House, Parfrey's publisher, also puts out "How to Become a Werewolf.") The anthology includes an interview with Karen Greenlee, confessed necrophile and "morgue rat," who details her sexual acts with cadavers. In "Frank Talk from a Psychopath," Parfrey celebrates a "self-confessed and self-promoting effing piebald fruitcake" identified only as Frank, the publisher of an alternative "fanzine." One issue features "Handy Hints for Messier Massacres," a guide for mass murderers. In "Handy Hints," Frank suggests the importance of "good shooting technique" and underscores the advantages of a confined area from which victims cannot escape.[27] Parfrey also collects "some recent examples of authentic schizophrenic writings," which are "not infrequently possessed of genius since [they] emerge from a dialogue between inner soul and outer surroundings unmediated by the burden of 'correct' societal conduct."[28] In "Aesthetic Terrorism" Parfrey defends *Pure* magazine, "a xeroxed vehicle which extols child torture, murder, and extreme misogyny." Its editor, Peter Sotos of Chicago, was convicted of possession of child pornography. Apparently, Parfrey says, *Pure* "tweaked too many civic-minded noses."[29]

My point in citing such examples of alienistic writing is neither celebration nor condemnation, but discrimination. We have seen that there are nuances of the power to hurt, varying strategies and performances of identification and alienation. We might well posit a continuum, ranging from coercive aggression through parabolic corrosion to critical description. Thus: psychic or physical torture, gratuitous cruelty, physical violence, emotional violation, intentional offense, disruption, shock, warning or alert, prophecy, watch, observation, representation. With tongue firmly in cheek, let us call this the Great Chain of Alienation. As in the Great Chain of Being, plenitude is one of the characteristics of this continuum. Thus alienistic qualities and performances, being theoretically infinite, are best revealed through a comparative, evaluative process— a practice that we have been calling virtue criticism. Again without being able to do them analytical justice, let me hypothetically locate the writings collected by Parfrey in the range of emotional violation and intentional offensiveness. Discriminating among strategies of alienation becomes of greater importance when we realize that writings like those collected by Parfrey have purposes and motives that resemble that of other resisters. Grimston's "Humanity Is the Devil," for example, is eerily reminiscent of gnostic dualism:

> Humanity is mean and corrupt, a liar blinded by its own deception . . .
> and humanity's home is the earth, and the earth is Hell.
>   Now there is nothing more evil in the universe than man.
>   His world is Hell, and he himself is the Devil.[30]

Thus does Grimston express a gnostic denunciation of humanity's blindness and corruption.

Yet any similarity between Grimston's theosophy and other gnostic strategies should only underscore the need for ethically nuanced languages to distinguish various alienistic strategies and performances. By means of virtue criticism we pursue an explanation of exactly how the particular gnostic virtues found in the early work of Eliot and of Gertrude Stein, for example, are distinct from the uncooked virulence of Robert de Grimston. We consider in what respects the parabolic discontinuities of Donald Barthelme are unlike the oppositional aphorisms of an institutionalized schizophrenic such as James Van Cleve.[31] We explain how the aestheticism of Nabokov's *Pale Fire* varies from the aesthetic cruelty of Artaud or Bataille. Such distinctions, though they seem apparent and intuitive, are best elaborated by coductions of the sort pursued in part 3 of this book. It is through such coductions, themselves auditions of performances, that practical, convincing, and perdurable judgments about virtues and vices will be articulated and refined.

⟶⟨⟶

In the process of these somewhat painstaking conversations about performances and strategies, we will often find that a distinguishing virtue of the writers we wish to embrace is concern for our prior and persisting concerns and for our fundamental well-being. One hesitates to insist on standards for alienistic strategies lest they lose their salt and be fit only to be thrown out and trampled underfoot. Balance, reciprocity, and trustworthiness seem at first blush rather bland and bourgeois virtues; yet it may be that the very essence of alienistic freshness—its characteristic power to hurt—depends on recognition of and respect for otherness. It is customary for twentieth-century art and artists to lay claim to the authenticity of the outsider. It is attractive, as Mann says, to think of art as always free, to see oneself as disenfranchised adversary, innocent of power.[32] The point of Mann's essay is the same one that lends sharpness to other thoroughgoing cultural critiques: it is not easy to remain exterior to power, especially when one's position, cause, or critique is historically grounded and politically urgent. Without a mode of noncoercive dialogue and coductive inquiry, strategies of alienation, authenticity, and resistance can usurp the role of progressivist power. Nemoianu describes this as a reversal of the proper cultural functions of the secondary and the principal; the results are not felicitous:

> The ugliness of adversarial subcultures when they grab for hegemony and set up
> their conforming and stifling rules is plain to see in different historical moments,
> and certain strands of European rightism in the 1920s and the 1930s, no less than
> areas of the American New Left from the 1960s on, could serve as excellent occasions for melancholy reflection. The charming secondaries lose their own validity
> without really gaining the stature of principals into which they are illegitimately
> propelled. They seldom do actual harm, but they always lose precisely the pleasant usefulness they earlier possessed.[33]

"To set one's hope on the secondary," Nemoianu says, "to try to raise it to the level of the principal, is exactly the most wrongheaded procedure. It means in effect to acquiesce in and strongly reinforce the stature of the principal and its supremacy over all things seen and unseen."[34] Nemoianu's caution about the secondary recalls Irving Howe's earlier caveat about oppositional literature:

"modernism must struggle in order not to triumph." Only the innocent and uncritical assume that one power is fundamentally different from another. Soon enough, self-satisfied and unreflective strategies of alienation become strategies of consolidation and control. To speak truth to power, alienistic strategies must appreciate the otherness of their adversaries and only gingerly partake of power themselves.

Charles Taylor suggests that this kind of appreciation, the genuine recognition of otherness, is a dialogical virtue often neglected in strategies of alienation. Respect for the other, however, is a virtue that is inseparable from the ideal of authenticity. Some alienistic practices and performances are driven exclusively by uncompromising and uncomplicated adversarialism: a confident and careless opposition to rules, social arrangements, moral traditions, linguistic rubrics, dominant culture, "the world." Taylor suggests that such zealous outsiders do not realize that alienistic transgression can be effectively foregrounded only against a background consisting of a more or less shared and homogeneous cultural milieu. Only a common culture can create what Taylor calls "horizons of significance"—those parameters of the social imagination that make alienistic performances possible and meaningful. Eliot understands the necessity of a received, conventional, and value-laden context for the transgressive action of "sinning mightily." But for simpleminded adversaries of civilization, a neo-Nietzschean, narcissistic understanding of value as self-created can fuel a power-seeking freedom. This merging of opposition, freedom, and power, according to Taylor, leads to our disastrous "fascination with violence in the twentieth century."[35] We have pursued a promiscuous infatuation with both freedom and power, and we have pretended that robust self-creation and political autogenesis can be achieved facilely, by simply ignoring the impediments of received traditions, communal moralities, and common practices. Our abandonment of the dialogue with that which is other and alien—whether it is the secondary refusing to acknowledge the principal or the principal ignoring the secondary—sets the stage, as Burke understands, for totalizing systems of domination and control. "Certainties will always arise," he noted prophetically in 1931, "impelling men to new intolerances."[36] The authenticity that we need is a strategy of alienation, to be sure, but it is a self-aware and self-critical strategy that is not limited to opposition but also includes dialogue with the hated powers that be.

The claims of Nemoianu and Taylor dovetail in a way that can assist our ethical differentiation of various alienistic strategies. Nemoianu suggests that elevating the alien and oppositional secondary to the status of historical and material dominance is self-defeating; Taylor suggests that privileging the virtue of authenticity at the cost of our dialogic ties to others is self-defeating. Both claims derive from a crucial intuition that seems self-evident but often goes unacknowledged: strategies and performances must keep their distance and their difference from the central processes of culture in order to practice the virtue of alienation. Nemoianu figures those central processes in historical terms—they are the courses of "the principal"; Taylor speaks of "horizons" of meaning and value that create the necessary context and background for expressions of authentic resistance. When an alienistic performance utilizes intimidation, coercion, emotional violation, or semantic terrorism as part of a cultural program or political agenda, it accedes to methods of cultural power and inadvertently reinforces, as Nemoianu says, the hegemony of the principal. When versions of resistance deteriorate into narcissism and license, Taylor suggests, they help create a flatter, more uniform, and ultimately more homogeneous world, more vast and yet more confining and airless. When the secondary embraces the machinations of the principal, the cultural theater becomes bland and featureless, devoid of genuine difference. We are left with a world in which the conditions of significance, most especially of significant opposition, have not been suppressed or contained by a dominant culture but abandoned by oppositionists themselves. It is yet another case of Pogo's "We have met the enemy and they are us." Alienation that is randomized and dispersed produces a kind of atomistic culture, a Hobbesian state of nature controlled by appetites, aversions, envy, malice—and fear. The most oppressive, seamless, and homogeneous "system" is the artless one in which the strategies of cultural alienation have been generally and thoroughly successful. The world's horizons and crevices are erased, the backwaters and eddies of the secondary disappear, and humanity's habitat becomes morally featureless— an infinite plain of power politics and murder.

If, with Kent, we would teach differences, then we ought to discriminate between nuances and variegations of the power to hurt. Neurotic acts of "resistance" or the compulsive performance of this or that "authentic" strategy may cultivate vices rather than virtues, infuse the world with more terror and cruelty, and cancel the very terms and conditions of alienistic expression and significance.[37] It may be that the very pervasiveness and adaptability of the white economy and global capitalism, now that "the eastern bloc" has all but imploded, will spawn strategies of alienation whose tactics will prove more intransigent and suspicious as we approach the millennium. In this fin-de-siècle context, it is tempting to reference some of the more public alienistic strategies of our time. One thinks of Heaven's Gate and the dazzling media coverage of the suicides, of the Unabomber and his rambling manifesto, of the Branch Davidians in Waco, the Oklahoma City bombing, the "Republic of Texas," and hundreds of other militia groups.[38] Remarkable too are increasing numbers of websites and electronic forums devoted to conspiracy theories and paranoiac alarms about NATO, the United Nations, and the U.S. government. It would seem that contemporary apocalypticism, marked by an obsession with global hegemonies or bedeviled by age-old disappointments with sublunary existence, is another strategy of alienation worthy of evaluation. What criteria are appropriate? What distinguishes a vicious, virulent alienation from a tonic one? Jean Bethke Elshtain suggests that Mary Douglas's discussion of purity and danger "helps explain why cults insist that all ties with family, friends, and other social institutions be severed." Such alienisms tend to calcify into fastidious dirt- and pollution-rejecting strategies. Instead of functioning as liminal performances, they evolve into "total meaning system[s] with no grounds for disputation and interpretation." Elshtain is wary of "a pattern of insulation, isolation, paranoia, and utter contempt for those outside," a lack of balance "between *amor mundi*—love of the world—and *contra mundum*—against or in opposition to the world." Without this balance, this "openness to new possibility," alienistic performances lose their bracing and beneficial freshness.[39]

It is well to judge strategies and communities empirically, by their fruits. And it seems especially important when evaluating the virtues and vices of alienisms to ask about the likely effects, the potential freshening or poisoning of the cultural well. Since the relationship between reader and writer is its own tiny culture, a little congregation for the transmission and exchange of values, we have looked to this relationship as a source and model of collaboration and performance. Since readers and writers practice particular relational and social virtues in the process of creating their temporal bonds, virtue criticism can ask of other writers, as we have of Eliot, Nabokov, and Barthelme, Does this writer show concern for a reader's concerns? Does she encourage us to practice Booth's "hypocrisy upward"? Does this alienistic performance allow for the next socially constructive myth—and, subsequently, additional freshening parables? Or does this writer poison the holding environment of performance itself, of myth *and* alienation? Does he break the implicit promise of nonsilent art—that what he has to offer is worth our while? Is her goal, like Jane's in *Snow White*, the unilateral injection of a corrosive or denaturing "u. of d."? Is he merely relieving himself by violating, offending, and controlling his implied reader? Asking such questions of a literary performance demonstrates the intimate connection between virtue criticism and communication ethics. And if Taylor is right, enacting the true virtue of authenticity, a viable power to hurt, requires reciprocity, empathy, and respect. Fortunately, there are many dialogic resisters, Strange Ones whose recognition of strangeness and otherness fosters a realization that their very alienation, their necessary authenticity, depends on a cultural holding environment. To be internally consistent, alienistic strategies must eschew violence, coercion, and the force of law. Authentic parable does not usurp myth but invigorates it. Aestheticism relies on mundane functional horizons and conventional patterns. Gnostic performances depend on sublunary law and material backgrounds. Thus contextualized, alienistic strategies can refresh culture in the process of resisting it and maintain what Nemoianu calls the "pleasant usefulness" of the secondary.

If one axis of alienation begins with "straight" representation and comfortable conventions, extending through verbal coercion and violation to semantic terrorism and cruelty, then the point at which coercion and offense are abnegated in favor of Burke's rhetoric of identification becomes critical. Those performed strategies that abandon the virtue of affiliation seem to foster a more sociopathic alienation, one that is also progressively more difficult to perform. I am thinking here not only of silent writers but also of silent persons; not only of the celebration of madness in story and song but of the isolated condition of madness itself; not only of Melville's "Bartleby the Scrivener" or Stern's "Bartleby the Scrivener by Herman Melville" but also of inarticulate refusal, physical withdrawal, biological death. When one thinks of Kleist and Lautréamont, Hölderlin and Artaud, Rimbaud and his infamous namesake Rambo, the consequences of alienation—the loss of friendship, association, congregation, and culture—become poignant.[40] And in these, the last days of the twentieth century, the consequences of alienation seem to press themselves into our collective sensorium with increasing frequency and immediacy. Recently I received a letter from a friend who had been reading an earlier version of chapter 10 while using city transportation. To her there was something eerie and apropos about being on the Broadway bus at 9:00 P.M. and reading about T. S. Eliot's gnostic strategy. She was auditing "The Fire Sermon" while witnessing a quite different strategy of alienation being performed by

> three "mentally disabled" people in full, fulminant glory. One woman was screaming about Asian women and "poor white trash" at the front of the bus, while an intoxicated young man farther back was yelling at her to "shut her ugly face" while he regaled us with a monologue that took in Marilyn Monroe, Betty Ford, Sammy Davis, Jr., and a re-enactment of his wife leaving him because he drank too much, complete with a falsetto rendition of her tirade. When things quieted down a bit, a

young woman sat next to me and proceeded to tell me about her recent release from the hospital after a suicide attempt, but that she was all better now because she was taking all her medication and did I think she could still get into heaven.[41]

For many of us who have attended to them, there is little doubt that these, too, are performances of identity. Such alienated and alienating auditions occur before an audience, real or imagined; they are often rehearsed performances, repeated enactments of fear, suspicion, and violation by persons who can no longer find solidarity and community in their world. Do strategies of alienation such as these performed on the Broadway bus "cause" social and personal dysfunction, or do various kinds of preexisting dysfunction manifest themselves through such performances? Appalled and shamed at scenes of such nightmare and suffering, most of us are quick to blame either the culture as a whole or the performers themselves. As a practical inquiry that addresses effects rather than causes, virtue criticism tells us little about who is to blame. What we can say is that strategies of alienation that sever the thread of dialogue, empathy, and respect typically engender performances that we recognize as pathological.

As a strategy of identification, virtue criticism presumes that literary performers can and do enjoy moments of solidarity, affiliation, and friendship. Gifts do, as Nemoianu says, have a moment of glorious flowering. Even those performers who choose public transportation or the spaces beneath freeway overpasses as their venues sometimes achieve an understanding and even a shared intimacy with their troubled audience. But Nemoianu is right to emphasize the sacrificial element inherent in the transaction and exchange of values. It is a sacrifice that the silent writer—with her "art so absolutely for its own sake that it is no longer art"—will no longer make, a gift that she will no longer give. She is, perhaps, so overwhelmed by the horror of alienation that she can no longer practice it. Perhaps violation is more likely to become violence when alienation itself is eschewed, when abnegation is abnegated. There are those who are so horrified of alienation that they are willing to pretend that it can be avoided altogether. Nemoianu discerns this horror of alienation in Marx, in Kierkegaard, and in Romanticism and its descendants—utopian socialism, aestheticism, populism, existentialism, and fascism. Yet, as Arthur Lovejoy demonstrates so convincingly, romanticisms, like alienisms, can and should be distinguished.[42] A Romantic such as Carlyle, for example, could recognize in Shakespeare the telltale signs of alienation and lost wholeness and yet remain thankful for the product. For Carlyle as for most of us, Shakespeare is emblematic of the autonomous, unencumbered "poet as hero"—the antithesis of the pleasing rhymesters and smiling panderers of his day and ours. Yet the bard, no less than the rest of Lord Chamberlain's Men (the company for which he wrote and acted and in which he owned equity), was obliged to perform "under cramping circumstances."[43] Carlyle mourns the artistic hero's sacrifice, but he endorses the gift. In the end the performer must ruefully embrace the alienation: the enaction of virtues and the transfer of values require it.

Like Carlyle's Shakespeare, Matthew's Jesus was also obliged to enter the world of cultural exchange and play the game. A parabolic figure, he nonetheless endured, in Trilling's words, "the inconveniences of undertaking to intercede, of being a sacrifice, of reasoning with rabbis, of making sermons, of having disciples, of going to weddings and to funerals, of beginning something and at a certain point remarking that it is finished."[44] The role of messiah, like the role of other subversives in history, is a gift that comes with encumbrances. "At the heart of their struggle," Zweig says of his subversive heretics, is "isolation—both psychological and social"; this isolation threatens to overcome their humanity.[45] But as alienistic performers, they respond to and for their audiences, taking us with them on a journey into the underworld, familiarizing us with their troubling news, turning their isolation into a transformative public ordeal.

As the work of Zweig, Jonas, Pagels, Schneidau, McFague, and countless others amply demonstrates, strategies of alienation are endemic to Western literature and culture—probably, as Nemoianu suggests, of all cultures. "Alienation cannot be totally rejected," he says, "without throwing out progress and evolution. It is too closely connected to liberty, which was often another name for it. It is too closely connected with analytical rationalism and abstract analysis; it is too closely connected with technological inventiveness." Religious concepts as well—individual salvation and guilt, Augustine's recasting of the human person, and concepts of difference, otherness, and interiority—are all "inextricably bound to estrangement" from the world, the community, or the divine.[46] The mixed blessings of alienistic art will always be necessary, because, as Burke says, "even a world rigorously schooled in doubt will be dogmatical enough."[47] So we dare not accept Nietzsche's project of isolating the "healthy"—those cheerful ones who go about their business—from the "sick."[48] Alienation is inseparable from function and even contributes, in its fashion, to healthy function. "The constructive vitality of alienating processes is plain to see at every historical moment," according to Nemoianu, "in antiquity, in the Renaissance, in the nineteenth and twentieth centuries."[49] Even wily Odysseus, supposedly part of hegemonic, logocentric Western antiquity, is the giver and receiver, the getter and begetter, of alienation. He is a man made for trouble, as his name suggests. And following Odysseus, alienistic performers play their parts like their own tough skins. Instead of relationship and love, they carry with them the very real and sometimes better gift of shared and shareable trouble. Transgression, resistance, self-reliance, subversive individualism, restlessness, recklessness, aesthetic innovation, parabolic ironies, authenticity—these strategies of alienation are tied to democratic governance, universal suffrage, and social justice. Strategies of alienation validate a whole host of freedoms, from speech to privacy to enterprise. They defend and guarantee, in their often perverse fashion, the Bill of Rights itself.

There is little doubt that fear and the appetite for power, symbiotic as they are, have become our principal cultural virtues. It is equally apparent that many of our strategies of alienation have denatured themselves by adopting methods of coercion, gestures of intimidation, and rubrics of violence: Everywhere the power to hurt meets with base infection. But we have learned from books that values can be transferred, friendships can be fostered, persons can be figured forth—that where alienation is, there shall ethics be. Were we permitted our own faint hope, it would be that an ethical criticism of alienation would challenge our practices, quicken our virtues, and freshen our performances.

Notes

1. Ralph Waldo Emerson, "Friendship," *Self-Reliance and Other Essays* (New York: Dover Publications, 1993), p. 50.

2. D. H. Lawrence, "Fenimore Cooper's Leatherstocking Novels," *Studies in Classic American Literature* (1923; rpt., New York: Viking Press, 1964), p. 62.

3. Ralph Waldo Emerson, "Thoreau," *Walden and Civil Disobedience*, ed. Owen Thomas (New York: W. W. Norton, 1966), p. 278.

4. Thomas LeClair, "A Conversation with William Gass," *Chicago Review* 30, no. 2 (1978), p. 98.

5. Walker Percy, "Diagnosing the Malaise," *Signposts in a Strange Land* (New York: Farrar, Straus, and Giroux, 1991), 204–21.

6. George Steiner, "On Difficulty," *On Difficulty and Other Essays* (New York: Oxford University Press, 1978), p. 42.

7. Ibid., p. 41.

8. Ibid.

9. Susan Sontag, "The Aesthetics of Silence," *Styles of Radical Will* (New York: Delta, 1970), pp. 4–5, 8.

10. Ibid., p. 52.

11. Vladimir E. Alexandrov, *Nabokov's Otherworld* (Princeton: Princeton University Press, 1991), p. 5. Tiutchev published "Silentium" in 1833.

12. William S. Burroughs quoted by Paul Mann in "Invisible Ink: Writing in the Margin," *Georgia Review* 39, no. 4 (1985), p. 819.

13. Mann, "Invisible Ink," p. 822. See also his monograph *The Theory-Death of the Avant-Garde* (Bloomington: Indiana University Press, 1991).

14. Mann, "Invisible Ink," p. 811, my emphasis.

15. Ibid., pp. 810, 811.

16. Thomas Carlyle, "The Hero as Poet," in *The Works of Thomas Carlyle*, ed. H. D. Traill (New York: Scribner's, 1896–1901), vol. 5, p. 79.

17. Mann, "Invisible Ink," pp. 814–20.

18. Ibid., pp. 820, 822, 821; George Herbert Mead, "Emergence and Identity," *The Philosophy of the Present* (Chicago: Open Court Publishing, 1932), pp. 33–39. We should acknowledge that a "silent writer" constitutes a performing readership of one and thus becomes an enacter of his or her unseen silent strategies. If those strategies become part of the silent writer's "pressing repertoire" of virtues, as we have said they do, then those strategies indirectly enter history whenever the silent writer interacts with others.

19. I am thinking of *ressentiment* as Max Scheler employed the concept in his early work (1912–15). See Max Scheler, *Ressentiment*, ed. Lewis A. Coser, trans. William W. Holdheim (1961; rpt., New York: Schocken, 1972). Scheler is elaborating and modifying Nietzsche's use of *ressentiment*, but Heinrich Heine had conjured with the term prior to Nietzsche. Basically, *ressentiment* "is a self-poisoning of the mind" manifested by "revenge, hatred, malice, envy, the impulse to detract, and spite" (p. 46). For Nietzsche, according to Lewis Coser, "*ressentiment* connotes impotent hatred, envy, repressed feelings of revenge, the inability to act out antagonistic impulses in open conflict" (p. 21). Nietzsche acknowledged that Heine had been an important stimulus of his thought about the concept—which he uses throughout *Thus Spoke Zarathustra*—and for Heine the key "distinction was between the 'Hellenes' and the 'Nazarenes,' between those who love life and those who deny it" (pp. 21–22).

20. R. D. Laing, *The Divided Self*, 2d ed. (Harmondsworth: Penguin, 1961), p. 39.

21. Paul Zweig, *The Heresy of Self-Love: A Study of Subversive Individualism* (1968; rpt., Princeton: Princeton University Press, 1980), p. 260.

22. Friedrich Nietzsche, *The Genealogy of Morals*, trans. Francis Golffing (Garden City, N.Y.: Anchor-Doubleday, 1956), p. 258.

23. Ibid., p. 259.

24. Ibid., pp. 258–61, Nietzsche's emphasis.

25. Adam Parfrey, ed., *Apocalypse Culture* (Los Angeles: Feral House Press, 1990). I bought my copy of this innocuous looking book during a Christmas shopping season at B. Dalton Bookseller in the glitzy Houston Galleria. Although *Apocalypse Culture* is a publication that one might expect to be underground, marginal, or "alternative," it was displayed as any other volume readily available for sale—not with the best-sellers but

not in a special or restricted section of the store either. This example of the commodification of alienation on the shelves of a mainstream retail outlet would seem to substantiate Paul Mann's claim that only silence can resist the engines of the marketplace. Still, it seems somehow appropriate that my copy's perfect binding began to crack and the book itself to disintegrate into separate leaves as soon as I began to read it. Could this disintegration be a strategy of "material alienation"?

26. Adam Parfrey, "Latter-Day Lycanthropy: Battling for the Soul of Feral Man," *Apocalypse Culture*, pp. 16–27.

27. Jim Morton, "The Unrepentant Necrophile: An Interview with Karen Greenlee," *Apocalypse Culture*, pp. 28–36; Frank, "Handy Hints for Messier Massacres," quoted by Parfrey in "Frank Talk from a Psychopath," *Apocalypse Culture*, p. 43.

28. Parfrey, "Schizophrenic Responses to a Mad World: Love, Lithium, and the Loot of Lima," *Apocalypse Culture*, p. 59.

29. Parfrey, "Aesthetic Terrorism," *Apocalypse Culture*, p. 51.

30. Robert de Grimston, "Humanity Is the Devil," quoted by Parfrey in "Infernal Texts," *Apocalypse Culture*, p. 40.

31. "Schizophrenic writing," Parfrey avers, "is not infrequently possessed of genius since it emerges from a dialogue between inner soul and outer surrounding unmediated by the burden of 'correct' societal conduct. . . . Collected here are some recent examples of authentic schizophrenic writings [including] James Van Cleve's *Love, Lithium, and the Loot of Lima*. . . . Van Cleve is in his late 70's and is still institutionalized in a home in upstate New York." "Schizophrenic Responses," p. 59.

32. Mann, "Invisible Ink," p. 816.

33. Virgil Nemoianu, *A Theory of the Secondary: Literature, Progress, and Reaction* (Baltimore: Johns Hopkins University Press, 1989), p. 152.

34. Ibid., p. 151.

35. Charles Taylor, *The Ethics of Authenticity* (Cambridge, Mass.: Harvard University Press, 1992), p. 67.

36. Kenneth Burke, *Counter-Statement* (1931; rpt., Berkeley: University of California Press, 1968), p. 113.

37. Arguably, there are more than a few such texts in circulation, and some of them are best-sellers. For example, some readers discover alienistic vices in Bret Easton Ellis's *American Psycho* . . . Now, having named one book, I find that my appetite is whetted for making a list of titles whose unearned and facile alienation (according to "some readers") crassly mocks the power to hurt. But the virtue criticism I have been espousing insists that worthwhile and responsible assessments require coductive elaborations that take time and require the adoption, identification, and empathy discussed in part 1. (Consequently, I probably owe even *American Psycho* an apology.)

38. In 1995 the Anti-Defamation League published and circulated a special report entitled "The Militia Movement in America" based on a national survey it conducted: "A continuing flow of information from ADL Regional offices around the country indi-

cates militias are operating in at least 40 states, with membership reaching some 15,000, and that these numbers could rise still higher." The report quotes a number of manifestos and manuals, including the Michigan Militia's, with its pledge to "stand against tyranny, globalism, moral relativism, humanism, and the New World order."

39. Jean Bethke Elshtain, "The Hard Questions: Heaven Can Wait," *New Republic*, 5 May 1997, p. 23.

40. David Morrell, who wrote *First Blood*, the 1972 action novel that introduced John Rambo, "named [Rambo] . . . after the 19th-century French symbolist poet Arthur Rimbaud." John Stark and Giovanna Breu, "Forget Stallone: A Peaceful Prof from Iowa Put Rambo on the Map," *People Weekly*, July 11, 1988, p. 103.

41. Suzanne Poirier, personal correspondence, 22 Feb. 1993.

42. Arthur Lovejoy, "On the Discrimination of Romanticisms," *Essays in the History of Ideas* (New York: George Braziller, 1955), pp. 228–53.

43. Carlyle, "The Hero as Poet," p. 79.

44. Lionel Trilling, *Sincerity and Authenticity* (Cambridge, Mass.: Harvard University Press, 1972), p. 172.

45. Zweig, *The Heresy of Self-Love*, p. 257.

46. Nemoianu, *A Theory of the Secondary*, pp. 147–48.

47. Burke, *Counter-Statement*, p. 113.

48. Nietzsche, *The Genealogy of Morals*, p. 261.

49. Nemoianu, *A Theory of the Secondary*, p. 148.

Coda: Not-Knowing

The following is an elliptically narrated performance piece. It is also one last try at a virtue criticism that is personal and vulnerable without being solipsistic and indulgent (though some readers will find in it both dubious qualities). As a confessional narrative, it can serve as an abstract or analogue of the book as a whole. Critical and biographical, the piece uses the occasion of Donald Barthelme's death and memorial service to contrast the ironic, alienistic author of Snow White, City Life, *"Brain Damage," and "The Tired Terror of Graham Greene" with "Uncle Don," the committed and conscientious citizen who directed the creative writing program at the University of Houston. The narrator has accused Barthelme in print of being an "authenticist"—that is, an alienist so obsessed with authenticity that he refuses to compromise and play the cultural game. By examining "On Angels," however, and "Not-Knowing," one of Barthelme's last and most revealing essays, the chagrined narrator wonders whether Donald Barthelme was in fact a moralist, an engaged reformer, an "Upton Sinclair." Like O'Connor's Hazel Motes—whose integrity, she says, lies in what he is not able to evade—Barthelme's work may reveal its ethical integrity precisely because he was not able to evade the commonality of language and the related exploitations of culture.*

—(—

The New York Times reported that God and Barthelme were dead, in that order, but never bothered to mention where they came from. This much we know: Barthelme was a Texan. As a young man he was a black sheep, a sojourner who left his own country to live among strangers. From thence he shall come to judge the living and the dead . . . and to build a writing program. However "creative," he knew it was an empire, even called it that—a place in the world with imperial encumbrances. For his students he became "Uncle Don" and "Dad," a prodigal father with an estate. He wore cowboy boots and drove a red Bronco to survey the back forty.

They had a memorial service in Ordinary Time, "the longest and hardest season of the liturgical year." Appropriate: he sought no escape from his Gulf Coast habitat, not even in July, not even in August. "We're writers," he told Ed Hirsch. "That's what writers do. They don't go places." Readings that twenty-fifth Sunday included a parable about serving two masters—"an earthly story," as the catechism puts it, "with a heavenly meaning." The bad steward was shrewd and won approval by using Mammon to make friends and to serve God: just so, the black sheep got good at what he ruefully called "the art business."

How would Don have rendered it? *"We must have a memorial now that Dad is dead," they told each other. Yes, and Oh yes, and By all means, they said. They memorialized and went back to their vats with greater equanimity, no longer sucking the mop.* Honestly grieving our loss, Cynthia Macdonald had trouble summoning it, but irony, irony, would not have forsaken him.

Mr. Hirsch said that he knew and loved the work before coming to know and love the man. He said, in the years to come, we might well grow to understand Don Barthelme's project as quasi-theological. Most of us never did get to know Don Barthelme. Now, not-knowing him will have to do. The would-be cognoscenti didn't really know him either. They liked to brandish him as a high priest of "the most significant strain of writing since 1945" or "ever"—there didn't seem to be much of a distinction. But how, how to denominate this new discourse? By finding or fabricating a term that would somehow suggest the recurrent and abiding urge to escape the ways of the world, to free oneself utterly from the gaze of the other. Yes, of course, quite obvious, the graduate students said, but what shall we call it? "Authenticism," one ejaculated. "It is a project of renunciation, a negative tropism. Forms and even form itself must be dissolved, eradicated, reduced, exaggerated, short-circuited, undermined, collapsed, rendered." Who in the world would do such things to literary form, job interviewers wanted to know. Not Joyce, surely you don't mean Joyce. Not Nabokov—no, no, no, Nabokov is in love with form. Oh, they said, you mean like Barthelme. Well, OK, in that case . . .

Thus Barthelme was reduced to exemplum. He was "wised-up," "off-beat," and rode with the Literature of Exhaustion gang: Burroughs, Federman, Sukenick, Sorrentino, and the dreaded Surfictionists. There was Barth in them there Barthelme. Yet here was Robert Coover to say that he had had his Barthelme epiphany only a year or so before: the guy in the boots was a tall, tale-telling Texan, "Don of the West." Still, if one had to divide the world into two kinds of people, and one did, then Barthelme would surely be one of the most up-to-date postmoderns, a self-conscious fictioneer, an authenticist.

Or so, not-knowing, we thought. But we were wrong, and Hirsch was right. You must understand our situation: How could we be expected to see comedy, to see Barthelme, when our solemn, self-aggrandizing quarrels would determine the answer to that most vexing and fundamental question for lovers of literature: Can I, will I, get a job? Tending vats of Chinese baby food? No p-problem, the Americanist stuttered, I'm your m-man.

Well, the phone rang, and a man said that there were some v-vats that needed t-tending down in T-Texas. There would be an interview with the department personnel committee. Isn't Donald Barthelme there, the candidate wanted to know. An affirmative reply, but no more; so one naturally assumed a Saul Bellow arrangement. You know, name prominently displayed in admissions viewbook and college catalog, but person not to be found. A face-card in the game of institutional prestige, not a presence in the halls.

But there he was—God, who else could it be?—sitting directly opposite the hot seat. "Linda Masterson." Hello. "John Etheridge." Hi. "I'm Don Barthelme." So it's Barth´-l-may. It is indeed a profound . . . no, no, you toady, can't say that. Exaggerated, false, manipulative, inauthentic, vacuous, etc. Just say, "Nice to meet you."

Sat awkwardly after the cordials were used up. A Chair would arrive shortly. Looked around the room, calculating angles and distances. Window too high and painted shut. One way out, though, cowardly but effective. "All that iced tea at lunch, y-know. Ha-ha."

Holy Shit! What if he read the dissertation? Why did you have to pick him to go after? *A writer like Barthelme can "register fifteen standard emotions and not share a single real feeling" with an audience.* No use leaping about on the platform, Tom Dooley. *Indeed, his fluidity of tone and texture, of satire and self-parody, succeeds so well that* Snow White *is scarcely a performance at all—or, rather, Barthelme's is a facile as opposed to a consistent performance, one that punishes rather than rewards the trusting reader.* Sometimes, Mr. Berra, it *is* over before it's over. *Snow White is a series of aesthetic airballs and turnovers.* Skewered like a bad cliché. Nothing to do now but empty yourself and take it like a Gnostic. No, too graphic; go back and "face the music."

The questions proceeded; for once the answers came when called. Someone asked about "career goals," someone about teaching. HE wanted to know if a paper on the romantic search for personal identity helped in the study of literature. Well, kinda. It was miraculously passing; hope was springing. Did HE have time for one more question? "Of course, Don." "Why, then, in your opinion, is Walker Percy not a better writer?" So tell the jury, Dr. O. Philosophy, when did you stop beating your . . .

"Uhh, maybe he lets ideas govern his stories too much." Yeah, that's it. "Maybe if he permitted images to engender his fictions just as the vision of Caddie's dirt-i-ness, the soiled drawers, motivated the linguistic pattern, the textual mosaic, which *is The Sound and the Fury* . . ." How the hell would I know, Don? Better than what? "Let me respectfully turn the question back to you, Professor Barthelme: Why do *you* think he's not a better writer?"

"He's not a better writer . . . because . . ."

Breathless, we waited. We waited breathless.

"Because Percy's talent is being absolutely stifled by his Roman Catholicism!"

The interview-ers strained to see if the interview-ee were still there. Yes. Though a tremor circulated through the room, the heavens did not part. Nothing in the building's architecture nor in the candidate's molecular structure had changed. Through the false azure of the windowpane, however, it was just possible to see fish leaping out of the fountain onto the Cullen Family Plaza. Many remembered feeling sorry at the time, watching them flipping and flopping around, getting fish slime on the legal pads and backpacks of the studious sun-seekers.

So we were right, after all. Barthelme was in fact and in person what he was in fiction and in essay: a postmodernist, a fulminator, an authenticist vehemently denouncing worldly contamination and institutional offense. (Now here was an ad hominem attack on Percy to go with his cavilling dismissal of Graham Greene.)

Still, there were unsettling testimonials. Don (they were afraid but they still called him "Don") was a generous, caring man and, moreover, a good university citizen. Impossible. Hadn't he told us what he thought of academic institutions in "Brain Damage" and "Porcupines in the University"? How could he *abide* those committee meetings? Meetings that not only required precious time but also imposed on one a profound sense of existential alienation, Kierkegaardian despair, and, what's worse, ordinary nausea. He even helped select the university's Rhodes Scholar nominees. The Rhodes: a sort of Miss America pageant (say no more, say no more) endowed by murderous, imperialistic, *colonial* exploitation. Throughout America, self-respecting, tenure-track teachers of English were being paid pretty good money to make students ashamed of Oxford, England, and themselves. Yet here he was, this Barthelme, showing up at the appointed time, doing his duty, coaching the nominees in the intricacies of self-presentation and desire.

Was the university in which he practiced good citizenship "constructed entirely of three mile-high sponges"? If not, why not? Did the "tentacle of the Department of Underwater Life Sciences devour a whole cooked chicken furnished by the Department of Romantic Poultry"? And did he, as others would, use those mock interviews, arranged by "the Department of Great Expectations," to persecute earnest undergraduates? What sardonic epithet did he use for *their* bogus disciplines? And with what irony did he designate his own? If, as he said, "you can hide in the universities but they are the very seat and soul of brain damage," what was he doing *here*? Why was he foregoing his personal book allowance to pay for the department's Canon copier? Had he become a supporter of re-production, a replicator of culture, a promoter of copies, a professor of brain damage?

Even in "Not-Knowing" there were the predictably arch epistolaries between Gaston and Alphonse, the silly talk about chastity belts and jazz banjuleles, and the celebrations of "the as-yet unspeakable, the as-yet unspoken." Another paean to silence or to infinite regress—more frames within frames, wheels within wheels. Far out. There was also a fashionable satisfaction taken in Mallarmé's absence from Bartlett's all-too *Familiar Quotations*. The essay articulated—yes, with brilliance and learning and poise—Don the Lamentator's sacred discontent with the world's corruption of the word, "the complicity of language" in our collective exploitations and atrocities. Another symptom: the hypersensitive suspicion of "existing rhetorics," of language as tool of the powerful, of grail as bomb.

Yet again, the disjunction: Had not Don become their don, the head of one of the great writing families, not Corleone but Barthelme—a godfather, a benefactor, a literary *agent*, for Christ's sake? Had he not become the functionary of Cecil Rhodes, assisting, as he did, in the grooming of the next generation of physicians and financiers, of managers and lawyers, of living mothers and undead fathers? For to teach was to cohabitate with the oppressors and their "busy functionaries," to help corrupt the word. If language was complicitous, then why those workshops encouraging pupils to "go on writing"? If, as he says, "even conjunctions must be inspected carefully," why urge common, ordinary people, who can't even be depended on to sniff the odorous adjectives, to compose? Why not follow the example of self-righteous authenticists in classrooms down the hall: pontificate, condemn, and say "*J'accuse!*" Wouldn't it be better if those creative writing students would please please please please please please please stop talking. And writing. Just cease, hush, and hold their respective peaces? Most of them are soon to become somebody's busy functionary, an architect or engineer of something, and soon they'll be going about their dirty little business of procreating, replicating, and contaminating. Why not just let them sicken and die unexpressed, let them croak like those gerbils in that other "School"?

Flannery O'Connor had the right idea. When they asked her if the colleges and universities weren't stifling "our young writers," she replied that, if they were, they weren't stifling enough of them. Yet it is said that while Barthelme's students read their work his face would become luminous with joy. That he never condescended, not even to the nontraditional "Nancy" relating in realistic representational terms the events of her day. Neither Percy nor O'Connor could bear to teach. No wonder: they, too, were perfectionists, easily bored. Yet Barthelme, an alienist, and thus surely an enemy of the people, persisted in this midwifery of discourse, this birthing of stories.

We never got the chance, found the time, to ask him how, how can you stand it. How can you justify the pollution of language. His "Not-Knowing" essay anticipated the query: "If words can be contaminated by the world, they can also carry with them into the work trace elements of world which can be used in a positive sense." Positive sense? But aren't you just supposed to go on, until you can't go on, just play, even though you can't, just write a silly sentence which goes on, and on, for seven pages, and then—scandalous!—*doesn't end with a period?* Isn't that what you do, all you can do, if you would avoid contamination?

Barthelme was willing to risk it. He wanted generativity: "The combinatorial agility of words, the exponential generation of meaning once they're allowed to go to bed together, allows the writer to surprise himself, makes art possible, reveals how much of *Being* we haven't yet encountered." After so much encouraging and supporting of students, so much caring and feeding of writers, there is bound to be some contamination. He must have known that if you keep practicing combinatorial agility long enough, something is going to get germinated. There's going to be conception and gestation and delivery and pretty soon you're going to have another little Presbyterian on your hands and she's going to be whining for a Cairn Terrier. Furthermore, isn't that . . . ? Yes, there it is, go check for yourself. Set in Janson typeface (with Caslon display headings) and printed by letterpress on 50 pound Warren Olde Style at Heritage Printers, Inc., Charlotte, North Carolina: a capital *B*.

While you're checking, go ahead and turn to page 522. Surely the author is pulling our legs, as it were, while ferociously frenching his own mucosa. "Flannery O'Connor, an artist of the first rank, famously disliked anything that looked funny on the page . . ." Walker Percy has been absolutely stifled by Roman Catholicism, and Graham Greene's terror is tired, exhausted, *boring*, but Mary Flannery O'Connor, daughter of Regina O'Connor, neé Cline, of Milledgeville, Ga., is not only elevated to the pantheon, she is allowed a "tough-minded put-down of puerile experimentalism." As the young were saying when Barthelme died—are they still saying it?—"Yeah, right." But this most wised-up of put-down artists persists: " 'Belief in progress,' says Baudelaire, 'is a doctrine of idlers and Belgians.' Perhaps. But if I have anything unorthodox to offer here, it's that I think art's project is fundamentally meliorative."

Time for a questionnaire to break the spell and short-circuit our willing suspension of disbelief:

In your opinion, dear reader, has the essay been
   A)   too fundamentally meliorative
   B)   just fundamentally meliorative enough
   C)   not sufficiently fundamentally meliorative.

While you've got your pencil out, please
CHECK ONE.
Is your narrator too smart-alecky ? (   )
Not smart-alecky enough? (   )

But Barthelme neglected to put a questionnaire on page 522. Can it be that he is going to encourage us to join in the dance, that he now realizes that there may be something, not much, but something, *good* in the simple act of singing anything, even "Me and my Winstons / Me and my Winstons"? His peroration, after all, sounds good—like a peroration should: "The aim of meditating about the world is finally to change the world. It is this meliorative aspect of literature that provides its ethical dimension. We are all Upton Sinclairs, even that Hamlet, Stephane Mallarmé." Ethical dimension? Meliorative aspect? Even that Beckett, Donald Barthelme?

Our blindness, our misidentification, might have been avoided. The eros, the love of life, was always there, in stories such as "The School" (performed that September Sunday by Richard Howard) and "On Angels" (read by Ms. Macdonald). Barthelme's angels, you see, had never experienced not-knowing. So they had never been curious; their souls had never been hungry. Comfortable, they had never turned answers into riddles, myths into parables. Never, that is, until "the death of God left the angels in a strange position"—our position, if the *New York Times* is to be trusted.

What to do, then, here at the eschaton, in these, the last days of the twentieth century? When Barthelme's angels faced not-knowing, they initially proposed lamentation. Plaint would now be their eternal function, as adoration had been formerly. But after a while their expressions of disappointment and despair did not seem quite lamentative enough. A new plan was proposed: it was agreed that "the mode of lamentation would be silence." Silence would be used to indicate dissatisfaction. But silence didn't work for long, either, because "it is not in the nature of angels to be silent." (*Nature?* Was the man going to turn out to be a closet essentialist as well?) Other angels wanted to try Chaos; still others suggested removing themselves from being: they would simply *not be*. But after some consideration, Not-Being was dismissed by Don's angels as a mistaken strategy, a gesture of spiritual pride. Some wanted to try "adoring each other, as we do," but gave up after a while because "they found it, finally, 'not enough.'" Still uncertain and at a loss, the angels continue, we are told, "to search for a new principle." We must assume that eventually, out of necessity, they will, if they haven't already, turn to writing.

Unlike Barthelme, Percy, O'Connor, and God, the novel *Wise Blood* "is still alive," or so Mary Flannery wrote in her note to the second edition. She thought of hers as "a comic novel about a Christian *malgre-lui*" named Hazel Motes. But comic does not mean unserious. "All comic novels that are any good," she writes, "must be about matters of life and death." For many readers, certainly, Mr. Barthelme's integrity, like Mr. Motes's, "lies in his trying with such vigor to get rid of the ragged figure who moves from tree to tree in the back of his mind." For other readers, the integrity of Hazel and Donald lies in their not being able to. "Does one's integrity ever lie in what he is not able to do?" Mary Flannery asks. "I think that it usually does," she answers, "for free will does not mean one will, but many wills conflicting in one man." Perhaps Barthelme's integrity lies in his inability to purge himself of the world's complicities. Did he, like his angels, find pure freedom, "finally, not enough"? "Freedom cannot be conceived simply," Mary Flannery says. "It is a mystery and one which a novel, even a comic novel, can only be asked to deepen."

Was Barthelme's parabolic integrity quasi-theological? Was he, like O'Connor, deepening cosmic mystery with every comic step? One might just as well ask, did Barthelme believe in angels? Like Hazel Motes's Church Without Christ (*That ain't anything but a way to say something. There's no such thing*), they were just made up. And yet, like us "in some ways," they go on. Even that angel, Stephane Mallarmé. Wouldn't Uncle Don want us to make the couplet, flawed yet heroic ("Even that Percy, Donald Barthelme"), and, bored with our customary doubts, speak the alienated question, "What shall we do now that God and Barthelme are dead"?

Silence? Chaos? Not-Being?

Not-Knowing.

Index

216, 223; desire to be, in Sartre, 83; and gnostic strategies, 80, 83–84; God-the-Mother versus God-the-Father tradition, 86n8; love of, 193n26; and the Upanishads, 148; ways of, justifying, 53; word of, 115n48. *See also* Being; Transcendence

Goethe, Johann Wolfgang von, 61, 92–93, 96, 99n15

Goffman, Erving, 36n37

Gold, Herbert, 104

Goldsmith, Oliver, 163

Goleman, David, 32n2

Good and evil, 72, 127–28, 145; and aesthetic strategies, 91; and Eliot, 141–42; and gnostic strategies, 80, 82, 84; and sexuality, 141–42

Gordimer, Nadine, 29

Gordon, Lyndall, 81, 142

Gospel of Philip, 84

Gossip: as cultural criticism, 126; as virtue criticism, 39

Grammar of Motives, A (Burke), 14, 20n3

Grand narratives, 4; and Barthelme, 178, 179; performances of alienation versus, 176. *See also* Myth

Greco-Roman era: and Gnosticism, 53, 79, 81. *See also* Pax Romana

Greene, Graham, 177, 189, 192n16, 218, 221; *The Comedians*, 177–78

Greenlee, Karen, 202

Grimston, Robert de, 203

Gunn, Giles, 89

Hall, Donald, 29

Hamlet (Shakespeare), 31, 221

Harassment: literary, as strategy of alienation, 121; in the literary classroom, 131n9

Harlequin romances, 35n21

Harrison, Bernard, 40, 106

Hassan, Ihab, 66–67, 79, 198–99

Hawthorne, Nathaniel, 29

Hayden, Sterling, 3

Heart of Darkness (Conrad), 119

Hebraism, 73

Hebrew Bible, 3, 62

He Do the Police in Different Voices (Bedient), 81, 135

Hegemony, 61, 125, 206–7, 210

Heidegger, Martin, 35n24, 40, 80, 98, 101

Helen of Troy: and sexual transgression, in Gnosticism, 82

Hellenism and Gnosticism. *See* Greco-Roman era

Heller, Joseph, 103, 105, 123, 129, 187

Hemingway, Ernest, 103, 107, 108

Hermeneutics of suspicion, 39, 177

Hermeticism, 2, 136, 139, 151, 198

Hermitism, 44, 84, 91; in Barthelme, 178; in Eliot, 136, 139; in Thoreau, 196

Hero: madman versus, 72; poet as, 95, 209

Heroism, 90, 113, 209–10; and antiheroes, 103; and Barthelme, 178–79, 190; and insanity, 104; and Nabokov, 158, 162, 165, 168

Herzog (Bellow), 94

Hesse, Hermann: as gnostic writer, 79

Heteroglossia, 17

Hinduism, 146–49

Hippolytus and Phaedra, 3

Hirsch, Edward, 216

Hobbes, Thomas, 180, 206

Hölderlin, Friedrich, 198, 208

"Hollow Men, The" (Eliot), 141

Holy Feast, Holy Fast (Bynum), 84

Homeopathy: alienism as, 7, 54, 74; allopathy versus, 77n53; and parable, 189

Homogenization, 102–3

Hope, 129, 130, 210

Howard, Richard: as virtue critic, 36n30

Howe, Irving, 65, 73, 89, 204–5

Huckleberry Finn, The Adventures of (Twain), 18, 104, 107, 117; as ritual of purification, 135

"Humanity Is the Devil" (Grimston), 203

Hume, Robert E., 146

Hunt, Leigh, 166

WILLIAM MONROE is an associate professor of
English and associate dean of the Honors College
at the University of Houston. His publications
include essays on Willa Cather and Flannery
O'Connor and articles on performance in
literature and medicine. His play *Primary Care*,
written with the collaboration of the historian
Thomas R. Cole, has been performed at
conferences, professional meetings, and theaters
in Texas, South Carolina, and Illinois. He directs
"Common Ground," a collaborative institute for
teachers of literature, and the Project for the
Study of Values in Civic Life and the Professions
at the University of Houston.